D1548430

Electrical Properties
of Cells
Patch Clamp for Biologists

Electrical Properties of Cells
Patch Clamp for Biologists

Louis J. DeFelice

Vanderbilt University Medical Center
Nashville, Tennessee

PLENUM PRESS • NEW YORK AND LONDON

Library of Congress Cataloging-in-Publication Data

DeFelice, Louis J.
    Electrical properties of cells : patch clamp for biologists /
Louis J. DeFelice.
        p.   cm.
    Includes bibliographical references and index.
    ISBN 0-306-45345-2
    1. Patch-clamp techniques (Electrophysiology)
2. Electrophysiology--Methodology.   I. Title.
    [DNLM: 1. Patch-Clamp Techniques--methods.   2. Cells--physiology.
QH 585 D313e 1997]
QH517.D44   1997
571.4'7--dc21
DNLM/DLC
for Library of Congress   97-14313
                                                                           CIP

ISBN 0-306-45345-2

© 1997 Plenum Press, New York
A Division of Plenum Publishing Corporation
233 Spring Street, New York, N. Y. 10013

http://www.plenum.com

To the memory of Ben,
for his enthusiasm and sense of fun

Preface

This book began in earnest in 1991 when I was on sabbatical at California Institute of Technology. The idea for the work came much earlier, soon after I published *Introduction to Membrane Noise* in 1981. It seemed then that a concise book patterned after Katz's *Nerve, Muscle, and Synapse* (McGraw-Hill, New York; out of print since 1991 but still worth reading) but updated to include channels, might have an appeal. With the appearance of *Ionic Channels of Excitable Membranes* by Bertil Hille, *Single-Channel Recording* by Bert Sakmann and Erwin Neher, and *Electrogenic Ion Pumps* by Peter Läuger, the need for such a book diminished. After spending a year away from the subject, and after speaking with biologists who used the patch clamp, I became convinced of the need for a simple text that covered the basics. Stephanie Canada at California Institute of Technology made it happen. She turned roughly penned drafts into legible text and sketchy math into manageable formulas. Her dedication to this project over the past 4 years was astonishing. I hope this book will assist biologists working with the patch clamp, and encourage them to become acquainted with more advanced texts. To aid in this transition, I refer to the following books throughout the present text:

IMN: *Introduction to Membrane Noise* (1981), Louis J. DeFelice, Plenum Press, New York, 500 pages.

ICEMa: *Ionic Channels of Excitable Membranes* (1984), 1st ed., Bertil Hille, Sinauer Associates, Sunderland, MA, 426 pages.

ICEMb: *Ionic Channels of Excitable Membranes* (1992), 2nd ed., Bertil Hille, Sinauer Associates, Sunderland, MA, 607 pages.

SCRa: *Single-Channel Recording* (1983), 1st ed., Bert Sakmann and Erwin Neher, Plenum Press, New York, 503 pages.

SCRb: *Single-Channel Recording* (1995), 2nd ed., Bert Sakmann and Erwin Neher, Plenum Press, New York, 700 pages.

EIP: *Electrogenic Ion Pumps* (1991), Peter Läuger, Sinauer Associates, Sunderland, MA, 313 pages.

Contents

Introduction

Let us suppose you are walking along and you see lightning strike the ground, and just at the place and moment where it hits, a basketball appears out of nowhere. That would be pretty amazing, and you would probably call it a magical event. However let us suppose that you make the same trip every day, and that *every* time lightning strikes a certain place, a basketball appears—that you could logically call science. Let me explain what I mean. Sometimes it would appear that the only difference between science and magic is that science repeats. If something happens once, then under the same circumstances, it will happen again. Science is no less magical than magic, it is just repeatable.

As strange as that may seem, there is something much stranger to consider. Suppose you walk to the place where you know lightning will strike and basketballs will appear, and you wait and watch. Let us say that over a certain period, lightning strikes 15 times, but a basketball appears only five times. It is not the first five times nor the last five times but just any five times out of the 15, and independent of how long you hang around and wait, basketballs appear about one-third of the strikes. I say about because it does not have to be exactly one-third. If you wait, say, ten times longer than you did when you saw 15 strikes and five basketballs, you may see 150 strikes (even that could vary) and only 46 basketballs. The next time you may see 52 basketballs and so on. At any rate you come to the conclusion, by making these observations a lot of times, that you obtain a positive result one-third of the time $(0.333 \pm$ whatever$)$. That means if you walk up with your friends and say "Here is the spot where it happens," then ask them to watch with you. Even though you cannot say whether you will see a basketball on the first strike, you can make a bet.

- HA, no ball! (First bolt of lightning)
- Just wait. (Two more blasts go by)
- There! (A shiny new Wilson appears)

And the longer you wait, the more certain you become that the chance of seeing a basketball has a certain value, though you can never say whether or not the next

Science or Magic?

bolt of lightning will produce a ball. I think it is science because it is a repeatable phenomenon, but it has a twist—probability. A lot of nature, most of nature, perhaps all of nature, behaves in exactly that way. Sometimes the probability of an event is so high that essentially no other outcome is possible; nevertheless many phenomena that appear perfectly regular up here where we live, when viewed in finer detail, are unreliable (except on average) at the bottom.

Let us switch to real science. Suppose you look at a hundred radioactive atoms located on a grid. You can be sure that after a certain time, half of them will have decayed, but you cannot say which ones will be gone and which ones will be left. Two atoms that are by all other measures identical, side by side, may have totally different lifetimes—one goes off in just a few seconds to become something else, phosphorous to sulfur, say, yet its neighbor (no different) waits years to do the same thing. What is it that selects one and spares the other? What decides which atom decays first? No one has ever explained this.

On a different level, no one has ever explained the simple laws of chance. If you flip a fair coin, you say that the odds of landing one way or the other are the same. But this is not something you can derive, this fifty-fifty probability, and it is not anything that obviously comes from some deeper sense of things. It just is. Of course the matter revolves around the word fair. When we say fair coin, we are already saying fifty-fifty, so there is really nothing to prove because we announced the outcome in the first place. What is behind all of this? Does a fair coin really exist? I think literally it does not. No matter how hard we tried to make it so, in the end there would always be some tiny difference in weight, air currents, or force of flip to make things different in one way or the other. Now all these odd tiny differences—most of which we would never know about—could cancel each other. In other words they could push events one way or the other but in the end leave the coin essentially (exactly?) fair. Another way of saying this is that all small perturbations could be random and could at least in principle add up to zero. These two examples—and they are extremes: exact sameness (the coin flip, etc.) and perfect randomness (the perturbations)—are what is needed to have exact fairness; in other words fairness does not exist.

But this is the very idealization that we assume exists at some ultimate level. Let us return to our previous example. Radioactivity—another kind of coin flipping—is assumed to be random. No one can predict which one of the many unstable phosphorous nuclei in UT ^{32}P in the tagged mRNA molecule that we use in our experiments will give up an electron to become sulfur. All we can say is that after about 2 weeks, half of the tagged molecules will be gone. Thus the process is totally random, totally fair in this sense of fair, but is this true? If you could do the ultimate experiment and measure and know everything about each one of the many ^{32}P nuclei, could you predict the eventual collapse of a particular atom? Modern physics is clear on this: The answer is no.

We assume that the same is true for ion channels. When we say that the open and close probabilities are random, we mean exactly that there is no way at all of telling what the individual channel is going to do. Like radioactive atoms, if we watch any channel for a long time, its future will not depend on its past. Even though by chance a particular channel happens to stay open for a very long time—assume that being open has a low probability—the chance that it will repeat this long opening next time it has an opportunity is just as low as ever. If we obtain heads ten times in a row (rare), the chance of obtaining an eleventh head is just the same as for the first head, exactly one-half. It is hard to believe.

Two issues have to be separated. One is the ideal notion of fairness, and the other is the practical absurdity of fairness; let us take these one at a time.

Ideal Fairness

What is going on in channel theory is this: By starting with the basic idea of a completely random opening and closing channel, it is possible to construct from at least two sets of such channels—say, Na and K—a nonlinear differential equation that describes the average behavior of many of these random events, i.e., excitability. Now here is another wrinkle that we have to correct before continuing: Choices for fairness are not confined to fifty-fifty. In other words you can have a fair coin (in the sense that we mean fair: unpredictable, event by event, and random) that is sixty-forty. (There is even another wrinkle that we are going to suppress for now: We are not confined to two outcomes. The coin could land on its edge, so we would have to consider fifty-nine, thirty-nine, two—more on that later in the book.) What does sixty-forty mean? It means that each time you flip the coin you do not know what is going to happen (it is fair), but on average you know that you will obtain heads more than tails, say, three-out-of-five times. Of course as the situation you consider goes more and more in this direction, say, seventy-thirty under one set of circumstances, eighty-twenty under another, ninety-ten, etc., you may justifiably feel more and more certain that you will obtain a head. This is what loaded dice are all about. But even in an extreme case, say, ninety-nine, one, you are really not *sure* that the next throw will be a head, you are only pretty sure—sure enough to bet, say, but not to bet your life. In that sense the lopsided coin that we are considering is still fair—it is just biased. Or maybe instead of fair, which implies fifty-fifty, we should say that the coin flip or the channel opening is a random event.

The intellectual content of regenerative excitability lies in this notion: The probability bias of opening depends on the voltage, the opening of a channel changes the voltage, and that new voltage changes the bias. That pretty much sums up the whole book. It is this loop, which is so much fun to think about, that is behind the whole process; it is also behind virtually all other electrical cell properties. Details may change: For example instead of voltage, serotonin binding may change the probability of the serotonin transporter opening, or D-flat may change the probability of a Na channel opening. A response can be an action potential in the cochlear nerve, a Ca wave, or cell division. In all these cases, the underlying principles remain the same, and there are not that many of them.

If you take the preceding point of view: Voltage changes the bias, and the bias changes the voltage, you arrive at something like the Hodgkin–Huxley (HH) equations very easily. By the HH equations (ICEMb, p. 44), we mean the entire set of these kinds of equations—numbering in the many dozens—that describe the action potential and its propagation in a variety of tissues. Let us call these different, nonlinear differential equations that describe action potentials in heart, brain, hair cells, etc., the HH set.

A typical member of the HH set is this equation:

$$\frac{C\,d^2V}{dt^2} = N_K \gamma_K(V)\,\{1 - \exp[-t/\tau_n(V)]\}^4 \left\{V + \frac{kT}{e}\ln([K]_{in}/[K]_{out})\right\}$$

$$+ N_{Na}\gamma_{Na}(V)\,\{1 - \exp[-t/\tau_m(V)]\}^3\,\{1 - \exp[-t/\tau_h(V)]\}$$

$$\times \left\{V + \frac{kT}{e}\ln[Na]_{in}/[Na]_{out})\right\} + N_{leak}\,\gamma_{leak}(V)\,V$$

The solution to this equation is an action potential. I wrote it in this elaborate way just to be provocative, without defining anything or telling you what I mean, but there is a point. Equations in the HH set are fairly complex, and they are capable of generating a lot of different solutions. The solutions we are thinking of are for the membrane voltage $V(x,t)$, because that is where we think the information is: What is the voltage across the membrane at a particular place at a particular time? Members of the HH set try to solve this problem, and ideal fairness underlies this equation and all equations like it. What these equations stand for however is the average behavior of many random events.

The Absurdity of Fairness

We will spend a lot of time showing how this equation is related to the underlying random opening and closing of ion channels because that is the way bioelectricity works. The heart beats spontaneously because ion channels open and close randomly. We see how this works later in the book when we assume that the cell membrane contains (among others) Na channels that are all identical—like the identical coins. But this is surely absurd; how can a large protein made up of thousands of amino acids embedded in a complicated structure like a lipid bilayer be exactly like its neighbor? Every amino acid, every turn, every angle, every dipole? I do not think so. Later on in the book I will try to convince you that the individuality of ion channels plays a role in how they do their job; I leave it up to you to decide about coins and electrons.

When something appears to be perfectly regular—or as we say, deterministic, like the HH equations or the Schrödinger equation—is it actually a random phenomenon at a certain probability? When something appears to be random, or as we say, stochastic, is it merely the chaotic behavior of deterministic equations? This is one of the deepest questions of physics, and how we look at the answer determines how we understand the electrical properties of cells.

1

Basics

van de Graaff Accelerator

A van de Graaff accelerator may seem like an odd place to start a book on the electrical properties of cells, but it is as good a place as any. Electricity is only charge (a mystery), the separation of charge (voltage), and the movement of charge (current). The van de Graaff machine illustrates these points about electrical charge: Charge piles up at one location, is placed on a moving belt, then it is transported to another place—a large metal dome. It builds up there and generates a large voltage difference—2 million volts in tandem machines—that is used to accelerate particles, like protons, to smash into the nuclei of atoms. If too many electrons are placed on the dome, exceeding the capacity of dome to hold them, you may say, the charge jumps off, sparks on the surrounding tank, then leaks to ground—more lightening (see Fig. 1.1). There you have it, all the essential ingredients for bioelectricity: charge (the essential element), separation of charge, movement of charge, then some secondary effects, like the storage of charge (capacitance) and the final resting place of charge (ground). Let us look at all of them in a little more detail.

The moving charge on the belt is a current, but what happens when the charge is scraped onto the dome? The dome is a metal full of its own electrons, which are free to move around. All of the dome (–) electrons are paired with (+) charges. When an extra one is added, it has no place to go, so the extra electron (–) tries to leave the dome. It goes to the surface, trying to get away from other electrons and looking for something to pair up with. The dome is surrounded by a gas with no free electrons, that is an insulator, so generally an extra electron cannot jump off. But eventually if too many electrons build up and the charge is very large, the mutual repulsion of the extra electrons for each other is too much, so a number of them jump off, then escape through the metal tank to ground. What is the ground? It is an ideal infinite domain where electrons may wander and pair up or not—just because it is so large and there is more room for unevenness in charge and potential.

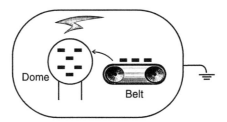

Figure 1.1. How a van de Graaff accelerator works

In other words it is a sink for electrons, sometimes called earth because that is where ground is.

The force driving electrons off the dome is an excess of charge, which can also be described as a voltage. These two attributes are essentially equivalent, but charge is more fundamental; nevertheless we usually think and work more in terms of voltage. In this book when we say that there are 12 million volts on the dome, we actually mean that compatible with the dome's capacity to hold charge with respect to the tank ground, a certain amount of charge has accumulated over the balanced amount that was already there. That may seem less familiar, but in the end it is the easier concept.

Capacitors

What is the relationship between charge and voltage? Let Q be the total charge that has built up on the dome (you may think of this as $Q = Nq$, where N is the number of electrons and q is the charge on one), let V be the voltage of the dome with respect to the tank. Let the tank's voltage equal zero, and let C be the capacity of the dome to hold charge with respect to the tank. This depends on how far away the dome is from the tank, the pressure of the gas between the dome and the tank, the relative areas of dome and tank, and other facts. In the end however it reduces to this familiar formula:

$$Q = CV$$

In words the extra charge on the dome is proportional to the voltage. But this seems backward if charge is the fundamental object. We can think of this formula in many ways: When we write

$$Q \propto V$$

then C is the constant of proportionality. But if Q is really the fundamental quantity, then we should write

$$V \propto Q$$

That is the voltage is proportional to the charge—just as we said before. In this equation the inverse capacitance $1/C$ is the proportionality constant that relates the two. We can also manipulate the formula to write

$$C = \frac{Q}{V}$$

where now the capacity of the tank is thought of as the charge held per unit voltage.

PROBLEM.   Let us think of a new unit of capacitance, called D, where $D = 1/C$. Then instead of $Q = CV$, we write $V = DQ$. We say voltage is proportional to Q and D is the proportionality constant; D depends on all the things C depends on. Everything would be fine, but we would have to give D a new name! (We do something similar later with R the resistance and G the conductance.)

Capacitance is one of the more difficult concepts in basic electricity. Let us try to make a capacitor: Twist two strands of electrical wire insulated in the usual way together. Scrape away a little of the insulation at two ends (see Fig. 1.2):

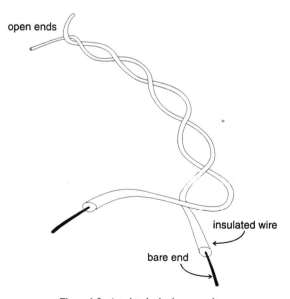

Figure 1.2. A twisted wire is a capacitor.

If you connect a capacitance meter to the two bare ends you have a real capacitor. Note: The *metal* wire ends on the other end of the twisted pair do not touch each other; the wires are separate at this end; they are far from the naked wires; and they are not directly connected. The nearness of the two metal wires makes the capacitor: They are close to each other, but they do not actually touch metal to metal.

A *capacitor* is two conductors separated by an insulator. Once it was common to find twisted-wire capacitors in radios; if the capacitance were off, you could give the wire another twist. In the twisted-wire capacitor, there are two insulators next to each other—but that is just one insulator. You need three regions to make a capacitor: a conductor, an insulator, and a conductor. We have made a capacitor, but we do not know how it works. According to theory even though the metal wires are not touching, current can pass between them. That is, we can push electrons from one metal wire to another but only in a special way.

What happens if we add an electron to one of the wires (see Fig. 1.3). The wire is electrically neutral. That is for every electron, there is an opposite charge somewhere else in the metal. Adding an electron to the metal unbalances this electroneutrality.

In Fig. 1.3 only the extra charge shows, so you must imagine the other (−)s and (+)s in the metal on the right and left. Note: The position of the extra electron is important. How did it reach the arbitrary middle point where I placed it? Though each electron in the wire is balanced by a (+) charge, some are free to move around. So when you add one to the end of the wire, it pushes the surrounding ones, and they push their neighbors, etc. Basically the electron is trying to find a (+) to pair with; all the electrons are. Imagine this situation: Initially each electron is paired off until extra electrons are added to the wire. Eventually the extra electron—not necessarily the one added to the wire—arrives at the insulation by pushing and shoving. The ideal insulator has no mobile electrons—that is what makes it an insulator. What is going to happen?

Up to now the electron has been displacing its neighbor, and the neighbor moves on, etc. But there is nothing to push at the insulator. The electron could wander

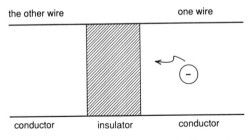

Figure 1.3. Adding an electron to one side of a capacitor

aimlessly around the wire forever if we had a wire (insulated or not) in empty space. In that case we could add as many electrons as we wanted, and they would all end up at the surface of the wire, trying to get out and pair up while all the other electrons in the core of the wire were paired off.

However when two wires are close to each other, there are electrons to push in the wire on the other side of the insulator; Fig. 1.4 shows what happens. The plus sign (+) represents the charge that *was* paired with the (–) on the left; now it is paired with the (–) on the right. We have a few more problems. First the (+) (–) pair are separated by a distance; however when the first electron was added to the wire, it too interacted with other electrons at a distance. Electrons can do this with any charge; if they could not there would be no spatial dimension. Second the electron on the right is fixed now, but the electron on the left is free to move; it can move around, pushing and shoving its neighbors as it tries to pair up.

Can the new free electron on the left pair up with the (+) to free the (–) on the right again? This could happen but there is some right-to-left force that causes electrons to pair more or less in one direction. What is this asymmetry? Simple—we just keep adding electrons to the original bare wire on the right; we could do this with a van de Graaff machine for example.

When we added the first electron on the right, one appeared on the left; if we add another electron we will have (+)(+)(–)(–), etc. For every (–) we add on the right, one (+) appears on the left. Note: No right electron ever crosses to the left; the electrons on the left were there already—they were just displaced as electrons on the right pushed them away from their partners. Now these electrons have to seek partners.

Recalling Fig. 1.2: If we add any number of electrons to the wire on the right, the same number appears on the left; however those on the left were never in the right-hand wire. Those on the right that accumulate at the insulator paired with the (+)s left behind are not the original ones we added, so no electrons actually *cross*

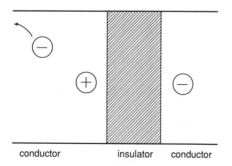

conductor   insulator   conductor

Figure 1.4. Displacement current

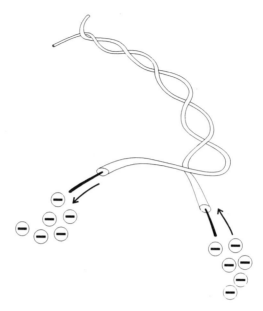

Figure 1.5. Electrons in, electrons out

the insulator. Nevertheless electrons enter on one side and exit from the other side (see Fig. 1.5); this constitutes a current, called the *displacement current*.

Dielectric Constant

Capacitance depends on the distance between conductors, i.e., the thickness of the insulator: the greater the distance, d, the smaller the capacitance; that is

$$C \propto \frac{1}{d}$$

This equation says that the capacitance is inversely proportional to the distance between conductors.

The apposition A defines the capacitance, i.e., the greater the area of apposition, the greater the capacitance. This seems obvious because of the tendency of extra electrons to go toward the available surface; we write this as:

$$C \propto A$$

This says that the capacitance is proportional to the area (of apposition between conductors). Putting these two equations together and letting ε be the *constant of proportionality*, we can write

$$C = \varepsilon \frac{A}{d}$$

Let us think of how to increase C. One way would be to use wires with thinner insulation on them. An easier way would be to give the two wires a few more twists.

What is ε? It is called the dielectric constant of the material separating the two conductors, so it is a property of the insulating *material*. Similarly the ratio A/d is a property of the geometry and sizes of the *insulated conductors*. The formula for C therefore divides into two parts: material and geometry; that is true for membranes as well as wires. Note: We never said that the insulator on the conductors had to be perfect. A perfect insulator is empty space. If there is no hope of freeing electrons to move around, that is as perfect as we can obtain. In such a case we use the symbol ε_o, the dielectric constant of empty space.

Let us think of a not-so-perfect insulation, like the rubber coating on the twisted wires or the lipid in a membrane. There is some chance of finding loose electrons. We write ε for that *particular* material. Note: ε does not depend on the shape or size of the insulator; it has the same value everywhere; the whole piece has the value ε, and so does any small part of it.

What about the value ε_o and its value for any material other than empty space? Let us consider its units. We introduce symbol θ, which stands for has the units of. Since:

$$C = \varepsilon \frac{A}{d}$$

and A θ area and d θ length, then A/d θ length and:

$$\varepsilon \, \theta \, \frac{\text{Capacitance}}{\text{Length}}$$

Therefore in whatever units we choose to use, the dielectric constant is the unit of capacitance (e.g., the farad) over the unit of length (e.g., the centimeter). What about the value? In some conventions we let $\varepsilon = K\varepsilon_o$, where K is a unitless constant for a certain material. Is K greater or less than one? In other words is empty space the best we can do in making a capacitor? You may assume that the dielectric constant is as large as it can be in empty space because there are no free electrons (it is empty!), while there may be some in rubber. But $\varepsilon = K\varepsilon_o$ is really a statement about the imperfect *insulating* property of the material between the conductors, not about the capacity. Actually K is greater than one (for more about ε, see IMN, p. 72). Even though there are no free electrons in rubber, there may be some charges that can move (a little). Thus materials can polarize.

To make this clearer, we now consider dipoles. Imagine a small dumbbell with a (+) and (−) attached to either end (see Fig. 1.6). The dumbbell is fixed, and so are

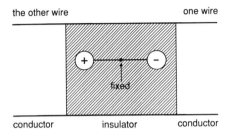

Figure 1.6. Dumbbell dielectric

the charges on it. It cannot translate, but it can rotate, so although the dumbbell charges are fixed, they can move a little. Now imagine that an extra charge rises from the conductor to the surface of the insulator. What happens? The extra electron we added to the right pushes on the fixed (−) charge on the dumbbell, so the dumbbell rotates (which is all it can do). When it rotates however, there is a small movement of the dumbbell (−) to the left; at the same time there is a small movement of the (+) to the right (see Fig. 1.7). A (+) on the right is just like a (−) on the left, so the electron in the conductor on the far left receives two pushes, one from the dumbbell (−) moving to the left and one from dumbbell (+) moving to the right. A positive shift to the right is electrically equivalent to a negative shift to the left. This property of insulators is called their *polarizability*; how many of these dumbbells are there, and how flexible are they about rotating? You now know the value of dielectric constants for different materials: $K = 1$ is a vacuum and $K > 1$ in something else; for example $K = 10$ for oil (and lipids), and $K = 80$ for water. If you use a conductor, like mercury, in place of an insulator, mercury has many free electrons, or salt water, which has many free ions, then the whole region shorts out and the capacitor can no longer function, or it is greatly diminished. Nevertheless, even two

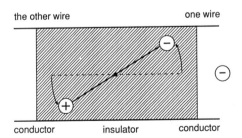

Figure 1.7. An extra charge in the conductor can move a fixed charge in the insulator.

conductors separated by a less-effective conductor (a relative insulator) defines a capacitance according to the rule capacitor = conductor, insulator, conductor.

Some materials make a better capacitor than others. How many dumbbells does empty space have? We cannot answer that question, but we do know the value of ε_o in terms of other properties. In the meters, kilograms, seconds, amperes (MKSA) system of units, the value of the dielectric constant is

$$\varepsilon_o = 8.854 \times 10^{-14} \text{ F/cm}$$

where *F* means farad, the MKSA unit of capacitance. Note: The A in MKSA stands for ampere (i.e., current), but current is charge/time, so time appears twice in the MKSA definitions—in S and A. There are historical reasons for this related to the standard of measurement for the basic units, but it would have been better to define an MKSQ system, where Q is the charge (coulomb). Although the M in MKSA stands for meter, we have expressed the value of ε_o in farads/centimeter, not farads/meter. Even if there is *nothing* between the two conductors, as suggested (but never true) by the symbol for a capacitor, ε_o is finite, and empty space is still polarizable!

Capacitive Current

How does time effect the properties we have discussed? Let us return to the original twisted wire (see Fig. 1.8). At this stage we are always dealing with a model, an approximation of the real thing. This is not only true of an explanation, but also of an experiment. To the extent that biology is more complex than physics has to model to a greater extent than physics.

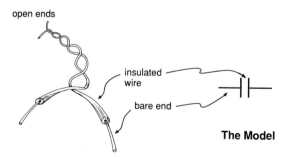

Figure 1.8. Equivalent circuit of a capacitor

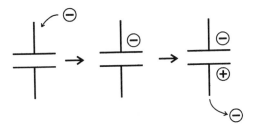

Figure 1.9. Charging the capacitor: Electrons enter the wire (left), collect on the plate (middle), and force electrons from the opposite plate, leaving behind a positive charge (right).

Suppose we add charges to the top conductor of the capacitor (see Fig. 1.9). The (−) charge Q moves quickly to the top plate (the surface of the conductor, which can have any shape). We call it $Q(-)$ because it stands for many (say, N) electrons, each with an elementary negative charge e. In time $Q(-)$ come in and $Q(+)$ go out, but after that, everything stops. If you place the whole object in a box, we would say that a current passed through the box. Of course we know the same Q did not actually go through—the $Q(-)$ coming out is *not* the same that went in because there is an impenetrable space between them. Note: The charge enters, causes an equal amount of the same sign to come out, then everything stops. If we add more charge to the top, more comes out the bottom, but something happens only when we *change* the charge (in time). We can add as much charge on the capacity as it allows, which we call C. Since the final static result is to separate the charge, we create a voltage V. We already know the relationship between these:

$$V = \frac{Q}{C}$$

We now write $Q = Q(-) = Q(+)$ to mean simply the charge (minus or plus) stored on one side (or the other) of the capacitor. If we add too much Q for a given C, V becomes too large, so that (possibly) a spark of charge jumps across the gap. (This is lightning if the cloud is one plate and the earth is the other. In this case Q comes from the cloud of water and dust, moving through the air.) If the opposing areas are large, more Q accumulates, and if they are far apart, it is more difficult for the charge to spark across the gap, as expressed by the following equation:

$$C = \varepsilon_o \frac{A}{d}$$

If we fill the gap with oil, then we replace ε_o with $10\,\varepsilon_o$, which makes C effectively larger and allows even more charge to accumulate. This is seen by combining the preceding equations:

$$C = \frac{Q}{V} = K\varepsilon_0 \frac{A}{d}$$

or

$$Q = \left(K\varepsilon_0 \frac{A}{d}\right) V$$

The charge that accumulates creates a voltage, and the proportionality between these two $[K\varepsilon_0 (A/d)]$ depends on the material separating the conductors $(K\varepsilon_0)$ and the geometry of the capacitor (A/d).

How do we formulate the time it takes for the charge on one end of the capacitor to displace the charge on the other end? If we change Q, which we denote by ΔQ, over a short time Δt, then using the equation:

$$Q = CV$$

we write

$$\frac{\Delta Q}{\Delta t} = C \frac{\Delta V}{\Delta t}$$

If Δ is very small, then we replace it with the differential from calculus d and write

$$\text{(the current =)} \frac{dQ}{dt} = C \frac{dV}{dt} \text{ (capacitance times the changing voltage)}$$

d/dt is the operator describing the time rate of charge of Q, and we see from the preceding equation that the rate of charge of V is proportional to the rate of charge of Q. Because a charge moving in time is a current, we write

$$I = \frac{dQ}{dt}$$

Therefore:

$$I = C \frac{dV}{dt}$$

This is probably the most important equation in bioelectricity—and one of the most misleading. The current I in this equation is fundamentally different than, say, the current in Ohm's Law, $V = IR$, but we use the same symbol for the two, and they can be treated in the same way. However I in the preceding equation does not report the movement of charge through anything—only the displacement of charge.

(For a detailed discussion of capacitive current, see IMN, p. 65). To go more deeply into this matter, we rearrange the preceding equation:

$$dV = \frac{1}{C} I dt$$

and

$$\int dV = V = \frac{1}{C} \int I dt = DQ$$

We have already seen that:

$$\frac{dQ}{dt} = C \frac{dV}{dt}$$

is derived from the following (more or less a definition):

$$Q = CV$$

This means that the voltage generated is proportional to the amount of charge. Thus voltage is a derived quality from the one fundamental quantity, charge. (We already have seen that $V = DQ$, see p. 9.)

Suppose we add a charge to the capacitor linearly, that is we add Q in the first second, Q in the second second (so $2Q$ in 2 sec), etc. (see Fig. 1.10). We assume that at time $= 0$ there is no charge on the capacitor, and at time $= t$ we stop adding charge. What equation describes this? Since the graph in Fig. 1.10 has two natural parts, before and after t_1 (we ignore what happens before $t = 0$), then:

$$Q(t) = \left(\frac{Q_1}{t_1} \right) t \qquad\qquad 0 < t < t_1$$

$$Q(t) = \frac{Q_1}{t_1} \qquad\qquad t \geq t_1$$

Between $t = 0$ and $t = t_1$, the charge rises with constant slope (Q_1/t_1)—this depends on how rapidly we add charge per unit time; at $t = t_1$ and thereafter, no more charge is added and the amount remains the same.

Since $V = (1/C)Q$ this is exactly what the voltage does. Let us consider how Q changes in time. We can think of $Q(t)$ as the current through the capacitor (though we know better) and write once again:

$$I = \frac{dQ}{dt}$$

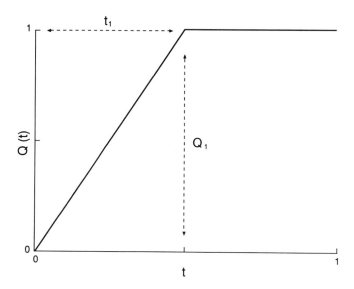

Figure 1.10. Charging curve of a capacitor

Therefore, as seen previously:

$$I = C \frac{dV}{dt}$$

Remember that equation $I = dQ/dt$ is general, but the particular form $I = C(dV/dt)$ is true only for a capacitor; therefore we call it I_c sometimes, but right now we call it I.

Then:

$$Q(t) = \left(\frac{Q_1}{t_1}\right)t \qquad I = \frac{Q_1}{t_1} \qquad 0 < t < t_1$$

$$Q(t) = Q_1 \qquad I = 0 \qquad t > t_1$$

Figure 1.11 shows $I(t)$. The constant *ramp* of Q in Fig. 1.10 gives a contact *value* of I in Fig. 1.11; when Q stops moving, the current goes to zero, as does dV/dt. The rule is that whatever Q does, V does, and whatever I does, dV/dt does.

Note: The equation relating the current through a capacitor and the voltage across can be reversed, that is

$$V = DQ$$

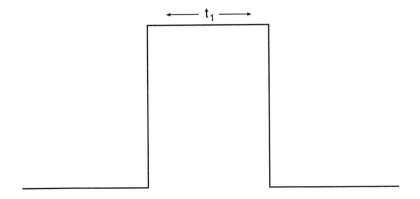

Figure 1.11. Current through a capacitor

yields

$$\frac{dV}{dt} = DI$$

We can imagine a certain (static) Q giving rise to a certain (static) V quite easily and that a changing Q (that is, I, the current) gives rise to a changing V (that is, dV/dt). But how does V generate Q and a changing V generate an I?

Batteries

To answer this question, we need a source of V, which is a battery. The symbol for a battery is the double bar, the long one for the plus (+) and the short one for the minus (−) side (see Fig. 1.12). The (−) ejects electrons and the (+) draws them in (IMN, p. 85). Note: The wires that connect elements (*horizontal lines* in Fig. 1.12) represent real wires meant to connect objects perfectly. Since a voltage follows every wire the voltage at every point along the wire is *exactly* (ideally) the same. Thus lines are ways of connecting voltages ideally.

In Fig. 1.13 a short wire with a dot at each end calls attention to the two parts of the circuit. We let the top part equal 1.2 V and we call the bottom part, which is connected to ground, zero. Remember that a voltage is always relative to something: $V = 1.2$ V is relative to ground. Note: We could also connect the two sides separately to ground, and there are other possibilities (see Fig. 1.22). In Fig. 1.13 the capacitor is said to be *charged*. The (−) and (+) signs are redundant, since the short and long bars of the battery already indicate sign. Let us calculate the charge Q on the capacitor C generated for voltage V:

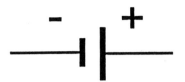

Figure 1.12. Equivalent circuit of a battery

$$Q = CV$$

EXAMPLE.   If $V = 1.2$ V (Note: We usually call a battery by its (+) name and let the diagram indicate which way it is placed.), $C = 1\ \mu F = 10^{-6}$ F, then:

$$Q = 10^{-6}\,(1.2)\ FV$$

$$= 1.2 \times 10^{-6}\ C$$

The coulomb (C) is the MKSA unit of charge; 1 C per second is 1 ampere (A), the A in MKSA. If we know that one electron has a charge:

$$e = 1.6 \times 10^{-19}\ C$$

Therefore:

$$Q/e = \frac{1.2 \times 10^{-6}\ C}{1.6 \times 10^{-19}\ C} = 0.75 \times 10^{13}$$

or 7,500,000,000,000 electrons. So 1.2 V places 7.5 trillion electrons on 1 μF.

Switches

We charge the capacitor by introducing a switch (see Fig. 1.14). Across the battery on the left, there is a voltage, but not across the capacitor; C is not really

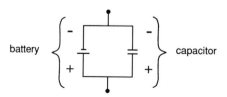

Figure 1.13. A battery and capacitor in parallel

connected to anything: One end is tied to ground, but the other is floating. The battery wants to push electrons from its (–) to its (+) end. If we close the switch, then electrons try to exit, but they run into an open space (or an insulator); that is they run into the capacitor. Thus there is a brief current in the wire from the battery to the capacitor, then things stop. Note: Electrons cannot escape through the ends with dots, since the dots are not connected to anything.

Figure 1.15 shows what happens to the voltage and current in time. At the beginning of our experiment, the switch is open, and at $t = t_1$ we close it. The voltage the capacitor *sees* (which is always in the battery) is called the voltage across C. The arrow represents a very large, brief current—sometimes called a *Dirac delta function* (δ; for a discussion of the Dirac delta function, see IMN, p. 63). We use this function because we assumed ideal conditions—the switch is infinitely rapid, so all the charge is transmitted in an infinitely short time, and the brief current is infinitely large.

To translate Fig. 1.15 into equations, we return to: $I = C(dV/dt)$ Recall that dV/dt is the *slope* of the charging $V(t)$, which at the ideal voltage step is vertical, i.e., infinite; so regardless of C, I is infinite too. We can actually write an equation for I in terms of the delta function. All you have to know is that $\delta(t)$ represents the function in general and $\delta(t-t_0)$ represents the function located at $t = t_0$ ($\delta(t)$ means located at $t = 0$, the origin). The units of the delta function are the inverse of its argument, in this case inverse time. Using this notation, no matter what x is, we can write:

$$\delta(x) \leftrightarrow \frac{1}{x}$$

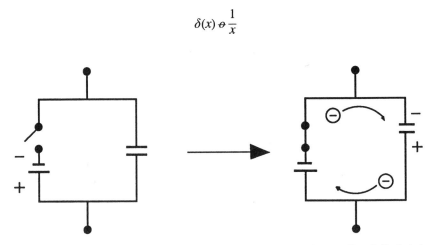

Figure 1.14. Closing a switch to charge the capacitor: Switch open, no electrons flow (left); Switch closed, electrons from the battery collect on the capacitor, forcing other electrons off the opposite plate that return to the battery (right).

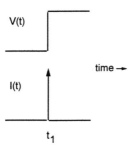

Figure 1.15. Step-voltage change leads to spike-current change: An instantaneous change in the voltage (top) corresponds to an infinitely brief current (bottom).

$$I = Q\,\delta(t - t_1)$$

which represents a sharp spike in current. Or we could write:

$$I = CV\,\delta(t - t_1)$$

We can give a value for $Q = CV$, but in this ideal world, δ is infinite so the product is too. We consider a more realistic case next.

Figure 1.16 shows a graded voltage switch. Using the capacitor equation for the current in the three regions:

$$I = C\frac{dV}{dt} = 0 \qquad\qquad t < t_0$$

$$I = C\frac{d}{dt}\left(\frac{t - t_0}{t_1 - t_0}\right)V_0 = \frac{CV_0}{t_1 - t_0} \qquad\qquad t_0 < t < t_1$$

$$I = C\frac{dV}{dt} = 0 \qquad\qquad t > t_1$$

Assume we have a function $f(x)$ with a peak at $x = a$. To move the curve just as it is to the right, we write $f(x - x_0)$, which means everywhere in the function that x appears, replace it with $x - x_0$, and the whole curve moves to the right by the amount x_0 (see Fig. 1.17). The rule works in reverse. To move the following equation to the *left* by the amount b:

$$f(x) = x^3 + \sin(x) - 3 + e^{-x}$$

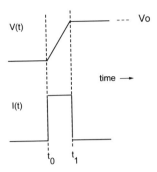

Figure 1.16. A graded switch produces a finite-width spike: A linearly graded change in the voltage (top) corresponds to a rectangular current pulse (bottom).

let $x \to x + b$ everywhere. Thus the left-shifted function is:

$$f(x + b) = (x + b)^3 + \sin(x + b) - 3 + e^{-(x+b)}$$

$f(x+b)$ looks exactly like $f(x)$, but it is located at $x = b$ units to the *left* (since we *added* b to x). We used this idea in Figure 1.16. We wrote, when we added Q to the capacitor (Fig. 1.10):

$$Q(t) = \frac{Q_1}{t_1} t$$

to describe charging a capacitor with a ramp. Now we have $V(t)$, not $f(x)$, but the ideas translate perfectly, thus $V(t)$ is "located" at t_0:

$$V(t) = \frac{V_0}{t_1 - t_0}(t - t_0) \qquad t_0 < t < t_1$$

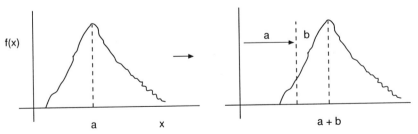

Figure 1.17. How to move a function $f(x)$ along the x-axis: A function of arbitrary shape "located" at position $x = a$ (left) moves without deformation to position $x = a + b$ (right), if we let $f(x) \to f(x - b)$.

Note: To think of t_0 as zero confuses matters in the general case. Watch out for zeros, which are also numbers; it is often better to include zeros than to omit them. Do not worry about what happens when $t < t_0$, i.e., do not try to use the formula:

$$V(t) = \frac{V_0(t - t_0)}{t_1 - t_0}$$

for $t < 0$; the formula is valid only in $t_0 < t < t_1$; before this time $V(t) = 0$. So we obtain a rectangular I for a ramp V; we would obtain another shape for $I(t)$ for another shape of $V(t)$.

Let us think about another way of rising to the value V_0, namely the shape shown in Fig. 1.18. Let $V_2(t)$ represent a yet unspecified function, with a break in the curve at t_0. For this situation:

$$V_1(t) = 0$$

$$V_2(t) = \text{whatever}$$

$$V_3(t) = V_0 \text{ (a constant)}$$

We can draw the following:

$$I_1(t) = C\frac{dV_1}{dt} = C\frac{d}{dt}(\text{zero}) = 0$$

$$I_2(t) = C\frac{dV_2}{dt} = \text{whatever the derivative is}$$

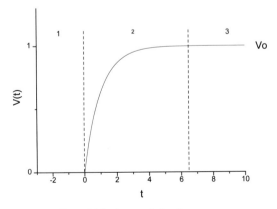

Figure 1.18. A general charging curve

$$I_3(t) = C \frac{d}{dt} (V_0 = \text{constant}) = 0$$

If $V_2(t)$ is a ramp, then $I_2(t)$ is a rectangle (Fig. 1.16), but other shapes yield other complementary shapes. We can almost guess the shape from Fig 1.18; since dV/dt is the slope, think of what the slope does: at first it is very sharp [$I(t)$ increases rapidly], then it tapers off [$I(t)$ decreases].

Let us ignore the possibility of a break between Region 2 and Region 3 in Fig. 1.18. We do this by considering the continuous function:

$$V_2(t) = V_0 \{1 - \exp[-(t - t_0)/\tau]\}$$

Note: Instead of writing $V_2(t - t_0)$ all the time, we write $V_2(t)$, which it is even though it shifted to the right from the special case $t_0 = 0$. Generally we write $V(t - t_0)$, etc., only to emphasize the shift. There is in effect no Region 3 now nor any break (unless you think of infinity), because $V_2(t)$ gradually rises to the value V_0. If $t = t_0$:

$$V_2(t) = V_0\{1 - \exp[-(t_0 - t_0)/\tau]\}$$

Therefore:

$$V_2(t) = V_0 (1 - 1) = 0$$

But at any other $t > t_0$ that is, in Region 2:

$$V(t) = V_0 - V_0 \exp[-(t - t_0)/\tau]$$

Thus think of Fig. 1.18 as the difference of two curves. We can imagine the function $V_0\exp-[(t - t_0/\tau)]$ as the shifted curve $V_0\exp(-t/\tau)$, which we have starting from the origin.

Let us use these ideas to find $I(t)$:

$$I_1 = C \frac{dV_1}{dt} = 0 \qquad \text{as before}$$

But:

$$I_2 = C \frac{d}{dt} (V_0\{1 - \exp[-(t - t_0)/\tau]\})$$

$$= CV_0 \frac{d}{dt} \{1 - \exp[-(t - t_0)/\tau]\}$$

Performing the indicated operation we obtain:

$$I_2 = CV_0 \exp[t_0/\tau][(1/\tau)\exp[-t/\tau]]$$

$$= \frac{CV_0}{\tau} \exp[-(t-t_0)/\tau]$$

We removed the constant factors from the operation (d/dt), used the notion that d/dt (constant) $= 0$ and the definition of an exponential:

$$\left(\frac{d}{dx}\right) e^{ax} = ae^{ax}$$

The slope of the exponential (that is, its derivative) is always proportional to its value, so the larger it is the faster it goes. (That is why we say numbers grow exponentially when we mean rapidly and in proportion to their size (see Appendix 4.) Note: The derivative rule takes care of the case when x has a factor, as seen above.

In math we often write e^x but do not specify x to make a general point. The x must be unitless; for example we cannot write e^t to mean $t =$ so many seconds, (t θ sec.) If $t = 5$ (no unit), then it is okay, but if $t = 1.37$ sec, then it is not. This is why we used τ in the following equation:

$$V_2(t) = V_0\{1 - \exp[-(t-t_0)/\tau]\}$$

Now τ θ sec, and it is the time constant of the rise (or the time constant of the fall if you look at 1 minus the exponent). Since t θ sec and $(t-t_0)$ θ sec, then the exponent (sometimes called the argument) in $exp[-(t-t_0)/\tau]$ is unitless, as required. In Region 2 in Fig. 1.18, voltage rises exponentially, and current falls exponentially. We have not yet said why voltage rises exponentially; we will come to that in Fig. 1.31.

In this analysis we used the equation:

$$\frac{d}{dx}(e^x) = e^x$$

where $e = 2.7182818\ldots$ is the only number for which this is true, i.e., the slope of the function e^x equals e^x itself at any x. Now e^x can rise more steeply (e.g., e^{6x}) or more gently ($e^{0.1x}$); see Fig. 1.19. In general, as seen above:

$$\frac{d}{dx} e^{ax} = ae^x$$

Another way of changing the rate of climb is to change the number being raised to the power. Thus 10^x rises more steeply than e^x, and 2^x rises more gently. In general for $N =$ any number and $x =$ any number:

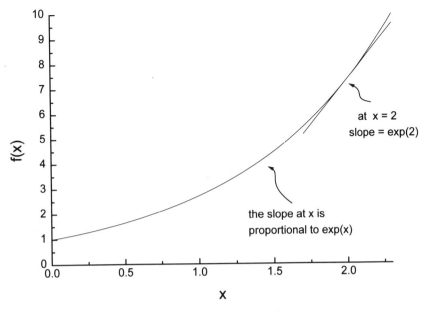

Figure 1.19. Function $f(x) = e^x$

$$\frac{d}{dx} N^x = N^x \ln N$$

Until how we had a simple circuit (see Fig. 1.14) consisting of a switch, a battery (that provides V), and a capacitor. We introduced a switch that lets C see V gradually (Fig. 1.16) rather than all at once (Fig. 1.15). If we close the switch in Fig. 1.14 at once, current flashes through C; if we close it gradually (say, exponentially, but any shape), then the current through C is a blip. We can introduce a *finite conductor* into the circuit to assist us in the analysis of this problem.

Conductors

What do we mean by finite conductor? We have been using infinite (i.e., perfect) conductors (the wires drawn between circuit electrodes). They cannot be real because if the voltage is the same everywhere along a wire, there is no voltage difference between them, so there is no force to move electrons from A to B. Secondly how could we have a perfect conductor? Superconduction does not exist under ordinary conditions for ordinary materials. So these wires are a fiction. They represent a point.

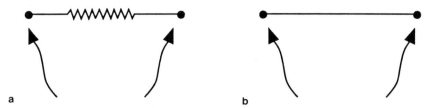

Figure 1.20. Real conductors: (a) voltage is different at these two points (when current flows); (b) voltage is always the same at these two points.

Real wires and other real conductors (salt solutions, for our purposes) have finite conductances. We draw these as squiggle lines instead of straight lines to indicate resistance (see Fig. 1.20). There is no special symbol for conductors (G) versus resistors (R), so we use the left-hand symbol in Fig. 1.20 for both even though one is the inverse of the other.

Let us recall that:

$$Q = CV$$

This equation states that the separation of charge Q (between any two points A and B, e.g., the plates of the capacitor) is proportional to the voltage (across the plates). The analogous equation for resistance is:

$$I = GV$$

This equation states that the flow of current (between A and B) is proportional to the voltage (between A and B); G, conductance, is the proportionality constant. Both equations work in the opposite sense. Just as we can think of Q as creating a V—or V as creating a Q, so too can we think of I as creating a V—or V as creating an I. If we force a current onto a capacitor (at a rate of Q charges per unit time), then there is a voltage across it. But what voltage? Where does it come from? Let us add (+) charges onto the conductor, as we did for capacitors but using the opposite sign (see Fig. 1.9) to see what happens. By convention current always goes from (+) to (−), therefore the voltage is as shown in Fig. 1.21. The voltage across is such that the top of the conductor is (+) and the bottom is (−). If we used (−) electrons, then the signs would be reversed, and the current arrow would point up. In Figure 1.21 the (−) side is connected to ground to give the (+) charges somewhere to go; the ground symbol is also used at the bottom. The *sign* of the voltage is *caused* by the current, but how large is the voltage? If we add so much Q per second and we know G, then we know I and the generated voltage (i.e., the V produced by the current flow):

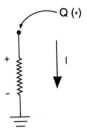

Figure 1.21. Conductor sign convention

$$V = \frac{I}{G}$$

If we call $(1/G) = R$, the resistance, then this is the familiar Ohm's law:

$$V = IR$$

But we added a twist: V created by an I, and we can also have an I created by a V. To discuss this we refer to the battery again and different ways of drawing the circuit (see Fig. 1.22). Current flowing around the loop (because of the impetus the battery V provides) is still $I = GV$. Note: We say loop (on the left-hand side of Fig. 1.22), so we really do not have to draw the ground. If we draw a simple element, such as a conductor, we must draw the ground so that the current has some place to go (Fig. 1.21). All the drawings in Fig. 1.22 are therefore equal: In an open circuit, no current can flow. (There are important exceptions; for example a local current can exist within G itself. This gives rise to Johnson noise; For more on this topic, see IMN p. 234.)

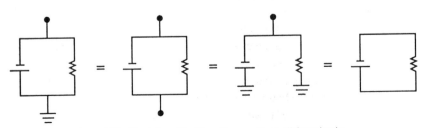

Figure 1.22. Ohm's law: $V = IR$ applies equally to all four circuits.

Comparing Capacitors and Conductors

Let us combine the following equations for capacitors and resistors.

Capacitors $Q = CV$ $V = DQ$

Conductors $I = GV$ $V = RI$

Note: We wrote $V = DQ$ for a capacitor even though the variable $D = 1/C$ is never used and is unnamed, and we wrote $V = RI$ for Ohm's law to emphasize that R is the proportionality constant between the two variables, just like the proportionally constants in the other equations. Because we usually do not work with Q but with I, we can take $dQ/dt = I$ and write

Capacitors $I = C\dfrac{dV}{dt}$ $\dfrac{dV}{dt} = DI$

Conductors $I = GV$ $V = RI$

Now everything is expressed in terms of I, V, and dV/dt. To obtain an I in capacitors, we need a changing V, but an I also causes a changing V. Likewise to obtain an I in resistors, we need V (even a steady V will do), but an I (even a steady one) also causes a V. In resistors I follows V exactly, but in capacitors, I follows dV/dt exactly.

To express the rules for Cs and Gs in terms of I and V only, i.e., not dV/dt, we solve the following equation for V:

$$\frac{dV}{dt} = DI$$

The answer is simple, symbolically at least:

$$V = D \int I dt$$

We can summarize the comparison of capacitors and resistors in the following way:

Capacitors $\int I dt = CV$ $V = D \int I dt$

Conductors $I = GV$ $V = RI$

We have replaced differentials with integrals so that our equations are given in terms of I and V.

Differential equations like $dV/dt = DI$ always have integral forms like $V = D\int I dt$, but what does the latter mean? Let us consider the expression for voltage across a capacitor for a given current through it. We force a constant current through C (see Fig. 1.23); now we want to find $V(t)$. According to the equation:

$$V(t) = D \int_0^{t_1} I_0 \, dt$$

where t_1 is the time we have waited so far. Note: $I(t) = I_0$, a constant, and the integral sign has limits, that is we are integrating from $t = 0$ to $t = t_1$. Since I_0 is constant, it comes out of the integral; therefore:

$$V(t) = D I_0 \int_0^{t_1} dt$$

$$V(t) = D I_0 \, [t]_0^{t_1} = D I_0 \, (t_1 - 0)$$

or

$$V(t) = D I_0 t_1$$

Recall that the antiderivative of the integrand is in brackets ([ ]); i.e., we ask

$$d[?] = dt \qquad \text{or} \qquad \frac{d}{dt}[?] = 1$$

The answer is $? = t$ in this case. In general we can write for any t:

$$V(t) = D \int_0^t I_0 \, dt$$

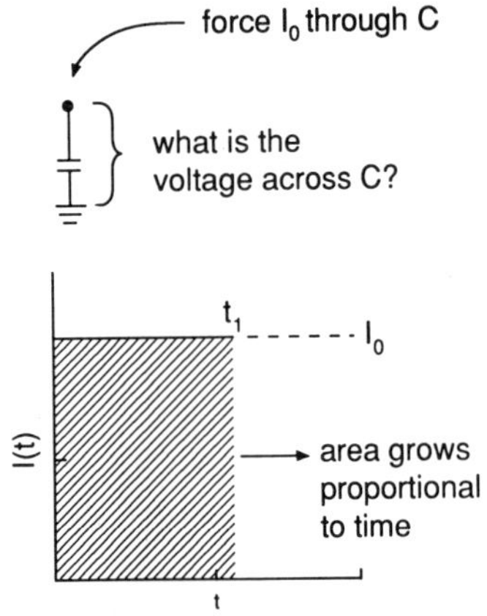

Figure 1.23. Constant current through a capacitor

Note: $I(t) = I_0$ = constant, and the limits of the integral range from $t = 0$ to $t = t$, that is to some *general* value of t (which we think of as a variable). Formally we had

$$V(t) = DI_0 \int_0^t dt = DI_0 \, [t]_0^t = DI_0 \, (t - 0)$$

or

$$V(t) = DI_0 t$$

This looks like a voltage ramp (see Fig. 1.16). So $V(t)$ is not constant but increases continually with t, because in general:

$$\int I(t)dt = \text{area under } I(t)$$

In this case $I(t) = I_0$, as time increases, the area increases proportionally.

We can check the reverse situation. Suppose we *forced* $V(t)$ to be a ramp. Going back to the differential form of the rule:

$$V(t) = V_0 t \qquad \text{(a ramp)}$$

then:

$$I(t) = C \frac{dV}{dt} = CV_0 \qquad \text{(a constant)}$$

If we identify CV_0 with I_0, we can go back and forth. It is easy with ramps, but what about more complicated wave forms? Let us try gradually increasing $I(t)$ (see Fig. 1.24):

$$I(t) = I_0 \, (1 - e^{-t/\tau})$$

In Fig. 1.24 the area again grows proportional to time; notice that the area grows rapidly at first, then more slowly. We can find out what the area, i.e., $V(t)$, is going to do by the equation:

$$V(t) = DI_0 \int_0^t (1 - e^{-t/\tau})dt$$

$$= DI_0 \int_0^t dt - D \int_0^t e^{-t/\tau}dt$$

We already know the first part of this equation; for the second part, we need:

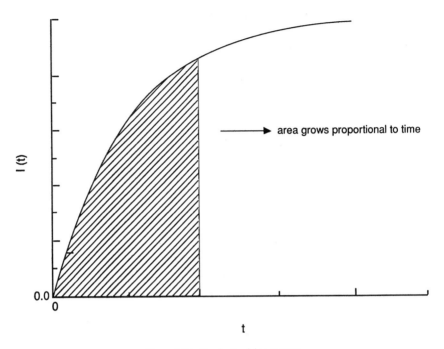

Figure 1.24. Gradually rising current

$$\int_0^t e^{-t/\tau} dt = [-\tau e^{-t/\tau}]_0^t$$

because:

$$\frac{d}{dt}[-\tau e^{-t/\tau}] = -\tau\left(-\frac{1}{\tau}\right)e^{-t/\tau} = e^{-t/\tau}$$

(Watch the minus signs.) Combining the two parts of the equation, we have

$$V(t) = DI_0 t - DI_0[-\tau e^{-t/\tau}]_0^t$$

$$= DI_0 t - DI_0 \tau(1 - e^{-t/\tau})$$

Note: Anything raised to the zero power is one. The graph of this equation has two parts: $DI_0 t$ and $DI_0 \tau(1 - e^{-t/\tau})$; the solid line shown in Fig. 1.25 is the difference between them. This means that if the current through C rises gradually, the voltage

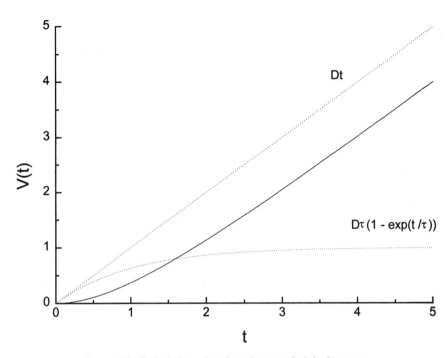

Figure 1.25. Gradual change in voltage due to gradual rise in current

across C starts to grow slowly, then picks up as I flattens out. Looking at the $I(t)$ graph, this makes sense—just think of adding areas for equal Δts.

Let us consider what happens when t becomes large:

$$I(t) = I_0(1 - e^{-t/\tau}) \rightarrow I_0$$

and

$$V(t) = DI_0 t - DI_0 \tau (1 - e^{-t/\tau})$$

$$\rightarrow DI_0(t - \tau)$$

At large values of t, $V(t)$ looks just like the curve Dt shifted to the right by τ, that is everywhere that t appears (as $t \rightarrow \infty$), we now have $t - \tau$ (see Fig. 1.17).

Suppose $I(t)$ decreases. Let:

$$I(t) = I_0 e^{-t/\tau}$$

Then

$$V(t) = D\int_0^t I_0\, e^{-t/\tau}\, dt$$

$$= DI_0[-\tau e^{-t/\tau}]_0^t$$

or

$$V(t) = DI_0\tau\,(1 - e^{-t/\tau})$$

We already know what this curve looks like. So as $I(t)$ decreases, $V(t)$s gain also decreases: For equal times, the bits of area we add are smaller and smaller. Even if we do not know the equation for $I(t)$, we can do the problem graphically (in other words, by computer). Even though $I(t)$ goes up and *down*, $V(t)$ goes up and *up*—only how fast it does so changes. The only way for $V(t)$ to decrease, is for $I(t)$ to become negative (see Fig. 1.26). The slope of V depends on whether I is negative or positive; if there is no change in I, then V stops whatever it was doing.

So far we have been forcing I through or V across a capacitor without saying how. Let us return to a specific model where all the elements are defined (see Fig. 1.27). The switch is all-or-none, and the conductor G and capacitor C obey the rules we have discussed. Note: E represents battery; when there was no G in the circuit, the voltage V of the battery appeared across C when the switch was closed. Now when we close the switch, electrons that move up through G generate a voltage

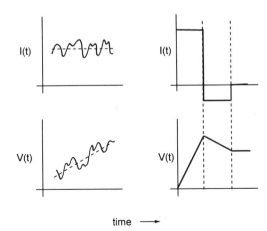

time

Figure 1.26. Voltage and current changes in a capacitor

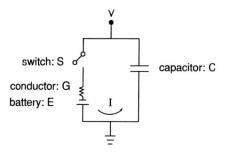

Figure 1.27. An equivalent circuit: Switch opens and closes

across G (sometimes called a voltage drop, but it can be a voltage rise too depending on direction Fig 1.21). Let us close the switch, give battery E a chance to work, and reserve the symbol V for voltage across the capacitor. Now when we draw the voltage V, we always mean with respect to ground. We must specify where the voltage is across, as we did with brackets in some diagrams. Remember: A voltage always needs two places to define it; when we show only one, the other is understood to be ground.

What is the voltage V across C when we close the switch? Let us think about what happens. Immediately electrons start to flow upward from the top of the battery E toward G. Think of the voltage below G in Fig. 1.27 as E; the voltage above G is V by the rule of wires. Even though we do not yet know what V is, we can use it symbolically in an expression for the current. Until now we have been careless about the *sign* of the current, but from now on we must be careful. Since by convention electrons are thought of as $(-)$, how they move is thought of as minus (i.e., $-I$); that is if we draw only the left branch of the circuit we are working on, then we draw the arrow pointing up to indicate that electrons are moving upward. Note: Another way of seeing this is to think of $+I$ as the direction of $+$ charges. This is just a definition. The $(+)$s and $(-)$s do not mean anything by themselves. All this becomes more important later when we deal with ions, which are $+$, $-$, and even $++$.

In a circuit there is no place for electrons to go except where we say they can. In Fig. 1.27 electrons must go up and around; they cannot escape at the top, because the top is not connected to anything. After they pass through C (by displacement), they go to ground, as drawn, but we could draw a loop just as well, as in Fig. 1.22. Then the electrons would return to the other side of the battery. The point is what goes through G must go through C. We need equations in V for both currents, set them equal, and solve for V. Since in Fig. 1.27, the voltage on the *low (bottom)* side of G is E and the voltage on the *high (top)* side of G is V, we write

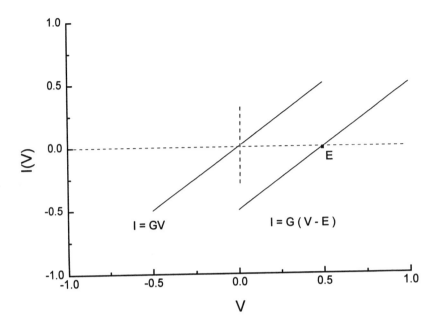

Figure 1.28. Shift theorem for current voltage curves

$$-I_G = G(E - V)$$

Note: If we wrote $I = G(V - E)$, which is exactly the same, we see that this is the rule for shifting to the right by E (see Fig. 1.28). [If you are accustomed to ion currents in membranes, $I = G(V - E)$ should look familiar.] Here we regard I as a function of V, that is $I = I(V)$, and also as a function of $V - E$, $I = I(V - E)$, as the shifted $I(V)$. Note: These last two equations illustrate the use of parentheses to mean *function of* as well as multiplication. In Fig. 1.28 the ( ) indicates multiplication, but in $I(V)$ the ( ) means function of. The shift theorem works for any function (Fig. 1.17). Fig. 1.28 illustrates shifting a straight line.

First-Order Differential Equations

In Fig. 1.27 the current through C is given by:

$$-I_C = C \frac{dV}{dt}$$

and $-I_G = -I_C$:

$$G(E - V) = C \frac{dV}{dt}$$

Now we have to solve this equation for V, which we think of as a function of time $V(t)$. Combining terms with the unknown V and moving them to the left yields:

$$C \frac{dV}{dt} + GV = GE$$

The V in this equation is the same V, that is the one at the top plate of the capacitor and at the top point of the conductor; it is also the one at the dot at the top of the circuit (see Fig. 1.27). Recall the rule of wires: Wherever the wire goes, the voltage goes too.

To solve the preceding equation, first divide both sides by C:

$$\frac{dV}{dt} + \frac{V}{C/G} = \frac{E}{C/G}$$

By inspection the units of C/G have to be time. Note: These are the same units as dt in the first term; the ds are unitless; since dV, V, and E are all measured in volts, then dt and G/C must all have the units of time. We can also see this directly from the definitions of G and C: We know that $G = I/V$ and $C = I/(dV/dt)$; therefore:

$$\frac{C}{G} \, \theta \, \frac{\text{amps}/(\text{volts}/\text{time})}{\text{amps}/\text{volts}} \, \theta \, \text{time}$$

Let $C/G = \tau$, a time constant. (We used τ before to represent a general time constant; now we mean something specific for this circuit.) Depending on what C and G are, so many farads and so many siemans, then C/G equals so many seconds. We can write:

$$\frac{dV}{dt} + \frac{V}{\tau} = \frac{E}{\tau}$$

If we consider:

$$\frac{d}{dt}(Ve^{t/\tau})$$

then use the rule that the derivative of a product is the first times the derivative of the second plus the second times the derivative of the first, then:

$$\frac{d}{dt}(Ve^{t/\tau}) = V\left(\frac{1}{\tau} e^{t/\tau}\right) + (e^{t/\tau}) \frac{dV}{dt}$$

This is almost the same as the left-hand side of the equation we want to solve. All we have to do is multiply by $e^{-t/\tau}$:

$$e^{-t/\tau} \frac{d}{dt}(Ve^{t/\tau}) = \frac{V}{\tau} + \frac{dV}{dt}$$

But the right-hand side just equals E/τ, so we can now write

$$e^{-t/\tau} \frac{d}{dt}(Ve^{t/\tau}) = \frac{E}{\tau}$$

or

$$\frac{d}{dt}(Ve^{t/\tau}) = \frac{E}{\tau}e^{t/\tau}$$

$$d(Ve^{t/\tau}) = \frac{E}{\tau}e^{t/\tau}dt$$

Integrating from 0 to t over both sides:

$$\int_0^t d(Ve^{t/\tau}) = \int_0^t \frac{E}{\tau}e^{t/\tau}dt$$

We rearranged the original equation to obtain a familiar form. By definition:

$$\int_0^t d(Ve^{t/\tau}) = V(t)e^{t/\tau} - V(0)$$

Note: The answer to the question $d(?)$ is contained in the ( ) because we arranged terms. To evaluate the integral, we substitute t and 0 for t, then subtract the two terms. The right-hand side of the equation is more complicated: first factor out E/τ because it is a constant. Then work on:

$$\int_0^t e^{t/\tau}dt$$

Thus we need the antiderivative:

$$\frac{d}{dt}[?] = e^{t/\tau}$$

But that is $\tau e^{t/\tau}$; therefore:

$$\int\limits_{0}^{t} e^{t/\tau} dt = [\tau e^{t/\tau}]_{0}^{t}$$

$$= \tau(e^{t/\tau} - 1)$$

Combining we have:

$$V(t)e^{t/\tau} - V(0) = \frac{E}{\tau}[t(e^{t/\tau} - 1)]$$

Solving for $V(t)$:

$$V(t) = V(0)e^{-t/\tau} + E(1 - e^{-t/\tau})$$

Note: We multiplied both sides of the equation by $e^{-t/\tau}$ to cancel the $e^{t/\tau}$ in the $V(t)$ term, then solved for $V(t)$. In summary if we close the switch in this circuit (see Fig. 1.29), then $V(t)$ changes according to the preceding equation. Closing the switch means that the voltage E appears all at once at G; it does not rise slowly, it is a step change. And our solution $V(t) = ...$ is true *only* for a step change in E. In this case E always exists, but we made it into a step by the switch. (For techniques to solve for $V(t)$ in the case of arbitrary changes, see IMN, p. 361). What does this equation mean? Let us discuss it term by term: In $V(0)e^{-t/\tau}$, $V(0)$ is the voltage that exists at $t = 0$, which means that if some voltage exists before we close the switch, then that voltage dies according to $e^{-t/\tau}$; Fig. 1.30 illustrates this. The $E(1 - e^{-t/\tau}) = E - Ee^{-t/\tau}$ means that at $t = 0$, voltage begins to rise to a new level E according to $(1 - e^{-t/\tau})$. We combine these two parts in Fig. 1.31. We indicated that before $t = 0$, some voltage $V(0)$ exits, then we close the switch, G sees E instantly, and the voltage V starts to rise across C like the solid line. Here *both* dotted lines,

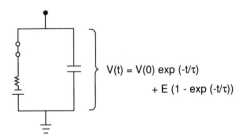

Figure 1.29. Closing the switch on an RC circuit

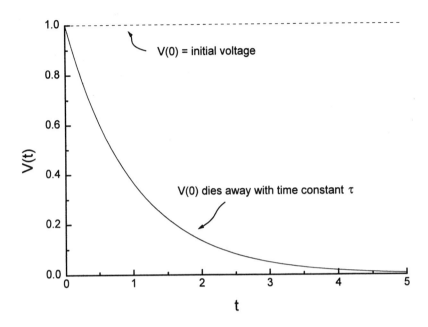

Figure 1.30. Exponential voltage decay

which represent the two terms of the equation, have the same time constant τ; it is a fixed parameter of the circuit, C/G.

An initial nonzero voltage means that there was some Q on C before we began. That is possible of course, but up to now we have not thought much about it. So $V(0)$ could be zero, and if so then the equation for $V(t)$ is simpler. What happens when there is so much charge on C that its initial voltage is larger than E? In other words:

$$V(0) = \frac{Q}{C} > E$$

In this case $V(t)$ actually drops, not rises [see Fig. 1.31, where $V(0) < E$]. When the switch closes, the voltage $V(t)$ can increase or decrease from any value, depending on initial conditions, i.e., on $V(0)$, which means on the amount of Q on C. Note: Do not forget the sign. There is an initial positive charge on C [so $V(0)$ is positive], but it could have been the other way around: I.e., the bold line in Fig. 1.31 could have *decayed* instead of risen, depending on the relative size of $V(0)$ and E.

It sometimes helps to redraw the circuit to see the step in E in a different way; this is illustrated in Fig. 1.32, where $E(t)$ is the input voltage and $V(t)$ is the output

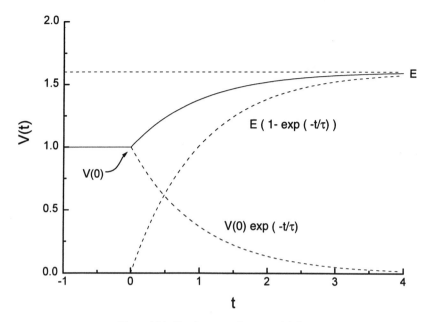

Figure 1.31. Steady-state and exponential rise

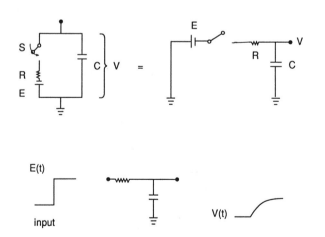

Figure 1.32. The RC circuit as input–output relations. Top: Parallel RC network redrawn to emphasize input–output; Bottom: A step change in voltage $E(t)$ as an input to an RC circuit gives an exponentially rising $V(t)$ as an output of the circuit.

voltage. Note: We moved the switch to the other side of the resistor so it looks like it controls the battery. That is a legitimate move in circuits. Figure 1.32 shows three different ways of looking at the same thing.

Having solved this problem, we can use the solution in different cases. Writing the switch–battery combination as a step input has some advantage, because we can think of $E(t)$ as any function of t, not just a step. As before the equation for the circuit becomes:

$$G(E - V) = C \frac{dV}{dt}$$

and (we skip some steps that we just completed):

$$d(Ve^{t/\tau}) = \frac{E}{\tau} e^{t/\tau} dt$$

when $\tau = C/G$. Now $E = E(t)$ is a general function of time; therefore when we integrate both sides of the equation, E cannot be placed outside of the integrand as a constant as it did before for the step; it has to stay within the integrand; therefore:

$$\int_0^t d(Ve^{t/\tau}) = \frac{1}{\tau} \int_0^t E(t)e^{t/\tau} dt$$

We have shown the exponential dependence of V and E on t. The solution is then:

$$V(t)\, e^{t/\tau} - V(0) = \frac{1}{\tau} \int_0^t E(t)\, e^{t/\tau} dt$$

or

$$V(t) = V(0)\, e^{-t/\tau} + \frac{e^{-t/\tau}}{\tau} \int_0^t E(t)\, e^{t/\tau} dt$$

If we know $E(t)$, we know $V(t)$. We have to calculate the integral:

$$\int_0^t E(t)\, e^{t/\tau} dt$$

then substitute into the formula for $V(t)$. If $E(t) = E$ (a constant), then we have the old answer, but if $E(t) = E \sin(\omega t)$ for example, then we have some work to do.

Let us consider one more easy case. Suppose $E(t) = \tau E\,\delta(t - t_0)$, that is the voltage input is a sharp spike of potential, in fact infinitely sharp, as expressed by the delta function located at $t = t_0$. Then we must calculate

$$\int_0^t \tau E\delta(t - t_0)e^{t/\tau}dt = E\tau \int_0^t \delta(t - t_0)e^{t/\tau}dt$$

To do this let us consider the graph of two functions in the integrand (see Fig. 1.33), i.e., $f(t) = \delta(t - t_0)$ and $f(t) = \exp(t/\tau)$. Since $\delta(t - t_0)$ is zero everywhere except at t

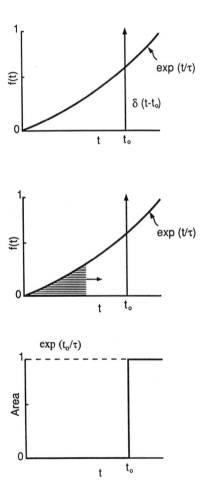

Figure 1.33. Graphic view of the delta function solution. Top: The two functions of the integrand; Middle: The shaded region represents integration; Bottom: The result of the integration.

$= t_0$, when we multiply these there is nothing left of $e^{t/\tau}$ except at $t = t_0$. First we integrate this function over all time from $0 \rightarrow t$; then:

$$\int_0^t \delta(t - t_0)e^{t'/\tau}dt = \exp(t_0/\tau)$$

This is a pure number; for example if $t_0 = 0.5$ sec and $C/G = 3$ sec, then $e^{1/6}$ is that number. What about $\int_0^t dt$? We want a function, not a number. Let us think graphically again. We want the area of this *product* (we show a finite, shaded region because otherwise there would be nothing to see) as t moves to the right (see Fig. 1.33 because we have zero up to t_0, then we have $e^{t_0/\tau}$, a number, which remains constant because integration after t_0 gives zero. We need a name and a symbol for this step function; it is $H(t - t_0)$, the Heaviside function (see IMN, p. 68). Using the H function we write somewhat formally:

$$\int_0^t \delta(t - t_0)\, e^{t/\tau}\, dt = H(t - t_0)e^{(t_0/\tau)}$$

This rule works for any function (not just $e^{t/\tau}$) that appears in the integrand. Assume there is no charge on C at $t = 0$, i.e., $V(0) = 0$, then if:

$$E(t) = \tau E \delta(t - t_0)$$

We obtain

$$V(t) = EH(t - t_0)e^{-(t - t_0)/\tau}$$

We normally express this as:

$$V(t) = Ee^{-(t - t_0)/\tau}$$

Therefore if we add a spike (of size E) at $t = t_0$, we obtain a decaying exponential at $t = t_0$ (see Fig. 1.34).

Now that we have established the response of a single circuit to a delta function, we ask how to generate one. This is accomplished by closing and opening the switch rapidly. This must be done *very* rapidly to obtain a true delta function, but we can idealize the motion. Note: In this idealization the size of the delta function is $E\tau_0$, not E, and we write $E\tau_0\delta(t - t_0)$ to indicate that the spike occurs at $t = t_0$. If the opening and closing is finite, then we have the progression illustrated in Fig. 1.35.

In all cases—finite and infinitely narrow—the area under the function is $E\tau_0$. In the preceding problem we close $\tau_0 = \tau$, but that does not have to be the case.

Let us review the procedure we used for the step function.

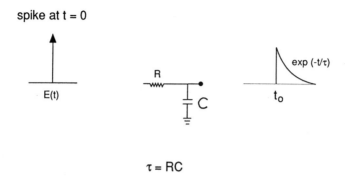

τ = RC

Figure 1.34. Input–output relation for a spike

1. We started with the circuit in Fig. 1.32.
2. We recognized that the solution for $V(t)$ was general for any $E(t)$.
3. We let $E(t)$ be a delta function.
4. We put the delta function in the circuit as a switch.
5. If S is closed briefly, the (S, E) combination is a brief pulse, and the voltage response across C is a decaying exponential.
6. If S opens and closes finitely, the response is a gradual rise and decline.
7. If we replace the (S, E) combination in our circuit with any $E(t)$, we can write an equation for $V(t)$. Therefore we think of (S, E) as the source, or stimulus, and the voltage across C, which is $V(t)$, as the response.

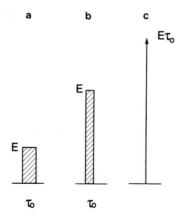

Figure 1.35. Real switch: (a) real, (b) more real, (c) ideal

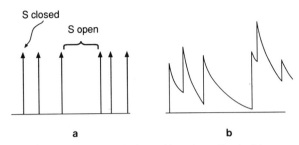

Figure 1.36. Random spikes as the input: (a) random spikes in, (b) response out

If S is a random switch (opens and closes randomly), what does V look like? Case 1: Assume S is open for random lengths of time, then closes briefly (see Fig. 1.36). Each little pulse gives a decaying exponential that starts at the pulse, then decays with a certain time constant τ. If the pulse is *infinitely* narrow, then τ reflects *only* the properties of the circuit (G and C); however if the pulse has any width at all, then the response reflects that too. The decay constant is purely $\tau = C/G$ only for a delta function. Note: In Fig. 1.36 two pulses come so close together that before one response decays, there is another pulse. Thus the two responses overlap and accumulate. This happens with Pulses 1 and 2, and it really happens with Pulses 4 and 5.

Case 2: Assume S is a switch that operates randomly but stays *open and closed* for random times (see Fig. 1.37). This of course is channel-like behavior. It is a little more complicated than a string of delta functions, but it is still straightforward. If the switch is open long enough compared to $\tau = C/G$, then the output reaches some flat plateau. If it is opened too briefly, then the voltage cannot rise to the top before it closes again—so the response is not so high as the others. As before two responses can overlap and accumulate. We return to this simple idea over and over, because it is the basis of excitability.

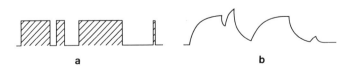

Figure 1.37. Random boxes as the input: (a) input, (b) output

2

Bioelectricity

Introduction

What does all of this have to do with bioelectricity? The answer is just about everything. From these few basic principles, we can derive almost all of the electrical properties of cells. Let us start with *resting potential*. Everyone knows that the inside of the cell is about -100 mV with respect to the outside (some cells, for example certain oocytes, have potentials that are much less: -10 mV). Historically the first cells measured had potentials in the -60 to -100 mV range.

We assume a cell has two parts, an inside compartment and a membrane, and that the cell floats in some outside medium, which is the third part of our system. Physically what are these three regions? The volume represented by Region 2 on Fig. 2.1 is the cytoplasmic fluid. Basically it is salt water, but not a simple salt solution, since the cell contains organelles and macromolecules. For now we assume that the volume of Region 2 is a salt water solution as is the volume of Region 1, the fluid outside the cell. The volume of Region 3 represents the very thin membrane that separates these two fluids; it is essentially a double layer of lipid molecules that does not allow any (that is, many) salt ions to enter. So we basically have two salt solutions separated by a thin lipid membrane; that is we have two conductors separated by an insulator. This is the definition of a capacitor—like our twisted wires (see Fig. 1.8). A capacitor need not be an excellent conductor or a perfect insulator (see Fig. 2.1). A salt solution is no where near so good a conductor of ions as a wire is of electrons, but it is better than the lipid.

We redraw the cell in Fig. 2.2 to show that the two salt solutions are electroneutral. Salt water by itself does not have an excess charge. If we look at the volume of Region 1 or 2, there are as many (+)s as (−)s. In a restricted volume, (+) and (−) charges are about equal, at least on average (see IMN, p. 33, for a discussion of ions moving in salt water). If there is a voltage difference between Regions 2 and 1 (as we said there was), then there must be a separation of charge. Since we stated that the cell is negative inside with respect to the outside, there must be more (−) charge

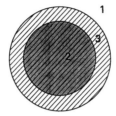

Figure 2.1. Compartmental model of a cell

on the inside. Where did this excess (−) come from, where is it located, and how much is there? We must answer these questions to understand the resting potential.

We said that the cell has a voltage across the membrane, so there must be a separation of charge, but the salt solutions in Regions 2 and 1 do not have excess charge. Conductors *can* have an excess charge—like the van de Graaff machine Fig. 1.1—but they do not want to, so they eliminate it if they can.

Let us assume that a hole in the membrane allows only (+)s to pass through (see IMN, p. 36). We also assume that the salt concentration outside is a lot weaker than inside, as in Fig. 2.3. Note: We indicate imbalance in the salt solution by adding (+)s and (−)s inside in Fig. 2.3. Both sides still have an equal numbers of the two charges, but the inside has more of both.

We know that objects move from concentrated to less concentrated, so the (−)s and (+)s inside try to pass though the hole to the outside. When the (+) near the hole passes through, there is a charge imbalance: 3 (+)s and 4 (−)s on the inside and 2(+)s and 1(−) on the outside. This indicates a separation of charge, so there must be voltage. The voltage sign must be negative on the inside, since there are more (−)s on the inside. Since there are still more (+) and (−) inside than outside, they want to move. However *after the first one moves*, the situation changes, so there is a reason for the (+)s to move (there are more of them) and a reason *not* to move: In summary, the (+) leaves behind an excess (−) that tries to draw back the (+). The

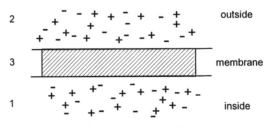

Figure 2.2. Electroneutrality

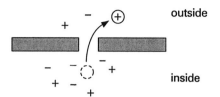

Figure 2.3. A selective hole

first (+) wants to pass through (and does) because there are more (+)s inside, but the second (+) cannot because the first one set up an opposing electrical force. To create a stable potential we need:

- Two salt solutions separated by a nonconducting membrane
- A stronger salt on one side
- A hole that lets only positive ions pass

The side with more (−) charge has a negative potential, so the side with the stronger solution is negative with regard to the other side. Note: If the hole let through (−)s and not (+)s, the opposite would be true. The cell we built has a negative resting potential due to the ion concentrations in the volume of the two regions (higher inside) and the hole connecting them which lets only (+) through.

Diffusion

But how much (+) charge actually moves? How large is the potential? To answer these questions, we need more information. A charge's desire to move does not depend on being (+) or (−); it is a property of number and thermal agitation (see ICEMb, p. 263): Particles are always moving at any temperature except absolute zero (there are some odd zero-point energies, but that is another issue). Basically there is no motion at $T = 0$ (−273 °C). At $T = 300$ °K all the molecules in a perfume bottle are moving around rapidly, and some come out, as indicated in Fig. 2.4. Most of them bounce off the walls of the bottle, but some probe the opening, and finding no barrier, they escape. If we heat up the liquid, molecules become more active, and more escape. Once in the air, the molecules continue probing their surroundings, left and right, up and down, in every direction.

What causes diffusion? Consider an abstract case of N particles near an imaginary interface (the dotted line in Fig. 2.5), with no particles on the other side. We do not want the particles to be charged, so that it is clear that electrical forces do not enter into diffusion (IMN, p. 33); therefore we draw the particles as dots without (+)s or (−)s. How many of the N particles escape is a statistical question.

Figure 2.4. Diffusion

Imagine that the number of dots extends to the left a long way, so the dots go only to the right: the *average* drift.

To gain insight into diffusion, consider the following problem. Suppose we have two concentrations a and b of some diffusable substance. Assume that a and b are kept constant at places far from a barrier that has a hole in it. The two concentrations mingle in the hole, then form a new concentration (IMN, p. 46). We can think of this as an average of a and b. If diffusion is the process, the average concentration in the whole is:

$$\text{Average diffusional concentration} = \frac{(a - b)}{\ln (a/b)}$$

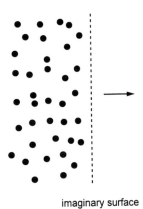

imaginary surface

Figure 2.5. N particles near an interface

This is a number between *a* and *b*, but it is not the usual average we think of (see Appendix 3).

Let us discuss the potential energy (PE) of a particle in the group of particles. What is the PE of this particle due to diffusion? It is proportional to the temperature of the group of *N* particles (and any one of them—we can think of *the* particle we selected as having that temperature); then the PE is

$$PE \propto T \quad \text{(right)}$$

If $T = 600$ °K, not 300 °K, the PE due to diffusion is twice as large.

The PE is proportional to the *number* of particles in the same set as the one we are considering, but if we try to write a proportionality like the one we made for temperature, we would be wrong:

$$PE \propto N \quad \text{(wrong)}$$

The PE increases as *N* increases, but it is not a simple proportionality as with *T*: *T* = 0 gives PE = 0, but *N* = 1 gives PE = 0. In other words if we have *N* particles at *T* = 0, the diffusional PE for one of them is zero. However we cannot say that we have *N* particles at $N = 0$ and find what the diffusional PE for one of them. We want the diffusional PE for $N = 1$ to be zero. We do this by letting *N* be the argument of a log function, the natural log; then:

$$PE \propto \ln N \quad \text{(right)}$$

Figure 2.6 shows the two graphs, PE proportional to *T* and PE proportional to $\ln N$. This gives us the correct idea about what is going on, but there is a price to pay. When we double *N*, the PE of diffusion is not doubled. To see how much doubling *N* increases PE, take the ratio:

$$\frac{\ln 2N}{\ln N} = \frac{\ln N + \ln 2}{\ln N} = \frac{1 + 0.7}{\ln N}$$

If *N* is such that $\ln N = 1$, then doubling *N* increases the PE 70% (not 100%). But if *N* is such that $\ln N = 100$, then doubling *N* represents an increase of only 0.7%.

Combining the two statements about *T* and *N*, we have:

$$PE \propto T \ln N$$

Therefore:

$$PE = kT \ln N$$

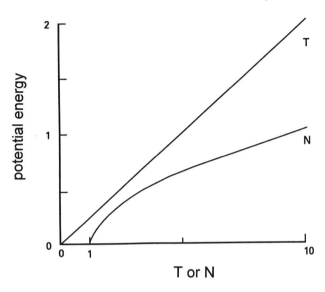

Figure 2.6. Potential energy of diffusion: Temperature and number

where k is a constant, called Boltzmann's constant (ICEMb, p. 7). Now k is a *very* small number; its value in the MKSA system of units is (where J is joule):

$$k = 1.38 \times 10^{-23} \text{ J/}^\circ\text{K}$$

If we have an Avogadro's number of particles, 6×10^{23}, at room temperature, then:

$$PE = (1.38 \times 10^{-23})\,(300)\,\ln(6 \times 10^{23})$$

$$= (4 \times 10^{-21})\,(\ln 6 + 23\,\ln 10)\,\text{J}$$

$$= (4 \times 10^{-21})\,(1.8 + 52.9)\,\text{J} = 2.2 \times 10^{-19}\,\text{J}$$

So even the very large number 10^{23} reduces to a mere factor 23; that is the power of logs. The PE required to move one particle by diffusion even in an Avogadro's number of particles is very small indeed.

The potential energy that one particle has to pass through the hole is:

$$PE = kT \ln N$$

where N is the number of particles on whose side the motion originates. Since the same is true for the other side, we number the two sides 1 and 2, then the PEs are $kT \ln N_1$ and $kT \ln N_2$; the *difference* in PE, which is what we are interested in, is:

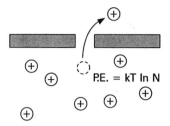

Figure 2.7. Diffusion through a selective hole

$$PE = kT \ln \frac{N_2}{N_1}$$

If $N_2 > N_1$, then PE > 0 and on average particles move from 2 → 1; if $N_2 < N_1$ particles move from 1 → 2 (see Fig. 2.7; Note: the PE still refers to the diffusional PE only).

Gravity and Diffusion Compared

We derived an expression for the diffusional potential energy of a particle located in N-like particles:

$$PE = kT \ln N$$

It is called a potential energy because it describes the desire (in units of energy) for a particle to move. In Fig. 2.8 we compare gravitational PE with diffusional PE where m is the mass of the particle on the table, g the acceleration due to gravity, and h is the height from which we measure the PE. Although we mean the PE with respect to two points, the top of the table and the floor, we do not always write:

$$PE = mg(h_2 - h_1)$$

We think let $h_1 = 0$ (reference) and let $h_2 = h$ and write the PE as mgh. We do exactly the thing for electrical potential: We let one reference point equal zero and do not subscript the other. The same is true for N, but it takes a different form; we must write $kT \ln N_2 - kT \ln N_1$, not $kT \ln(N_2 - N_1)$, which reduces to $kT \ln(N_2/N_1)$. So in diffusion the *ratio* of the number of particles is important, not the literal difference. This plays an important role in our thinking, and we use this fact many times.

Still comparing the two potential energies of gravity and diffusion, we assume that:

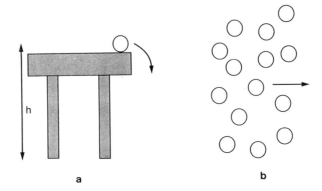

Figure 2.8. Gravity and diffusion compared: (a) PE = *mgh*, (b) PE = kT ln N

$$m = 1 \text{ kg}$$

$$h = 1 \text{ m}$$

$$g \cong 10 \text{ m/sec}^2$$

Then:

$$PE \text{ (grav)} = 10 \text{ kg}\frac{\text{m}^2}{\text{sec}^2} = 10 \text{ J}$$

A measure of how badly a 2.24-lb (1-kg) object wants to get off a 3-ft table on earth is 10 J. How many particles do we need to obtain this impetus from diffusion. We keep the same 10 J and solve for N at room temperature:

$$10 = kT \ln N$$

$$\ln N = \frac{10}{kT}$$

$$N = \exp(10/kT)$$

At room temperature:

$$kT = (1.38 \times 10^{-23} \text{ J/°K}) (300 \text{ °K})$$

$$\sim 4 \times 10^{-21} \text{ J}$$

Therefore:

$$N = \exp[10/(4 \times 10^{-21})]$$

or

$$N > e^{10^{20}}$$

which is more particles than in the entire universe! In our world diffusion is a weak force—even compared to gravity, which is weak compared to electricity—yet this weak force of diffusion accounts for most of biology.

We have demonstrated the similarity between the concept of PE in gravity and the same concept in diffusion: When something moves or wants to move, we define the *potential* for its desire to do so. The potential for a mass m at height h in a gravitational field is mgh; the potential for a particle in a group N particles is $kT \ln N$. Suppose these are opposing forces, i.e., there are many particles on the floor but only a few above. We think of these particles on the floor as diffusing upward, but since they have mass, gravity opposes them. Consider one particle at height h. Two forces act on it, diffusion (upward) and gravity (downward). Eventually these forces balance one another, as illustrated in Fig. 2.9. If these two forces balance, then the sum potential energy is zero:

$$mgh + kT \ln(r) = 0$$

In this equation r is the ratio of particle density at height h to particle density at ground level. At what height is the air only 1% of its density at ground level; i.e., let $r = 0.01$, then solve for h:

$$h = -\frac{kT}{mg} \ln(0.01)$$

If $m = 10^{-25}$ kg, which is the approximate mass of an air molecule, and $T = 300\,°K$, then:

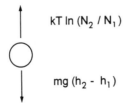

Figure 2.9. Gravity balances diffusion

$$n = -\left[\frac{(1.38 \times 10^{-23} \times 300)}{(10^{-25} \times 10)}\right] \ln (0.01) \sim 20000 \text{ m}$$

That is over 10 miles, which is about as high as the atmosphere on the earth, so these formulas work. The layer of air on the earth balances the desire of air to diffuse away with earth's desire to keep the air.

Membrane Potential

The same sort of balance occurs at the discriminating hole; Fig. 2.10 shows a cation at a (+) hole that wants to go out (up) because of diffusion but wants to go in (down) because of an electrical force (more negatives on the inside). When one particle moved up, it did so because it had the potential given by:

$$kT \ln N_2$$

It has the potential to move back given by:

$$kT \ln N_1$$

The particle leaves a space when it moves, an extra (−) that is now unpaired. This creates a voltage, and the sign of the voltage is such that it *opposes* any further movement of charge. We need to know the electrical *potential energy* created to oppose further movement. The (−) left behind pulls the (+) toward it with an energy equal to:

$$eV$$

where e is the charge on the ion and V is the voltage between them; that is

$$V = V_2 - V_1$$

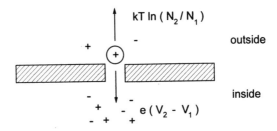

Figure 2.10. Electricity balances diffusion

The potential that is generated in Fig. 2.10 lasts forever. If these two forces are balanced, we write:

$$eV + kT \ln N_2/N_1 = 0$$

and therefore:

$$V = -\frac{kT}{e} \ln(N_2/N_1)$$

The symbol e reminds us that the fundamental unit of charge is the electron; the $(-)$ on the anion means an extra electron just as the $(+)$ means a missing electron.

Let $N_2/N_1 = 100$ then:

$$V = -\frac{kT}{e} \ln(100)$$

or at room temperature:

$$V \cong -115 \text{ mV}$$

Thus we see that a cell membrane potential is a balance between diffusion and electrical forces. If we were talking about a perfectly selective K channel for example, these ideas would lead to the Nernst potential (IMN, p. 36).

Exercise: Imagine a sheet of glass with a hole separating two KCl solutions. What material do you place in the hole to make it K-selective? Try to answer the question, then consider the quote from Erlanger and Glasser's *Electrical Signs of Nervous Activity* (Univ. Penn. Press, 1937):

> A physical chemist desiring to reveal the greatest potential difference which the two concentrations of the electrolyte could possibly produce would place between them, as the intervening partition, a sheet of metal corresponding to the cation which the solutions have in common. His potentiometer would then show a voltage determined by the expression: $E = 58 \log c_1/c_2$, where E is the potential in millivolts and 58 is a constant holding for room temperature and univalent ions. (pp. 133–35)

The answer is potassium: Place K in the hole to make a K-selective hole, Ca to make a Ca-selective hole, etc.

Membrane Capacitance

The cell potential is -115 mV on the inside with respect to the outside if the ratio of hole-selected cations is 100 to 1 inside to out. But the number of charges that actually move depends on the capacity for storing. They are stored just underneath the membrane, because the cytoplasm (a conductor) does not want extra charge; thus the extra charge moves to the surface near the membrane.

Suppose the capacitance of the membrane is C. We already know that:

$$V = \frac{Q}{C}$$

In this case we write Nze for Q to keep track of the number of negative ($z = -1$) charges making up Q under the membrane, so:

$$V = -\frac{Ne}{C}$$

where N is the number of ions and e is the charge on one. This is the same V we had before, so for N ions we have

$$-\frac{Ne}{C} = -\frac{kT}{e} \ln(N_2/N_1)$$

Therefore:

$$N = \frac{CkT}{e^2} \ln(N_2/N_1)$$

This is the number of negative ions N that we can store on a capacitor C to obtain a certain voltage. We already know the voltage, -115 mV, so we can take a shortcut:

$$N = \frac{C}{e}(115 \text{ mV})$$

We need to know only the C of the cell! The formula for C is:

$$C = \varepsilon \frac{A}{d}$$

And $\varepsilon \cong 10\, \varepsilon_0$ for a lipid bilayer (p. 15). Therefore:

$$C = 10\,(8.85 \times 10^{-14} \text{F/cm}) \frac{A}{100\text{Å}}$$

And $A \cong 300\,\mu^2 = 300 \times 10^{-8}$ cm^2 for a typical cell that is $10\,\mu$ in diameter (that is $10\,\mu \times 10\,\mu \times$ six sides if we imagine a cube about the size of a cell). Thus a cube doubles the correct answer (see Fig. 2.11). Therefore $C \cong 3$pF, and:

$$N \cong \frac{3 \times 10^{-12}}{1.6 \times 10^{-19}}(10^{-1}) \cong 2 \times 10^6 \text{ ions}$$

We calculated the preceding to have a potential of -115 mV across the membrane; we need two million ions per $300\,\mu^2$ or about 7000 ions per μ^2.

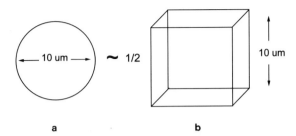

Figure 2.11. Typical cell surface area (the art of approximations): (a) $314 \, \mu m^2$, (b) $600 \, \mu m^2$

Let us try to calculate the number of particles underneath the cell membrane more directly: Since we assume that the concentration is 100 to 1 inside-to-out, we have (thinking of potassium as the cation that moves):

$$V = -\frac{kT}{e} \ln\left[\ln(K_{in}/K_{out})\right] \cong -115 \text{ mV}$$

We also know that:

$$V = \frac{Q}{C}$$

Since $C = 1 \, \mu F/cm^2$ for a biological membrane (which in effect we calculated above):

$$\frac{Q}{C} = -115 \text{ mV}$$

$$Q = (1 \, \mu F/cm^2)(-115 \text{ mV})$$

$$= -115 \times 10^{-9} \text{ C/cm}^2$$

A 10-μ diameter cell has $\sim 300 \times 10^{-8}$ cm^2 surface area, and a single anion has -1.6×10^{-19} C; therefore the number of electric charges on the inside is:

$$N = \frac{Q}{e} \text{ (Membrane Area)} = \frac{(115 \times 10^{-9})(300 \times 10^{-8})}{1.6 \times 10^{-19}}$$

or

$$N = 2.2 \times 10^6$$

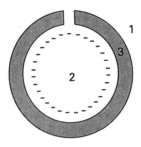

Figure 2.12. A cell stores excess charge near the membrane.

which is about two million negative charges left under the membrane because K moved out (Fig. 2.12).

Thus a small cell, $10\,\mu$ in diameter with a resting potential of around -100 mV, negative with regard to the outside, has about millions of charges just underneath the membrane. In principle to determine potential, there is no restriction on where, how large, or how many holes exist when we have only one type of selective pore. Now let us consider a more complicated situation.

Ion Selectivity

Let us assume we have two holes, one passes only (+), and the other passes only (−); we can think of KCl in water as the source of these (+) and (−) ions (see Fig. 2.13). The ions can move in both ways, up or down (in or out), but the corresponding (−) in the (+) hole or (+) in the (−) hole cannot move in either direction. If we add a 100:1 KCl solution, inside with respect to outside, both kinds of charge wants to escape, but only the (+) goes through the top hole, while only the (−) goes through the bottom hole. Even though we have drawn these as separate channels, imagine that they both exist on the same cell. What happens? The first guess is that there is no potential: The (+)s give −115 inside with respected to outside, and the (−)s give +115 inside with respect to outside, so they cancel. Right, but also wrong! It depends on how *well* ions can move through these two kinds of holes. With only one type of hole, it did not matter if ions moved easily or with difficulty through many holes or one, but now it does. If we have the *same* number of holes, say, one each, and ions can move through both of them *equally well*, then one (+) escapes, leaving a (−), and one (−) escapes, leaving a (+); thus the extra (−) and the extra (+) cancel, and there is no potential. Note: Before when one (+) escaped, it set up a potential that opposed the next (+) escaping. This would occur also if there were only the (−) hole (only the sign of the potential would change). In the cell we first created (see Fig. 2.12), around 2 million (+)s escaped (due to the

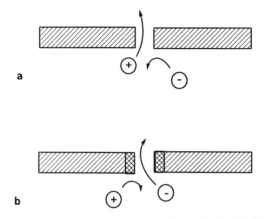

Figure 2.13. Ion selectivity: (a) potassium channel, (b) chloride channel

particular *C* used); Here it is different: No potential is set up because both (+)s *and* (−)s can move in the same cell, albeit through different holes, so there is no reason for more charges of both kinds *not* to move. In this case of (+) and (−) holes, the concentration difference eventually disappears: The (+)s and the (−)s escape is always matched, and never a potential (on average), until the concentration gradient is finally gone.

Channel Density

Does it matter how many holes exist of each kind, or how well the (+)s and (−)s move through them if there is more than one kind of hole? Nature plays with channel density to make different kinds of cells (see ICEMb, p. 330). Assume we have two (+) holes and one (−) hole with equal *ability* to pass a charge, as indicated by the equally sized holes in Fig. 2.14. Except for ion selectivity—one moves (+) and the other moves (−)—we assume they have the same conductance, i.e., they can carry their respective charges equally well. Because of the number of holes, it is easier *overall* for the (+)s to escape than for the (−)s.

Note: The three holes, 2 (+) and one (−), are in the same cell. We also assume that there are many more (+) and (−) charges inside (down) than outside, as before.

We ask what happens when all three changes escape from the cell, as they wish to do? Two of the channels cancel out as before, but now we have an extra (+) escaping through the third channel. This is a combination of the two preceding situations, and we have a potential; however the potential eventually disappears, as does the concentration gradient.

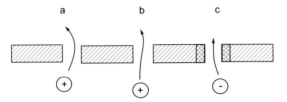

Figure 2.14. Channel density: (a) and (b) both admit positive ions, (c) admits only negative ions.

Let us assume that the actual number of ions inside the cell (down, in Fig. 2.14) is so large that we need not consider those that have escaped when we calculate the cell potential. Another way of picturing the potential without gradient depletion is as the *initial* potential—before too many ions escape or as an ion pump that somehow puts back into the cell all the ions that come out of the cell (EIP, p. 12). We can assume that the pumps are nonelectrical, but in fact they are electrical (EIP, p. 47), as we see in Chapter 3.

Let us assume there are N_+ (+) holes and N_- (−) holes, i.e., N is the actual number of either type of hole, and the subscript indicates which type. Note: We now use N for the number of channels; before we used N for the number of ions. What is the potential across the membrane now? A fraction of the potential is due to the (+)s and a fraction to the (−)s; the rule for the cell potential V is

$$V = \frac{N_+ V_+}{N_+ + N_-} + \frac{N_- V_-}{N_+ + N_-}$$

That is the total voltage V is the weighted sum of the voltages V_+ and V_- due to the (+) and (−) pathways (IMN, p. 86). We also know that:

$$V_+ = -\frac{kT}{e} \ln \frac{[+]_{in}}{[+]_{out}}$$

$$V_- = +\frac{kT}{e} \ln \frac{[-]_{in}}{[-]_{out}}$$

In these formulas the [ ] stand for the concentration of the respective ions. If we have only (+) holes but no (−) holes, then $N_- = 0$ and $V = V_+$. (The same for V_-, if $N_+ = 0$). If $N_+ = N_-$, then:

$$V = \frac{1}{2} V_+ + \frac{1}{2} V_- = 0$$

as it should, since V_+ and V_- are equal and opposite in this example (we saw this in Fig. 2.13). However if $N_+ \neq N_-$ and neither is zero, then the weighted sum formula holds. For $N_+ = 2N_-$, as in Fig. 2.14:

$$V = \frac{2}{3}V_+ + \frac{1}{3}V_-$$

Since we know the actual values for the example of a 100:1 ratio of a KCl solution inside:outside, then in Fig. 2.14:

$$V = \frac{2}{3}(-115) + \frac{1}{3}(+115) = -77 + 38 = -39\ \text{mV}$$

Note: So far all the channels are the same *except* for selectivity, and there are twice as many (+)s as (−)s, therefore the potential is negative inside with respect to outside, but not so large as if we had all (+)s. Remember that the ion gradient is being depleted, and this −39 mV is only the initial value, or the value when the KCl gradient is somehow maintained.

Now we have a way of determining the potential for any combination of discriminating holes, (+) or (−).

Channel Conductance

In the preceding calculations, we represented a greater (+) connection between inside and outside cells by a greater number of equally conducting holes, but suppose one type of hole is inherently more conductive than another. Let us represent this difference in conductivity by drawing one hole larger than the other, as in Fig. 2.15, where the (+) hole is twice as wide as the (−) hole. Note: Although channel conductance may vary quite a bit from type to type, the range is perhaps narrower than you imagine (ICEMb, p. 333). Let us start with two holes as before and indicate the situation as graphically as possible by letting two ions go through one hole, while only one goes through the other, as illustrated in Fig. 2.16. This looks only a little different than our last case, but it has some interesting features. First we must now introduce a measure of how well an ion can pass through a hole. Let γ_+ be the measure for the (+) hole and γ_- be the measure for the (−) hole. We have the same kind of formula, namely:

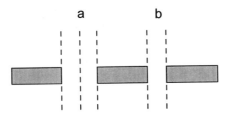

Figure 2.15. Channel conductance: (a) more conductive, (b) less conductive channel

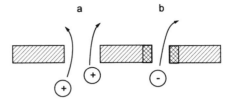

Figure 2.16. Channel conductance: (a) wide enough to admit two ions, (b) wide enough for only one ion

$$V = \frac{\gamma_+ V_+}{\gamma_+ + \gamma_-} + \frac{\gamma_- V_-}{\gamma_+ + \gamma_-}$$

This is the voltage across two holes that conduct only (+) and (−) ions, respectively, with one (the + in this example) twice as permissive as the other. If $\gamma_+ = 2\gamma$ as we assumed, then as in our previous example:

$$V = \frac{2}{3}V_+ + \frac{1}{3}V_-$$

Note: We did not take into account the possibility of different numbers of holes of either kind; we do that in the following section.

Channel Number, Channel Conductance, and Membrane Potential

The preceding examples show that the *number* of channels and channel *conductance* play the same sort of role in determining voltage across a membrane; in fact at this level of discussion, there is really no way of distinguishing these two cases. Note: The *conductance* describes what we previously referred to as the permissiveness or ability of the channel; conductance is the correct electrical term.

What does Ohm's law $V = IR$ mean? Let us assume we fasten two clips to a wad of paper soaked in salt water (see Fig. 2.17). Note: We use a wad of paper to focus on the arbitrary geometry of the conductor. We want to pass a current through the wad of paper—it has ions from the salt water (IMN, p. 31), so it should conduct electricity. The two extremes at the end of the wire clips are the defining points of the system. If we have a voltage V between the two clips, then the current through the wad of paper is

$$I = \frac{V}{R}$$

Figure 2.17. Wad of paper soaked in salt water

where R is the resistance of the paper wad. It depends on how much salt water (and the salt concentration, kind of salt, and drying rate, etc.) we used on the paper, as well as how tightly we wad the paper and (a related factor) where we place the wire clips. Since this problem involves so many variables, we simply say that the paper wad has a resistance R (with respect to the two clips). We define:

$$G = \frac{1}{R}$$

and write:

$$I = GV$$

which is Ohm's law for current; G is the conductance (the permissiveness of ion movement). The G depends on many factors, the object's physical properties, its shape, and the direction of current flow, etc. A channel is similar.

We use γ to describe the conductance of a single channel, and not G, to be able to include the *number* of channels too. The more channels there are, the easier ions are able to move, so let us define:

$$G = N\gamma$$

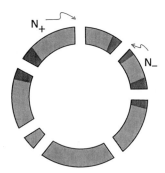

Figure 2.18. Voltage across a cell membrane with a different number of different channels

This is similar to what we did for charge (see Fig. 2.12) when we wrote $Q = Ne$; that is the total conductance of N channels is the sum of all individual conductances. Note: $G = N\gamma$ is a shorthand for $G = \gamma + \gamma + \gamma + \ldots \gamma$, with N terms on the right-hand side (multiplication is just shorthand addition). Now combine these concepts in Fig. 2.18. The formula for the voltage across a cell idealized in Fig. 2.18, when we have N_+ of γ_+ type channels and N_- of γ_- type channels is

$$V = \frac{N_+\gamma_+V_+}{N_+\gamma_+ + N_-\gamma_-} + \frac{N_-\gamma_-V_-}{N_+\gamma_+ + N_-\gamma_-} \qquad \text{(correct)}$$

where N is the number and γ is the conductance of the (+) or the (−) channel and V is the voltage of the (+) or the (−) channel. Note: We do not write

$$V = V_+ + V_+ + \ldots V_- + V_- + \ldots \qquad \text{(incorrect)}$$

i.e., the sum of all the voltages. It is wrong even if $N_- = 0$ [no (−) conducting holes] because the correct formula in that case is not the sum of all the V_+s, but:

$$V = V_+$$

This equation is true even if there are *thousands* of the N_+ type hole. The equation says that the voltage across any number of the same type of channels (in parallel with each other) is the same as the voltage across one of those channels. The voltage across many channels of two different types is the *weighted sum* of the two kinds of voltages that each channel type generates, and so on for three channels.

Channel Conductance and the Random Switch

We assume that all the conductance γ is in the hole itself, i.e., γ belongs to the holes in Fig. 2.18, not to the lipid membrane holding it, and not to the surrounding solution; it is a property of the hole, just like V_+ is a property of the (+) hole. The γ for the channel depends on channel geometry and whatever is inside the channel, as well as the physical–chemical forces acting on the ion moving through the hole. But these considerations are too complex for now, so we group them together into the index γ, just as we grouped together the complexities of the paper wad (see Fig. 2.17) into a conductance G.

The holes that we are interested in have another important property—they open and close randomly; this is true not only for voltage-gated but also for ligand-gated channels (SCRb, p. 397; ICEMb, p. 140). It is this randomness that explains most of the interesting electrical properties of cells, like action potentials and propagation (see Chapter 3). We can think of random opening and closing as a flap on the hole: The channel is either open or closed. We need a measure of how often the hole is open, and how often it is closed, which is the *probability p* of being in the open state.

Let us assume a channel stays open and closed for random (with no particular pattern) periods. Figure 2.19 shows what we might see if we took pictures of the hole every second. The hole is first open (O), then open in the second picture, then closed (C) in the third picture, etc.; we represent these states as OOCCCCO in Fig. 2.19; the state of the flap appears above the row. After a number of snapshots, we do not notice a pattern of open or closed channels, so we conclude that the process is random—the channel opens and closes randomly. However, if on average half the snapshots show the channel open, then we can state that the channel is open half the time. But how do we evaluate whether between every snapshot the channel is closed (or open) all the time? If we assume that between views of the channel state, the channel behaves just as it does when we are photographing, then our initial interpretation was correct. This is a sampling problem, and we are always limited by our sampling of events; however on paper we can sample continuously, as in

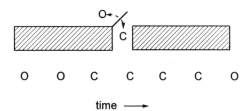

Figure 2.19. Random switch: one channel, many snapshots

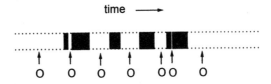

Figure 2.20. Sampling: one hole with continuous viewing

Fig. 2.20, where a dark band means the hole is closed. We still see no pattern to the behavior, but now we can add up when the flap is open, when it is closed (dark), then generalize. If the total time we viewed the flap is $T = 1000$ sec and the total time the channel is open is $T_0 = 500$ sec, then without measuring we know that $T_c = 500$ sec because we have only two states. In this particular case we can define the fraction of time the channel is open by:

$$\frac{T_0}{(T_0 + T_c)} = \frac{T_0}{T} = \frac{1}{2}$$

The total time is $T = T_0 + T_c$, i.e., the channel is open 50% of the time. We could obtain the same result, 50%, from a number of channel behavior patterns (see Fig. 2.21). In the first case the channel opens and closes at regular intervals; in the second, it is closed during the first half of an experiment and open during the second half.

In our case of a randomly opening channel, there is no pattern, so we want to determine from T_0/T the probability p of a *single channel* being in the open state (SCRb, p. 404). In fact for one channel, we can write

$$p = \frac{T_0}{T}$$

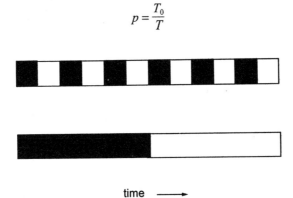

Figure 2.21. Two other ways of obtaining a 50% flap opening

Note: This definition also works for the two cases shown in Fig. 2.21, which are obviously not random, as well as for the random case. Even though we do not know in the random case whether a channel opens or closes at a particular time (as we would certainly know in a regularly opening channel), we can still determine what the probability will be. In our example in Fig. 2.19, if we sample a lot, we obtain a good measure of the overall behavior; how fast we sample depends on how fast the channel we are watching actually changes from one state to the next.

Probability

With these ideas in mind, we introduce a new feature in our channel—a random switch with a probability p of being open. The *effective* conductance of the channel is now not merely γ (although it is still γ when it is open), but $p\gamma$, and the overall conductance of N channels is not $N\gamma$, but $Np\gamma$. In our example the working conductance is half of what it is when the channel is open because $p = 1/2$. There are a number of ways of looking at these relationships. Let us think of $(pN)\gamma$ instead of $N(p\gamma)$. While there is no numerical difference in these two expressions, grouping them in this way makes a point: Up to now we have discussed *one* channel's behavior over time, and, its open-channel conductance is γ, and its open probability is p; therefore $p\gamma$ makes sense and N of these channels gives an overall average conductance of $G = N(p\gamma)$. But if instead of looking at one channel we look at all N channels at once, we have the situation in Fig. 2.22. Imagine that we are looking down on a membrane full of channels but only for 1 microsecond, and we see that half of them are open and half are closed. For the case that $p = 1/2$, (p is a property of one of the channels), this is what we expect. In the next snapshot, taken, say, 1

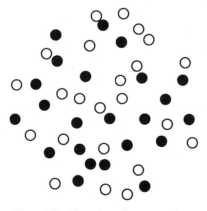

Figure 2.22. Many channels, one snapshot

second later, we also see that half the channels are open, but these are a different set of channels, with perhaps some overlap with the last set but in general a different set. We could have defined p differently by looking at the behavior of only one channel, as we did in Fig. 2.19; we could have looked at the number of open channels N_0 in a population of N channels. Again we would have obtained $p = N_0/N$ = 1/2; that is of the N channels that exist, only a fraction are open, and that fraction is pN. The effective number of channels that are working to give a conductance G is therefore $(pN)\gamma$. The difference between $(pN)\gamma$ and $N(p\gamma)$ is the difference between looking at one channel over time, then generalizing about many channels (at one time) and looking at many channels at the same time, then generalizing about one channel (for all time). This concept is embodied by the Ergotic theorem, which says that the two ps defined in these two different ways (looking at one over and over and looking at many at once) amount to the same thing.

Membrane Potential Revisited

With this feature in mind, we can now use p. The equation for the voltage across two different kinds of channels (one cation, one anion) in a cell is:

$$V = \frac{N_+ p_+ \gamma_+ V_+}{N_+ p_+ \gamma_+ + N_- p_- \gamma_-} + \frac{N_- p_- \gamma_- V_-}{N_+ p_+ \gamma_+ + N_- p_- \gamma_-}$$

The formula is clumsy, but its contents are essential: N is the number of (+) or (−) channels; p is the probability that a channel is open, with a different value for the (+) and the (−) probability, in general; and γ_+ and γ_- is the open-channel conductance for each type of channel, again not necessarily the same.

Let us try to look at the limits of this equation, then give some examples of its use. In effect we have redefined our definition of membrane conductance to account for random channel openings and closings. If all the channels of a certain type are open, then total membrane conductance is $N\gamma$. If we have two types, say, one for (+) ions and the other for (−) ions, then total membrane conductance is:

$$N_+ \gamma_+ + N_- \gamma_-$$

Then if one channel type is the dominant pathway, we could cover the first term or the second term to show only the operating channels, and that is what p does. So total conductance is:

$$G = p_+(N_+ \gamma_+) + p_-(N_- \gamma_-)$$

Note: We list p first to emphasize that it controls the relative value of each term; of course the weight of each term also depends on how many (+) and (−) channels we have (N) and how large the (+) γ is relative to the (−) γ value. If we assume there are about the same number of Ns and the γs are not too different, then total conductance is:

$$(p_+ + p_-)N\gamma$$

Membrane voltage is:

$$V = V_+ \left(\frac{p_+}{p_+ + p_-} \right) + V_- \left(\frac{p_-}{p_+ + p_-} \right)$$

Note: This particular formula is true only for $N_+\gamma_+ \sim N_-\gamma_- = N\gamma$.

As an example let us assume K channels and Cl channels in the membrane, with high KCl inside and low KCl outside. If concentrations do not change over time, we can write:

$$V_+ = V_K = -\frac{kT}{e} \ln \frac{K_{in}}{K_{out}}$$

$$V_- = V_{Cl} = +\frac{kT}{e} \ln \frac{Cl_{in}}{Cl_{out}}$$

For a tenfold concentration difference:

$$(KCl)_{in} = 10 \, (KCl)_{out}$$

Then:

$$V_K \cong -58 \text{ mV}$$

$$V_{Cl} \cong +58 \text{ mV}$$

Note: In real cells $Cl_{in} < Cl_{out}$, so V_{Cl} is actually a negative number too.

In this case under our special assumption $N_+\gamma_+ \sim N_-\gamma_- = N\gamma$, total potential across the cell membrane is:

$$V = \frac{p_K}{p_K + p_{Cl}} (-58 \text{ mV}) + \frac{p_{Cl}}{p_K + p_{Cl}} (+58) \text{ mV}$$

If we assume all Cl channels are closed, then $p_{Cl} = 0$, and no matter how many K channels are open (at least one must be open):

$$V = -58 \text{ mV}$$

So if $p_K = 0.001$, i.e., only a tenth of a percent chance of being open, then we still have essentially the full K voltage if all Cl channels are closed; an analogous situation is true for Cl channels.

Looking at other cases, if $p_K \sim p_{Cl}$, then net voltage is about zero; if $p_K \ll p_{Cl}$, then we move approximately toward +60-mV membrane potential (see Fig. 2.23). Note: Figure 2.23 includes time. Let us assume we can turn a knob to adjust the relative value of the two ps in question; thus we can obtain a potential we want between the two extremes, but *cannot* obtain a potential outside this range. That is in the two batteries, the K and the Cl concentration differences combined with the K- and Cl-specific pathways limit the potential our system can give, but within this ±60mV range, we can have any shape voltage. We can also obtain any voltage shape by controlling the ps; for example we can achieve the situation in Fig. 2.24, where at some time we change the probability of the channel opening from all p_K to all p_{Cl}. Then at some other time, we do the reverse. Note: The ps have values between 0 and 1, i.e., $p_K = 1$, $p_{Cl} = 0$ to $p_{Cl} = 1$, $p_K = 0$; however Fig. 2.24 implies that $p_K \gg p_{Cl}$ or $p_{Cl} \gg p_K$ is the actual requirement.

Now we imagine that the change in potential occurs in a more complex way, as in Figure 2.23. If we assume in Fig. 2.24 that we never have all p_K or all p_{Cl}, so we never reach the two extremes, we are always somewhere in between—sometimes $p_K = 0.78$ and $p_{Cl} = 0.11$, at other times $p_K = 0.23$, $p_{Cl} = 0.37$, etc. We assume the two ps are adjusted so that the resulting voltage changes, as shown in Fig. 2.25, to have an action-potential shape. Here we see that the action-potential shape results

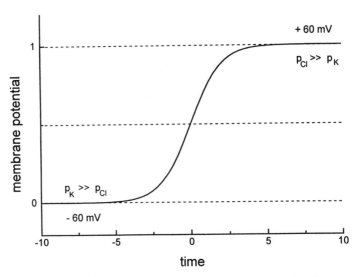

Figure 2.23. Membrane potential depends on open-channel probability.

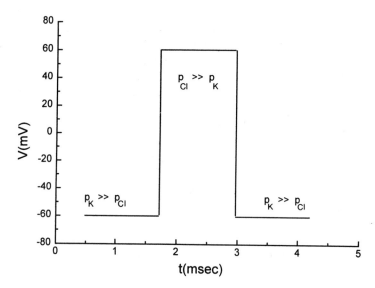

Figure 2.24. Membrane voltage due to rapidly changing probabilities

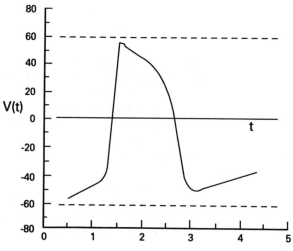

Figure 2.25. Real action potential

from the balance of ion channel probabilities changing in time. Proof that the underlying cause of action potentials (= excitability) is a change in membrane conductance was demonstrated by Curtis and Cole in 1939 (see ICEMa, p. 28).

Let us summarize: So far we considered three conditions of one case that ranges from simple to more complex. Note: $V = V_2 - V_1$, that is the inside potential minus the outside potential is the transmembrane potential.

CONDITION 1. One (+)-selective hole:

$$V = -\frac{kT}{e} \ln \left([+]_{in}/[+]_{out} \right)$$

Here $V = V_+$, that is the potential due to the (+)-selective hole. Remember: (inside minus outside) = minus (inside divided by outside), which is always true for positive ions.

CONDITION 2. One (+)-selective and one (−)-selective hole:

$$V = \frac{\gamma_+ V_+}{\gamma_+ + \gamma_-} + \frac{\gamma_- V_-}{\gamma_+ + \gamma_-}$$

where γ is the conductance of the (+)- or (−)-selective hole. Here the potential is a weighted sum of the relative conductances, and the two holes are always open.

CONDITION 3. Many (+)-selective and (−)-selective holes that open and close randomly:

$$V = \frac{N_+ p_+ \gamma_+ V_+}{N_+ p_+ \gamma_+ + N_+ p_+ \gamma_+} + \frac{N_- p_- \gamma_- V_-}{N_+ p_+ \gamma_+ + N_+ p_+ \gamma_+}$$

In Condition 1 it does not matter how many holes we have, since we have only one kind. In Condition 2 we are restricted to two selective holes, one of each kind, but we have not introduced the probability of opening yet. With two different kinds of selective holes, it *does* in general matter how many we have of each type. Condition 3 includes all the effects described so far, explains all kinds of graded potentials across membranes, including action potentials. In Chapter 3 we generalize to more than one type of (+)-selective channel (hole), (−)-selective channel, or mixed-selective channel.

Diversity in membrane voltage depends on probability, which changes with time; it also depends on the relative values of N and γ, which help determine the contribution of each ion channel class, (+) or (−). But probability describes the action. How much charge actually moves across the membrane to give the specific voltage is always given by:

$$Q = CV$$

To determine the actual number of ions, we use

$$Q = Ne$$

where e is the charge on one ion and N is the number of ions. Note: N sometimes stands for the number of channels and sometimes for the number of ions. In Condition 1 Q is easy to calculate because only one type of charge moves across, the (+) type; there is no question of which charge you are calculating. In Condition 2 there are two types of charge, (+) and (−). You may think that since both types move, there is no real charge left over, but that is not true except when all the γs for (+) and (−) channels are identical; in that case there is no voltage either. There is no voltage difference, such as that implied in Condition 2, without a net separation of charge.

Let us look into this more deeply. In Condition 2 there are only two channels, but each one has different conductance, i.e., a different willingness to let the (+) and the (−) pass; furthermore there is a higher concentration of KCl on the inside (2) than on the outside (1). Let us assume $\gamma_+ > \gamma_-$, as in Fig. 2.26. That is the (+) charges (K in our example) moves more easily through their channel than the (−) charges (Cl in our example) move through theirs. Note: The two (+)s that have escaped leave two (−)s behind, but at the same time in the (−)-selective channel, only one (+) is left behind; that difference creates the net separation of charge. We calculate the extra charges as before, using $Q = CV$. However we use the *sign* of V for the *kind* of extra charge, that is extra (+) or extra (−). In Fig. 2.26 $\gamma_+ > \gamma_-$ and except for what has escaped or been left behind (the charges in the circles), there is an equal number of (+) and (−) inside and out. The net V is negative, i.e.:

$$V_2 - V_1 < 0$$

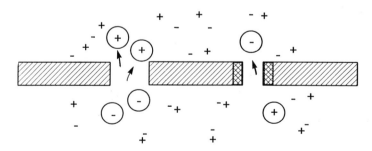

Figure 2.26. There is no voltage without a charge separation.

Since V is negative, so is the excess charge on the inside of the membrane. Thus there is some net extra equal and opposite (−) on the inside, which we can now calculate from $Q = CV$. We usually ignore the net extra charges on the outside by connecting the outside bath to ground and letting the excess flow away. This amounts to letting $V_1 = 0$ (i.e., letting it equal the reference potential).

Note: We let the differential desire to separate the charge equal different γ, but γ_+ and γ_- could be the same, with, say, two γ_+ holes and one γ_- hole; the result would be the same. However there is a subtle difference: We assume γ can vary continuously and the number of channels (N) can vary only discretely. With many channels of both kinds (Condition 3), the same is true; we substitute values for the γs, Ns and ps, then calculate V. If V is negative, then $V_2 < V_1$, and there is an excess (−) on the inside; if $V_2 > V_1$, the opposite is true. In many cases we can determine the sign of the potential without knowing the actual value of N_+ or γ_-, etc. We use $\gamma_+ = 2\gamma_-$ or some similar relation, so that the γs cancel one another. Likewise the Ns may cancel.

What happens during an action potential? At rest there is an excess (−) on the inside, and at the plateau there is an excess (+) on the inside (see Fig. 2.27).These two situations alternate as the membrane voltage changes sign. The membrane capacitance holds this transient charge, and $Q = CV$ is valid at every moment in time; p controls the entire process. That is N and γ are essentially constant and do not change over the small time scale; instead the ps are always changing.

The ion flow is linked, i.e., when one ion moves, another one wants to. Let us assume equal conditions caused by either N or γ; in Fig. 2.28 one (+) escapes and one (−) escapes, so there is no net charge left behind, i.e., no potential generated.

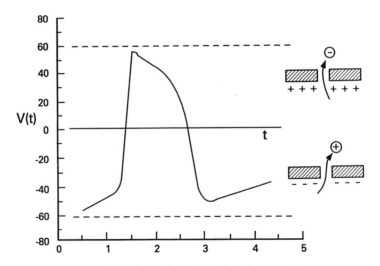

Figure 2.27. Excess charge during the action potential

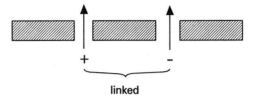

Figure 2.28. When a cation (+) escapes from solution, an anion (–) escapes.

Note: *When* the (+) escapes, the (–) *has to escape*; they must escape together. It does not matter how far away they are from one another if they are in the same conducting volume—they may be very close or on opposite sides of the cell—this rule must be obeyed. No excess charge in the bulk solution is a property of any ionic conductor, including the cytoplasm inside the cell (see Fig. 2.28).

The same is true if we have, say, two N_+ channels to every one N_- channel, or $\gamma_+ = 2\gamma_-$. The movement of (+) and (–) is still linked, but charge is left behind, so that a potential is generated. To unite these concepts we must discuss membrane *capacitance*, the lipid bilayer holding these selective holes.

The idea that a charge movement is linked to another charge movement is not a special property of membranes but a general property of electrical conductance; it does not even require a membrane to operate, as we shall see below.

Diffusion Potential

Suppose we have a material that lets (+) ions move faster than (–) ions. In Fig. 2.29 the (+) ion would like to move faster, but the (–) ion constrains the (+) ions

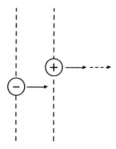

Figure 2.29. The diffusion potential: The plus ion wants to escape more rapidly; the diffusion potential retards it.

from actually doing so. Note: Arrow length represents the desire to escape; a double arrow on the (+) ion indicates that it would move more rapidly if it could. *Both ions must escape together:* The tug-of-war between the natural tendency of the (+) ion to escape (diffuse) first and the (−) ion to retard its movement results in a charge separation and hence in a potential, as when we considered a membrane. The distance between dotted lines represents the average separation between charges; the result is the diffusion potential (see IMN, p. 38).

What material lets some ions escape more easily than others? Think of KCl in solution: Water interacts differently with K^+ than it does Cl^-; K^+ ions move about 3% more easily through water than do Cl^- ions. If we have a glass pipette containing 3-M KCl dipping into a lower salt concentration, say, 100-mM KCl, then we have the situation in Fig. 2.30 (compare with SCRa, p. 38.) The diffusion potential between the inside of the pipette (Region 2) and the outside (Region 1) is given by a familiar equation:

$$V = \frac{\gamma_K V_K}{\gamma_K + \gamma_{Cl}} + \frac{\gamma_{Cl} V_{Cl}}{\gamma_{Cl} + \gamma_K}$$

As before V_K is the Nernst potential that exists *if only* K could flow, and V_{Cl} is the Nernst potential *if only* Cl could flow, so once again:

$$V_K = -\frac{kT}{e} \ln(K_2/K_1)$$

$$V_{Cl} = +\frac{kT}{e} \ln(Cl_2/Cl_1)$$

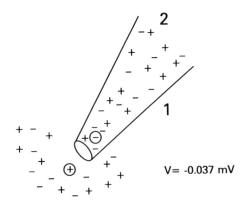

Figure 2.30. Tip potential

Therefore we can write

$$V = \frac{\gamma_K}{\gamma_K + \gamma_{Cl}}\left[-\frac{kT}{e}\ln(K_2/K_1)\right] + \frac{\gamma_{Cl}}{\gamma_K + \gamma_{Cl}}\left[+\frac{kT}{e}\ln(Cl_2/Cl_1)\right]$$

Now because of local neutrality, no matter where we look along the pipette, the K concentration equals the Cl concentration (on average); therefore at every position:

$$[K] = [Cl] = [KCl]$$

We cannot have extra K; if we momentarily do Cl ions move to balance K ions. The 3-M KCl inside the pipette means 3-M K^+ and 3-M Cl^-; therefore $[KCl] = n$ represents the anion or cation concentration on either side. We substitute this information into the above equation for V, factor, and rearrange; then:

$$V = \frac{kT}{e}\left(\frac{\gamma_{Cl}}{\gamma_K + \gamma_{Cl}} - \frac{\gamma_K}{\gamma_K + \gamma_{Cl}}\right)\ln(n_2/n_1)$$

This is a famous equation. To see what happens when $\gamma_K = \gamma_{Cl}$, i.e., both K and Cl ions move in the same way through water; then $V = 0$. But if $\gamma_K > \gamma_{Cl}$ even by only 3%, then we obtain some small potential (IMN, p. 39). Let

$$\gamma_K = 1.03\,\gamma_{Cl}$$

Since $kT/e \cong 25$ mV at room temperature:

$$V \cong (25\text{ mV})\left(\frac{\gamma_{Cl} - 1.03\gamma_{Cl}}{1.03\gamma_{Cl} + \gamma_{Cl}}\right)\ln(3/0.1)$$

$$= -1.2\text{ mV}$$

This small voltage is part of what is called the *tip potential* of the glass microelectrode. Even if K and Cl do not move at the same rate in water, the tip potential is obviously zero if $n_2 = n_1$. Generally the tip potential exists if two adjacent solutions have different concentrations and contain ions with different mobility.

Anyone who works with microelectrodes knows that -1.2 mV is nonsense. So what is going on? Charged surfaces make these problems more complex than we have indicated. A good example is that the tip potential in a glass electrode (see Fig. 2.30) is always much larger than the few millivolts we calculated, because the glass is charged and that adds another dimension to the problem, as shown in Fig. 2.31, where the negative signs *fixed in the* glass (*in circles*) indicate a preferred pathway for (+) ions near the glass—a sort of K channel. Negative charges create a preferred avenue for K ion flow, and that selectivity

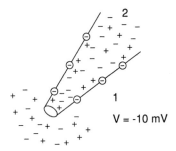

Figure 2.31. Tip potential with negatively charged glass

provides a potential. As we expect $V_2 - V_1 = V$ is negative because of it. For microelectrodes filled with strong KCl solutions, the tip potential is about -10 mV. For an extended discussion of glass microelectrodes, including the effect of pressure on mixing the solutions, see IMN, pp. 52, 54.

Before going further into this problem of parallel pathways, we must understand where the basic equation comes from:

$$V = \frac{G_+}{G_+ + G_-}(V_+) + \frac{G_-}{G_+ + G_-}(V_-)$$

Note: We write G *instead of* $N\gamma p$ to emphasize the form of the equation, not how G is composed. Let us consider a selective hole as a conductor, a battery, and a switch (see Fig. 2.32). Thinking of channels again, the conductance G stands for the hole (or a group of N holes), its individual conductance γ, and the probability that the hole is open p. There is no order in where we place G, E, and S. Also we use G (= $1/R$) instead of R. Voltage V represents, say, V_+ or V_-, the specific Nernst potential for that hole. In general we consider two holes (or two sets of holes, N_+ of one kind and N_- of the other kind) side by side, or, as we say, in parallel.

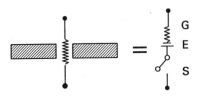

Figure 2.32. Selective hole and its equivalent circuit

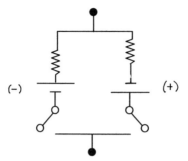

Figure 2.33. Two selective holes

We make the following assumptions: the Gs and Vs have specific meanings, (+) or (−); total V equals V_+, say, only if V_+ is the *only* pathway; we connect the two pathways with wires representing the cytoplasm and the extracellular plasma, which for the moment we assume to have no resistance.

We draw an electrical circuit to represent two selective pathways side by side because we can use existing rules for such a circuit. We want to know the voltage across the two pathways. To solve this problem we note that there is *no net* current from dot to dot. Why is this? If we have a cell in a dish (see Fig. 2.34), the current must go somewhere—in a loop, or as we say in a *circuit*. There is no external circuit here, only the cell and the solution. What leaves a cell must go back in; there is no where else for it to go, so eventually it returns to where it started—to close the loop, as it were.

The simple consequence of this is that in our case of two pathways in parallel, whatever goes up one branch must come down the other—or vice versa (see Fig. 2.35). Thus the *current* arrows must be equal and opposite even though the ion movement arrows are not, which is exactly the condition that we have already set.

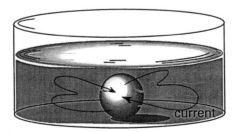

Figure 2.34. A cell in a dish

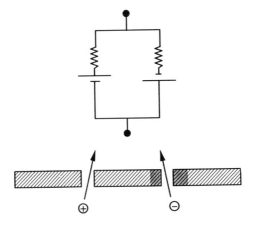

Figure 2.35. Two channels in parallel

Figure 2.35 shows that (+) and (–) charges *must move together*, and a (–) moving up is the same electrically as a (+) moving down. We can also have (+)s moving oppositely; we do not have to have (+)s and (–)s balancing one another. Suppose there is a lot of KCl inside relative to outside and a lot of NaCl outside relative to inside, and there are *no* Cl holes but two kinds of (+) holes, one set for K and the other for Na. Then K and Na are the only permeabilities. Now K escapes and Na enters (in the *electric circuit* arrows of current direction are always taken as how (+) charge moves). Anyway—whether we have a (+) coupled to a (–) (both escaping) or a (+) linked to another (+) (escaping oppositely), the result must be no net current: The two movements must cancel one another. To determine the voltage V between the dots (see Fig. 2.35), given Gs and Vs for each branch, we use Ohm's law to write for the loop:

$$V = \frac{\text{Total current}}{\text{Total conductance}} = \frac{I}{G}$$

Note: This is just a version of the formula $V = IR$. The total current is the sum of the two currents:

$$I = I_+ + I_-$$

Total conductance is the sum of the two conductances:

$$V = \frac{I_+ + I_-}{G_+ + G_-}$$

We can use Ohm's law again for each branch; therefore:

$$I_+ = G_+ V_+$$

$$I_- = G_- V_-$$

Then:

$$V = \frac{G_+ V_+ + G_- V_-}{G_+ + G_-}$$

or to show the weighted terms individually:

$$V = \frac{G_+ V_+}{G_+ + G_-} + \frac{G_- V_-}{G_+ + G_-}$$

We see this is a form of Ohm's law and addition. Voltage across the entire membrane from the two channels (or the two sets of channels if there is more than one of each type) is the weighted sum of each voltage, a piece of V_+ [the $G_+/(G_+ + G_-)$ fraction] and a piece of V_- [the $G_-/(G_+ + G_-)$ fraction]. The V_+ and V_- limit our total voltage, and we have all of one *only* if all of the other one is zero; thus V equals V_+ only if $G_- = 0$, etc.

When we add that $G = N\gamma p$ for each type of pathway in our cell, we really have all the formalism necessary to construct a cell membrane potential. The G_- equals zero if $N_- = 0$ (there are no channels of this type), $p_- = 0$ [there are (−) channels, but none are open], *or* $\gamma_- = 0$ [there are (−) channels and they are open, but they do not let any ions escape—this situation actually occurs]. Electrically these three situations are identical; physically of course they are very different. We can obtain any voltage between V_+ and V_- by adjusting the relative values of p_+ and p_-, but, V_+ and V_- are all we have to work with—we cannot go outside these values.

More Realistic View of Cell Potential

Let us consider three holes in a cell, where each one stand for *a set* of similar holes, N_K, N_{Na}, and N_{Cl} in number (see Fig. 2.36). There are more K ions inside than outside and more Na ions outside than inside. Voltage across this cell membrane is

$$V = \frac{N_K \gamma_K p_K}{\Sigma N \gamma p} (V_K) + \frac{N_{Cl} \gamma_{Cl} p_{Cl}}{\Sigma N \gamma p} (V_{Cl}) + \frac{N_{Na} \gamma_{Na} p_{Na}}{\Sigma N \gamma p} (V_{Na})$$

Total voltage is the weighted sum of individual potentials. Note:

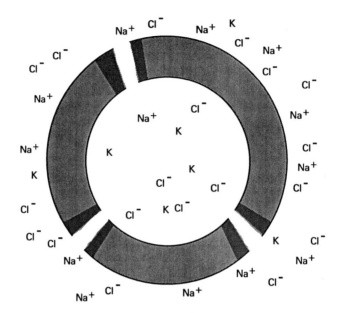

Figure 2.36. A more realistic cell

$$\Sigma N \gamma p = N_K \gamma_K p_K + N_{Cl} \gamma_{Cl} p_{Cl} + N_{Na} \gamma_{Na} p_{Na}$$

We assume that each hole is selective—it passes only one kind of ion and no other. Thus each pathway has a perfect Nernst potential. If there were equal Cl inside and outside as Fig. 2.36 suggests, then $V_{Cl} = 0$. If we assume there are large $(-)$ charged molecules inside the cell to balance the $(+)$ charge and the large $(-)$ molecules cannot move through Cl holes, these large $(-)$ charges take the place of Cl^- ions and thereby balance the charge, so that we have less Cl inside than outside. We set these values:

$$V_K = -\frac{kT}{e} \ln(200\text{-mM K}/2.5\text{-mM K}) = -110 \text{ mV}$$

$$V_{Cl} = +\frac{kT}{e} \ln(55\text{-mM Cl}/200\text{-mM Cl}) = -33 \text{ mV}$$

$$V_{Na} = -\frac{kT}{e} \ln(10\text{-mM Na}/200\text{-mM Na}) = +75 \text{ mV}$$

The concentration in the numerator of the log argument is the concentration on the *inside* in each case. Note: Each Nernst potential also represents inside minus outside, i.e., we could write:

$$V_K = V_{K(2)} - V_{K(1)}, \text{ etc.}$$

We do the same with the overall potential $V_2 - V_1$, calling it simply V; otherwise there are too many symbols and the equations are more complicated.

Note: V_K is going to be negative (inside with respect to outside) because the natural ratio (200/2.5) is greater than 1, so $ln(\ ) > 0$ and therefore $V_K < 0$. But in V_{Cl}, there is a (+) outside the (kT/e) term because the sign of Cl (the valence) is opposite to K; therefore Cl has the opposite effect of K. Now the log ratio 55/200 is less than 1, so that term is negative. Even though Cl is distributed *opposite* to the K ions, their negative charge makes the V_{Cl} sign the same as V_K. Na has a (–) factor, like K, but it is distributed like Cl, i.e., the log term is negative; therefore overall V_{Na} is positive. We show these three potentials as if they were moving along in time (in Fig. 2.37). We think of each term of the equation for V as pulling the voltage toward its own potential, e.g., V_{Na} tries to make the V go to that particular voltage. It pulls with the relative strength:

$$\frac{N_{Na}\gamma_{Na}p_{Na}}{\Sigma N\gamma p}$$

which represents some fraction of the total. Now it is easier to understand the more compact equation:

$$V = \frac{G_K V_K + G_{Cl} V_{Cl} + G_{Na} V_{Na}}{G_K + G_{Cl} + G_{Na}}$$

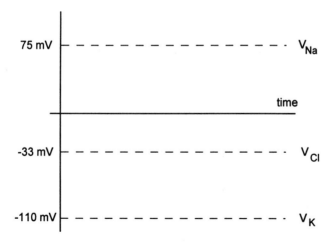

Figure 2.37. Na, K, and Cl potentials

For example, Na ions contribute an amount:

$$\frac{G_{Na}}{G_K + G_{Cl} + G_{Na}}$$

If all Gs are equal, then each ion pathway has one-third pull, i.e.:

$$V = \frac{1}{3} V_K + \frac{1}{3} V_{Cl} + \frac{1}{3} V_{Na}$$

However that is a special case; at any moment or condition, some ion usually dominates. Note: The pull of membrane potentials can change but never exceed the bounds in Fig. 2.37 unless there is another (*dotted line* above Na or below K) source of potential.

What does the current do under the conditions we have discussed? We know that $I = 0$ [this is the total (net) current taking the sign of the current into account]. Remember the cell in the dish in Fig. 2.34: There is a potential (a separation of charge) but no current (no net current). Total current must be zero, but individual ionic currents are not zero. Mathematically we express this by writing

$$I = I_K + I_{Cl} + I_{Na}$$

But we also know that:

$$I_K = (V - V_K)G_K$$

$$I_{Cl} = (V - V_{Cl})G_{Cl}$$

$$I_{Na} = (V - V_{Na})G_{Na}$$

Why $V - V_K$, etc.? To answer this, let us look at any branch as in Fig. 2.38. The V_K is an *opposing* voltage—the one created to prevent the Ks from escaping. Therefore when we say $V_K = -110$ mV, we mean an *opposing* force to the motion of K (*little arrow*), but the V across the whole element is a voltage that tries to move K ions (*large arrow*). The total effect of these two voltages is:

$$V - V_K$$

Note: V_K is *opposing*, and V is *encouraging*; in the end all the currents have to balance, so from $I = 0$ we have:

$$(V - V_K)\, G_K + (V - V_{Cl})\, G_{Cl} + (V - V_{Na})\, G_{Na} = 0$$

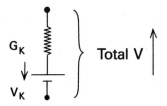

Figure 2.38. The K branch of the cell

Therefore the separate currents that we draw going in and out actually exist, but they add up to nothing in an isolated cell (see Fig. 2.36).

Let us see if we can solve our new equation in V; factoring we have:

$$V(G_K + G_{Cl} + G_{Na}) - (V_K G_K + V_{Cl} G_{Cl} + V_{Na} G_{Na}) = 0$$

or:

$$V = \frac{V_K G_K + V_{Cl} G_{Cl} + V_{Na} G_{Na}}{G_K + G_{Cl} + G_{Na}}$$

which is our old equation. In other words the above equation and $I = 0$ are equivalent.

We can even divide the total separation of charge across the membrane into its parts by writing:

$$Q_K = CV_K$$

$$Q_{Cl} = CV_{Cl}$$

$$Q_{Na} = CV_{Na}$$

If $C = 10$ pF, which is typical for a small cell (p. 60), then assuming -110, -33, and 75 mV for each of the three potentials, the charge deposited on the *inside* of the membrane is:

$$Q_K = -1.1 \times 10^{-12} \text{ C}$$

$$Q_{Cl} = -3.3 \times 10^{-13} \text{ C}$$

$$Q_{Na} = +7.5 \times 10^{-13} \text{ C}$$

Letting $Q = N(1.6 \times 10^{-19} \text{ C})$, where N is the number of ions of a particular type:

$$N_K = 6.9 \times 10^6 \quad \text{Potassium ions on the outside}$$

$$N_{Cl} = 2.1 \times 10^6 \quad \text{Chloride ions on the inside}$$

$$N_{Na} = 4.7 \times 10^6 \quad \text{Sodium ions on the inside}$$

Since we have a cell of $1000 \, \mu^2$, we can divide these numbers by 1000 to determine the number of each type of ion per μ^2:

$$N_K/\mu^2 = 6900 \quad \text{Negative charges left behind inside}$$

$$N_{Cl}/\mu^2 = 2100 \quad \text{Positive charges left behind outside}$$

$$N_{Na}/\mu^2 = 4700 \quad \text{Negative charges left behind outside}$$

There is a net distribution of 4300 negative charges/μ^2 on the inside. These ions are spread over the entire *inner surface* of the cell; they do not accumulate near their respective channels. In the end there must be net charge on one side of the membrane: All the other ions in the two domains on either side of the membrane but far from it are in $(+)$ and $(-)$ pairs, so they cancel, but there is a net $(-)$ on the inside near the membrane. That is a separation of charge and a voltage. Can you calculate the cell voltage in this case? So even though we think of each ion as contributing to the net charge separation (and it is correct to do so) in the end what matters is $Q = CV$, where V is total potential and Q is the net charge separation (or V is the net potential and Q is the total charge; these are equivalent).

Throughout this discussion we used $G = N\gamma p$, but since a particular ion can pull the net potential to its own potential, e.g., K ions can pull V toward V_K:

$$\frac{G_K}{\Sigma G} = \frac{N_K \gamma_K p_K}{N_K \gamma_K p_K + N_{Cl} \gamma_{Cl} p_{Cl} + N_{Na} \gamma_{Na} p_{Na}}$$

$N_K \gg N_{Cl}$ could create a pure V_K potential (i.e., more K holes than another type), but there are other mechanisms: p, γ, or all three. To see the relative effects we can write

$$\frac{G_K}{\Sigma G} = \frac{1}{1 + G_{Cl}/G_K + G_{Na}/G_{Na}}$$

Now it is obvious that if $G_K \gg G_{Cl}$ and $G_K \gg G_{Na}$, then the K term (V_K) dominates.

We have shown a fairly complete picture of how monovalent cations and anions [the $(+)$ and $(-)$ respectively in the preceding discussion] contribute to a cell's resting potential. We saw that the parameter p can control how much each of the inherent potentials V_K, V_{Cl}, or V_{Na} contributes to the overall potential. We generally assume that N and γ are constant for each subtype; e.g., there are a fixed number of K channels, and open conductance is fixed at γ_K. What about divalent ions?

Using our standard drawing (see Fig. 2.39), we begin with Ca^{++}, a common divalent cation that moves through membranes, with a lot of Ca outside the cell compared to inside—the case in most cells. Figure 2.39 shows only the charges that represent Ca^{++} and those that balance Ca^{++}, that is the (−) and the (−). The selective hole now passes Ca^{++} and no other ion. The Ca^{++} wants to move into the cell by diffusion; when one Ca^{++} moves in, it leaves two (−) charges behind, unbalanced. Thus twice the opposing potential builds up. That means only half as many Ca^{++} move as, say, K^+ if this were a K^+-selective hole. So the PE for diffusion is the same (for an equal ratio of Ca or K ions), but the opposing force builds up when only half as many ions move; therefore (region 2 is inside):

$$kT \ln(Ca_{in}^{++}/Ca_{out}^{++}) = -2e\,(V_2 - V_1)$$

Therefore if $V_2 - V_1 = V_{Ca}$:

$$V_{Ca} = -\frac{kT}{2e} \ln\,(Ca_{in}^{++}/Ca_{out}^{++})$$

So for the same ratio of ions (say, 10:1), the Ca ion gradient generates only half the potential as the K ion gradient; however the ratio of Ca is usually much greater than for any other ion, so its potential turns out to be large. Substituting some typical values:

$$V_{Ca} = -\frac{kT}{2e} \ln\,(10^{-7}\text{-M Ca}/10^{-3}\text{-M Ca})$$

$$V_{Ca} = -\,12.5 \times \ln\,10^{-4} = +\,115 \text{ mV}$$

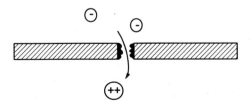

Figure 2.39. Charge balance as Ca ion moves through a Ca pore

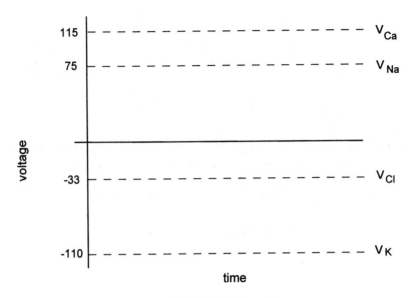

Figure 2.40. Potential cell potentials

The Ca potential is much greater in general than the other large (+) potential found in cells, e.g., the Na potential. We can add this fourth potential to our drawing (see Fig. 2.40). In a membrane full of holes that passed only one of these ions, say, K, V would equal V_K. If we enhance any one of these contributors to the potential, say, add something to open Cl channels, then V moves toward V_{Cl}. If we open Ca channels on the other hand, V moves toward V_{Ca}, etc. All of these potentials (even some that are not shown) contribute to the final potential V across the membrane. Not only the V_x of that channel type matters but also its G_x, and that means its N_x, p_x, and γ_x. Let us look at p in more detail.

Channel Opening Probability

So far we explained that p is a random switch, as shown in Fig. 2.41, that has only two values, 0 and 1; yet we use it as if it were a continuous variable, $0 < p < 1$, that governs the amount of available G: $G = Np\gamma$. We can think of p as continuous because for most cases N, the number of channels, is large. Since p is a property of each channel, e.g., let 90 out of 100 channels be open, then $p = 0.9$. Note: 90 is an average, so in time we have the situation shown in Fig. 2.42. The actual number of

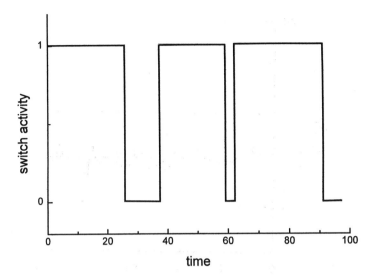

Figure 2.41. Random switch in time

open channels fluctuates; when we write $G = Np\gamma$ we are talking about the *average* p.

What happens as N becomes smaller. If $N = 10$ and the fluctuation mechanism that makes an individual channel open and close randomly stays the same, we have the situation shown in Fig. 2.43. Although these figures look the same, there is an important difference: The average decreases from 90 (for 100 channels) to 9 (for 10 channels), and absolute fluctuation (or, as we say, the noise) decreases, but not by the same proportion. If $N = 1$ (Fig. 2.41) the channel is open more often than closed; in fact it is open about 90% of the time. However the hypothetical experimental trace looks somewhat noisier than it did at $N = 100$, at least in relative terms; it is noisier. What is the rule? If we have two channels, the probability that both are open at the same time is $(0.9)(0.9) = 0.81$ or 81%; the probability that one is open and one is closed is $(0.1)(0.9) = 0.09$ or 9%. This can happen in *two* ways: Channel 1 open, Channel 2 closed *or* Channel 2 open, Channel 1 closed, so there is actually an 18% probability this state (one open, one closed) occurs; the probability that both channels are closed is $(0.1)(0.1) = .01$ or 1%.

Probability (%)	Status
81	Both open
18	One open, one closed
1	Both closed

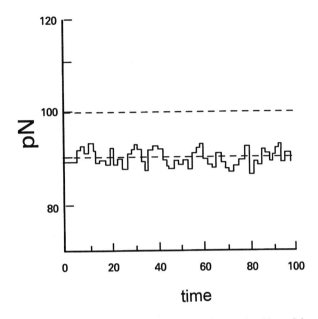

Figure 2.42. Steady-state fluctuations from 100 channels with $p = 0.9$

The two histograms in Fig. 2.44 summarize these results for $N = 1$ and $N = 2, p = 0.9$. For $N = 3$ there is a $(0.9)^3 = 0.729$ probability that all channels are open; for two channels open, one closed, the probability is $(0.9)^2(0.1) = 0.081$, which can happen in one of three ways, so 0.243 is total probability. For two channels closed, one open, $p = (0.1)^2(0.9) = 0.009$; again there are three possibilities so 0.027 represents this probability. For all three channels closed, $p = (0.1)^3 = 0.001$.

Probability	Status
0.729	Three open
0.243	Two open, one closed
0.027	Two closed, one open
0.001	Three closed

The histogram in Fig. 2.45 shows the $N = 3$ case. Note: As N increases the relative weight of each point shifts; that is the *ratio* of three open channels to two open, one closed is not so large as the ratio of two open channels to one open, one closed was for $N = 2$. The ratios gradually shift as N changes.

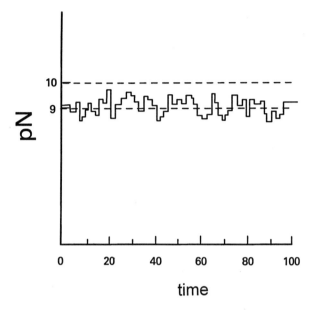

Figure 2.43. Steady-state fluctuations from 10 channels or one channel with $p = 0.9$

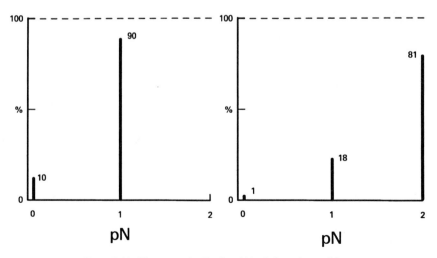

Figure 2.44. Histograms for $N = 1$ and $N = 2$ channels, $p = 0.9$

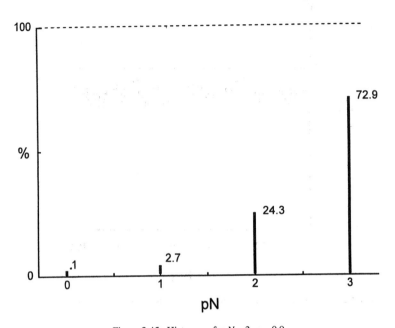

Figure 2.45. Histogram for $N = 3$, $p = 0.9$

In general, there are N channels, and each channel has only two states. The probability of being open is p. What is the probability that a set of channels is in a particular situation? The chance of all channels being open is:

$$p^N$$

If $p = 0.9$ and $N = 3$, $(0.9)^3 = 0.729$, or 72.9% of the time all three channels are open. The probability of all the channels being closed is:

$$(1 - p)^N$$

So for $p = 0.9$ and $N = 3$, $(1 - 0.9)^3 = 0.001$, or 0.1% of the time all channels are closed. Note: $1 - p$ represents the probability of a channel being closed because a channel is only open (p) or closed ($1 - p$). The number one represents 100%.

If at some time, N_o channels are open, that means $N - N_o$ are closed. The chance of finding a *particular* situation is:

$$p^{N_o} (1 - p)^{N - N_o}$$

If all channels are open, $N_o = N$, so we are back to p^N; if all channels are closed, $N_o = 0$, so we are back to $(1 - p)^N$. If $N = 3$:

Probability	Status
$p^3 (1 - p)^0$	Three open
$p^2 (1 - p)^1$	Two open, one closed
$p^1 (1 - p)^2$	One open, two closed
$p^0 (1 - p)^3$	Three closed

The exponents in each product must equal three, the total number of channels. But how many *ways* can each situation occur? For the first and the last, there is only one way, but for the second situation, we could have Channel 1 closed and the other two open, Channel 2 closed and the other two open, or Channel 3 closed and the other two open (we number the channels for this discussion). The general equation is:

$$\text{(number of possible states)}^{\text{number of objects that can assume these states}} = S^N$$

For our particular problem, the number of states S is two (open or closed), and the number of objects N is three; Therefore the total number of possibilities is:

$$(2)^3 = 8 \text{ total configurations.}$$

Since all-open or all-closed channels are unique, there are three ways of achieving each of the two middle situations $(6 \div 2)$.

Configurations	Probability	Status
1	$p^3 (1 - p)^0$	OOO
3	$p^2 (1 - p)^1$	OOC, OCO, COO
3	$p^1 (1 - p)^2$	OCC, COC, CCO
1	$p^0 (1 - p)^3$	CCC

Note:

$$1p^3 + 3p^2 (1 - p) + 3p (1 - p)^2 + (1 - p)^3 = 1$$

which says that everything is somewhere.

Now let us ask, how many ways can we have *exactly* two channels open. To answer this we must ask a slightly different question: If there are N channels, and each channel has two states, how many ways can we obtain exactly N_o? We must

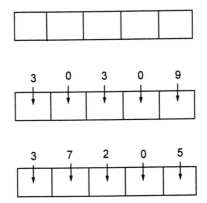

Figure 2.46. Zip codes. Top: Each digit can have 1 to 10 objects. Middle, Bottom: Two possible locations.

think of combinations in different ways; for example how many unique zip codes are there in the United States? A zip code has five digits, and each digit can have 1 to 10 objects, 0, 1, 2 . . . 9 (see Fig. 2.46). In this situation we can have multiple numbers, e.g., 22222; that is 2 or any number can appear more than once, and order also counts. Then we can have all the combinations:

00000

00001

00002

.

.

.

99999

which is exactly 10^5, or 100,000. We can divide the United States into 100 thousand unique zip codes, about one zip code for every 2500 people. The number 10^5 (99999 + 1) is *one* of the possible combinations. Note: We give each combination a *name*, and that name stands for *how many*, so 100 in the set 00100 is both a *selection* and an *amount*, as is 6307. This seems trivial, but if we look at the binary system, base two, you will see the point. Consider a 5-place zip code system in this base.

$$00000$$

$$00001$$

$$00010$$

$$00011$$

.

.

.

$$11111$$

Each place can have only 1 or 0. Thirty-three unique zip codes are possible. Note: We have no names for these numbers; we would have to say that 11111 is 32, because $S^N = 2^5 = 32$, and $32 + 1 = 33$.

We have a physical concept in mind when we say there are three channels, each having two states, because for channels we *do not* consider that OCC is different than COC; however we do consider 011 to differ from 101. For channels *order* in combination possibilities does not matter, or so we assume. Therefore when we calculate that $2^3 = 8$ probabilities for three, two-state channels, we group some of them together, namely those with two channels open (no matter where they are) and two closed (no matter where they are). That is the basis of writing

$$OOO$$

$$\left. \begin{array}{l} OOC \\ OCO \\ COO \end{array} \right\} \text{ Assumed the same}$$

$$\left. \begin{array}{l} OCC \\ COC \\ CCO \end{array} \right\} \text{ Assumed the same}$$

$$CCC$$

We think that OOC carries the same current as OCO, since these are supposed to represent two channels open in parallel, and this would certainly be true for ordinary resistors in parallel.

We now want to know how many of these same types exist for a given situation. If there are three channels and each has two states, what is the equation for *three* with two open and *three* with two closed? What is the probability of having two open of the 2^3 cases? Consider three distinguishable objects: A, B, and C. How many ways can we arrange three distinguishable objects?

ABC

ACB

BAC

BCA

CAB

CBA

There are three possibilities in the beginning, $(3 - 1)$ ways of arranging the second object, then $(3 - 2)$ ways of arranging the third object; that is $3(3 - 1)(3 - 2) = 6$ ways. This is called factorial, or 3! Thus:

$$3(3 - 1)(3 - 2) = 3 \times 2 \times 1 = 3!$$

In general, we can arrange *N distinguishable* objects, *N!* different ways. Note: There is no repetition in this example, i.e., no AAB. This is *not* like determining the number of ways of arranging three objects when each can have x number of states (like zip codes). Under such conditions given three spaces to fill when *each space* can take the value A or B for example, we have the following possibilities.

AAA

AAB

ABA

ABB

BAA

BAB

BBA

BBB

To summarize: If there are N objects, each of which can have S states, the total number of possibilities is:

$$S^N$$

If $S = 1$ and there are 100 channels, there is only one possible outcome:

$$1^{100} = 1$$

We assume that no matter how we arrange these channels (at some level they are distinguishable), we always have the same outcome. Thus A-red next to A-blue next to A-green . . . is the same as A-blue next to A-white next to . . . If we think of two states, A-open next to A-open next to A-open . . . is the same as A-open next to A-closed next to A-closed . . . as long as the total number of open and closed remain the same in each file. For channels this means that the two situations shown in Fig. 2.47 are the same, which seems unlikely (open circles mean open, and solid circles mean closed).

Assuming that the two situations shown in Fig. 2.47 are functionally equivalent, we want to combine the idea of: S^N and $N!$; that is we relax the idea of order among N distinguishable objects, i.e., it does not matter if we have AB or BA of the two potentially distinguishable arrangements of A and B ($2! = 2$), we have only one state (but we have it twice). If order matters, we have $N!$ possibilities: N_o open and N_c closed. There are $N_o!$ ways of having open channels and $N_C!$ ways of having closed channels; since $N_c = N - N_o$ we have the following number of possibilities:

$$\frac{N!}{N_0!(N - N_0)!}$$

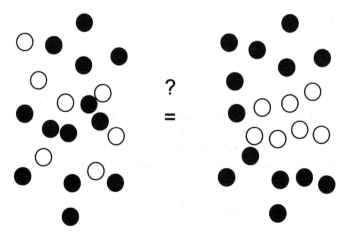

Figure 2.47. The strange assumption of channel groups

We removed redundancies (i.e., AAB, ABA, and BAA), which are all treated as the same state. If $N = 2$, with one open, then $2!/1!(1!) = 2$ possibilities; if $N = 3$, with one open, then $3!/1!(3 - 1)! = 3$, etc. To summarize if we have N distinguishable objects, $N!$ is the number of ways of arranging them if order does not matter. If N_o objects are open, $N_o!$ is the number of ways of arranging these open (and for the moment distinguishable) channels, and $N_C!$ is the number of ways of arranging N_C channels. Thus we can arrange the Os *and* the Cs in $N_o! (N - N_o)!$ ways. Note: $0!$ $= 1$, by definition. If we arrange objects in any way ($N!$), then remove the *order* ($N_o!$ and $N_c!$), for $N = 3$ and $N_o = 2$, we have (see p. 99):

$$\frac{N!}{N_0!(N - N_0)!} = \frac{3!}{2!\ 1!} = 3$$

This equation means that of the combinations ⊙OC, O⊙C, ⊙CO, OC⊙, C⊙O, CO⊙ (circles with dots help to define the "distinguishable" opens), only three survive because *order does not matter*. Then we can think of the above equation as the degeneracy: It indicates how many states are left out of the possible $N!$ *if order does not matter*. For $N = 2, N_o = 1$:

$$\frac{N!}{N_o!(N - N_o)}! = \frac{2!}{1!\ 1!} = 2$$

which means two ways of having OC out of a total of $2^2 = 4$ states. For $N = 3, N_o = 1$:

$$\frac{3!}{1!\ 2!} = 3$$

which means three ways of having OCC out of a total of $2^3 = 8$ states. For $N = 4$, $N_o = 2$:

$$\frac{4!}{2!\ 2!} = 6$$

which means six ways of having OOCC; these are OOCC, OCCO, COOC, OCOC, COCO, and CCOO. Work out some examples of your own.

Now we can get back to our problem asking what's the chance that 10 are open, that 9 are open, ..., etc. The probability that N_o channels are open when $N = 10$ channels taking into account the redundancy factor, is:

$$\frac{N!}{N_o!(N - N_o)!}\, p^{N_o}(1 - p)^{N - N_o}$$

So for $N = 10$ and $N_o = 10$ (then 9, 8, etc.), if we assume $p = 0.9$:

$$\frac{10!}{10!\ 0!}\ (0.9)^{10}\ (0.1)^0 = 0.348678 \Rightarrow 34.9\%$$

$$\frac{10!}{9!\ 1!}\ (0.9)^9\ (0.1)^1 = 0.38742 \Rightarrow 38.7\%$$

$$\frac{10!}{8!\ 2!}\ (0.9)^8\ (0.1)^2 = 0.19371 \Rightarrow 19.4\%$$

$$\frac{10!}{7!\ 3!}\ (0.9)^7\ (0.1)^3 = 0.05740 \Rightarrow 5.7\%$$

and so down to:

$$\frac{10!}{0!\ 10!}\ (0.9)^0\ (0.1)^{10} = \text{small} \Rightarrow \sim 0\%$$

Figure 2.48 shows the number of distinguishable states for a particular N_o when open channel order does not matter. When N is small, say, $N = 1$ or $N = 3$, there is only a monotonic change (Figs. 2.44 and 2.45), but when N is large (Fig. 2.48), the

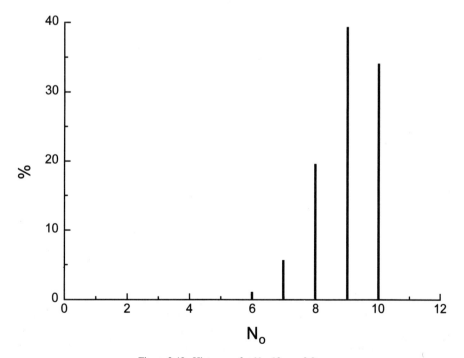

Figure 2.48. Histogram for $N = 10$, $p = 0.9$

highest part of the curve is no longer at the highest value of $pN = N_o$, which in this case is 10; instead it occurs at 9. For $N = 10$ and $p = 0.9$, we have the greatest number of functionally equivalent states when nine channels are open. The redundancy factor caused this; of course if p were another value, say, $p = 0.1$ (the reverse situation), then we would get a different result. Topics in this section and the following fall under the Bernoulli distribution; for a discussion, see IMN, p. 302 and ICEMb, p. 322.

We have argued for the existence of an equation that predicts the probability of finding a certain number of channels open, given that: (1) each channel has two states, open and closed; and (2) channels are independent (order does not matter):

$$\frac{N!}{N_o!(N-N_o)!}\, p^{N_o}(1-p)^{N-N_o}$$

where N is the number of channels, N_o is the number of open channels, and p is the probability that a channel is open. These variables are static; they do not change with time. Let us reconsider the case of three channels, then diagram them. Note: The two states enter the equation in two ways: Only N_o and $N - N_o$ are considered, and only p and $1 - p$, are considered. We list the states:

OOO

OOC   → ⎫   Order is not important;

OCO   → ⎪   These three are the same $\left(\dfrac{3!}{2!\,1!} = 3\right)$.

So are   ← OCC   ⎪

these three   COO   → ⎭

$\left(\dfrac{3!}{1!\,2!} = 3\right)$.   ← COC

← CCO

CCC

Note: We could have used number of N_cs, and not N_os in our formulas. For two states it does not matter; in this example 1 N_o is equivalent to 2 N_C. End points are given by $N_o = 3$ and $N_o = 0$, which has the same chance as $N_c = 0$ and $N_o = 3$. This means that of the original eight possibilities ($2^3 = 8$) only four are left: all open; all closed; two open, one closed; one open, two closed. So in an experiment, we see

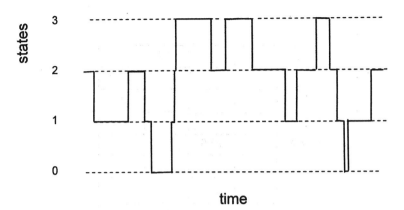

Figure 2.49. Eight possibilities, four levels

only four levels of current, as in Fig. 2.49. If $p = 0.9$ as before, then we know how often to expect *three channels* to be at, say, the third level:

$$\frac{3!}{2!\,1!}\,(0.9)^2\,(0.1)^1 = 0.243 = 24.3\%$$

Or at the first level:

$$\frac{3!}{0!\,3!}\,(0.9)^0\,(0.1)^3 = 0.001 = 0.1\%$$

If we examine a very long record, we see the hypothetical channel recording at the third level about 24% of the time and at the first level about 0.1% of the time, etc. Of course, the same two channels are not always open at the third level but any two of the three, and so for the other levels. We need a sense of how things vary with N_o and p; you can do by completing the table in Fig. 2.50. Let us use the Bernoulli equation (p. 104) for predicting how many channels we expect to find open (and therefore how often we find the set at that level over a long period) with the following equation:

$$N_o = pN$$

But can we find p from a record of many channels? The answer is yes—but only by fitting the percent distributions to:

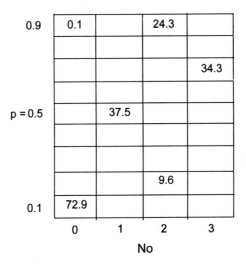

Figure 2.50. Score card for $0 < p < 1$ and $1 < N < 4$

$$\frac{N!}{N_o!(N-N_o)!}p^{N_o}(1-p)^{N-N_o}$$

which means we must know N.

The connection between the total number of states and the total number of degenerate states is:

$$2^N = \sum_{N_o=0}^{N}\frac{N!}{N_o!(N-N_o)!}$$

The 2 on the left-hand side of the equation represents two states, N_o and $N_c = N - N_o$. Thus for $N = 3$:

$$8 = 1 + 3 + 3 + 1$$

The factorial function (the degeneracy) is connected to the binomial theorem; to show this, we expand $(x + y)$:

$$(x+y)^2 = x^2 + 2xy + y^2$$

$$(x+y)^3 = x^3 + 3x^2y + 3y^2x + y^3$$

The coefficients in each term of the expansion are exactly the numbers in the factorial distribution; in general we write:

$$(x+y)^N = x^N + \frac{N!}{0! \, (N-1)!} \, x^{N-1}y + \ldots y^N$$

Instead of writing out the factorial terms in detail, we sometimes use the notation:

$$\binom{3}{2} = \frac{3!}{2! \, (3-2)!} \, , \text{etc.}$$

These are called the binomial coefficients. Pascal's triangle:

$$
\begin{array}{c}
1 \\
1 \; 1 \\
1 \; 2 \; 1 \\
1 \; 3 \; 3 \; 1 \\
1 \; 4 \; 6 \; 4 \; 1 \\
1 \; 5 \; 10 \; 10 \; 5 \; 1
\end{array}
$$

also gives the binomial coefficients (see Appendix 4). Thus if a channel has two states and the order (which, we recall translates into relative position in the membrane, see Fig. 2.47) does not matter, then there are rules about the combinations, how many there are and how many are degenerate.

We have used the symbol N_o in two different ways. We define the probability p of a channel being open as:

$$p = \frac{N_o}{N}$$

But N_o means the *average* of open N_o (this can be the same-time-average of many or the average-over-time of one). We should write:

$$p = \frac{<N_o>}{N}$$

where $< >$ means one of these averages. In the same way, we should write:

$$<I> = <G><V>$$

Many of the properties we discuss and symbols we use are really averages, but we do not always use $< >$, for example, when we write:

$$N_o = pN$$

The N_o in $N!/N_o! (N - N_o)!$ does not mean the average N_o but the *exact* number, like $N_o = 2$ or $N_o = 3$. We cannot substitute $N_o = pN$ into $N!/N_o! (N - N_o)!$, because the N_os stand for different properties in the two expressions, although the N_os are related. We think of $<N_o>$ as a number around which the actual N_o fluctuates. The Bernoulli distribution helps determine how large this fluctuation is; i.e., what is the likelihood of obtaining exactly $N_o = 104$ if $<N_o> = 100$, etc.

The problems we discuss in the remainder of this chapter and in Chapter 3 are based on these ideas. In these problems I, p, and V affect each other—when one changes, this affects everything, including the fluctuations themselves. When a channel opens, that opening changes the local current, which in turn changes the local voltage. Voltage changes the probability p that the channel is open; thus an opening changes the probability of opening, etc. We explore these relationships in detail in Chapter 3.

Channels in Membranes

We have not considered the time it takes for voltage to change as a result of channels opening; that time involves the membrane capacitance. Let us consider a Na channel in a lipid bilayer. We consider only a certain amount of lipid around the channel, not the rest of the lipid in the cell (see Fig. 2.51). In a normal cell there is more Na outside than inside, so Na wants to enter the cell when the channel opens: Na flows down its concentration gradient. Consider one of those Na ions to see what happens with respect to the capacitance it sees.

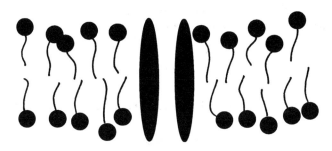

Figure 2.51. Na channel in a lipid bilayer

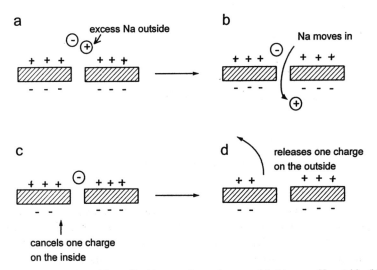

Figure 2.52. Open Na channel in a cell with a negative resting potential: (a) excess Na outside, (b) Na moves in, (c) cancels one charge on the inside, (d) releases one charge on the outside.

In Fig. 2.52 there is a net negative charge on the inside of the cell membrane, which means it has a (−) resting potential inside the cell with respect to outside. This could be due, say, to K channels that are (on average) open, but we ignore those K channels for now and accept the resting potential as just being there. The (+) Na ion, which is paired with a (−) ion, moves in because it wants to rebalance the unequal Na concentration. It *also* moves inside because the cell is (−) inside and (+) Na ions go to a (−) place; thus it moves for two unrelated reasons. When the Na ion moves inside, it changes the charge imbalance that the K channels had set up. The Na ion that enters removes one of the (−)s near the membrane, and these two ions move to the neutral cytoplasm.

If there were six extra charges on the inside of the membrane when we begin and one (+) Na enters and one (−) is left behind, two events occur: The (+) Na ion surely cancels one of the (−) surface charges giving the resting potential and, a new unbalanced (−) is created on the outside of the membrane (see Fig. 2.52). Note: Although we usually show only the excess (−) on the inside, we should show the cell as (−) inside and (+) outside. There are no *excess* free charges, just a *separation* of free charges (free means free to move). For example, we can think of the six (+)s as the K ions that escaped. The (+) Na ion that enters leaves behind a (−), which it was paired with and which in the end cancels one of the (+)s on the outside. Thus everything begins neutral and ends neutral, as it must, but in the process one Na (+) moved inside and decreased the initial separation of charge. Thus either a (+) escaped somewhere or a (−) entered somewhere because an Na ion cannot enter the

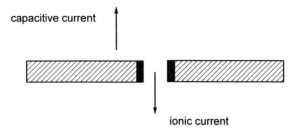

Figure 2.53. Capacitive current can balance ionic current.

cell by itself. A K^+ channel could cause the (+)-balancing move, or a Cl^- channel could cause the (−)-balancing move, but even without these permeabilities, there is another possibility: Capacitive current flowing through the lipid can balance ionic current through the channel (Fig. 2.53). Even with only *one* channel, there is always the possibility of an opposing current. If the ionic current enters (*down arrow*), the capacitive current, which releases stored charge on the membrane, must exit (*up arrow*). Compare Fig. 2.53 with Fig. 2.52.

Classes of Selective Holes

When we first discussed selective holes (Fig. 2.13), we distinguished between *one* kind of hole (or many holes of the same class) and two or three kinds of holes in a membrane. With one (or many of one type), only the selected ion moves, builds up a separation of charge, then stops. With two different holes, the current never stops (as long as there is a gradient) because the charge can be balanced by other charge. Many combinations are possible; Fig. 2.54 shows two. If *both* the K and Na gradients are high inside and low outside (not so in real cells), then we have a

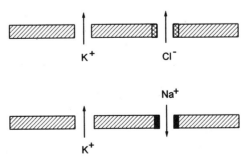

Figure 2.54. Ionic current can balance ionic current.

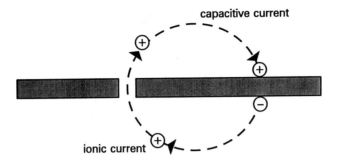

Figure 2.55. Current flows in a loop.

special situation. In this case too the movement of ions comes to a halt as soon as enough charge separates to build up the appropriate voltage. In general however if one *countercurrent* balances the other current, then ions keep moving as long as a concentration imbalance exists.

When we considered a single hole with the paired (−) charge left behind (say, K^+ escapes, leaving Cl^- behind), a counter current was actually moving across the lipid bilayer that holds the channel. That is the (+) escapes, pushing a (+) onto the outer membrane surface, then that (+) pushes a (−) charge off the inner surface (the capacitance) toward the place where the (+)s are leaving the interior (see Fig. 2.55). Current cannot move by itself; it has to move in a loop.

The knock-on, knock-off current through the lipid bilayer is the capacitance current, *but it can work only when the charge is changing.* While (+) ions are escaping, the counter current, i.e., the capacitance current, is entering; this makes the loop. However as (+)s accumulate on the outside and create a potential, it becomes more difficult to add charge; eventually enough charge accumulates to stop further ion movement. Then the countercurrent stops, so all current stops because the counter capacitance current works only when charges are *moving*; it is related to the equation for capacitive (stored) charge: $Q = CV$. A change of charge dQ causes a change in voltage dV in a certain time dt; then:

$$\frac{dQ}{dt} = C\frac{dV}{dt}$$

We call dQ/dt the capacitance current I_C; thus (p. 17):

$$I_C = C\frac{dV}{dt}$$

Capacitance current takes time because of the fundamental difference between the two laws:

$$I = GV$$

and (p. 31):

$$Q = CV$$

In the first law $I \propto V$, but in the second $Q \propto V$; therefore $I \propto dV/dt$. It becomes more difficult to build up the separation of charge because of the already-existing charge.

Total Membrane Conductance and Potential

We now consider the movement of ions through a pore in the membrane, paying attention to the entire membrane, including the lipid; the membrane holding the pore plays an important role too. If there are, say, more K ions inside a cell than outside, K ions move through the K-selective pore. But this hole must be located in something with the properties of an insulator—if it were not an insulator, (+)s pass not only through the pore but through that part of the membrane too. Remember: An insulator separated by two conductors (the regions *from which and to which* the ions move) is a capacitor Fig. 1.3. Thus the hole is located in a capacitor, more or less by our definition of the problem; this is true for a hole in a piece of glass, Saran Wrap®, or in a lipid bilayer. This introduces time into the problem: If we consider the hole by itself as a simple resistor, then time does not enter into the problem; the rule for the resistor is $V = IR$, where V is the voltage across the hole and I is the current through it. If we vary V, I follows V without delay; if we vary I, V follows it (see Fig. 2.56). If we change the slope of V, we change the slope of I in the same way: When V changes, i.e., moves in time, say, from 0–100 mV in 1 msec, I moves with it; I and V always follow each other.

The same is true for capacitors if we consider the charge, because: $V = Q/C$. But to have current, we must change V in time (see Fig. 2.57). As long as V is moving, I is flowing, but the shape is different. If we change the *slope* of V, we change the *level* of I. If V changes uniformly and continuously (a ramp), I is flat; if the V ramp goes from 0–100 mV in 1 msec, then:

$$\frac{\Delta V}{\Delta t} = \frac{100\,\mathrm{mV} - 0}{1\,\mathrm{msec} - 0} = 100\,\mathrm{mV/msec}$$

If we know the capacitance of the membrane, say, 100 pF, then:

$$I_{\mathrm{C}} = (100\,\mathrm{pF})(100\,\mathrm{mV/msec}) = 10^4\,\mathrm{pA} \qquad \mathrm{or} \qquad 10\,\mathrm{nA}$$

Note: I and V *still* follow each other *exactly* even though the shape is different: When one curve moves, the other moves with it. Figure 2.58 shows the two rules side by side for more complex shapes.

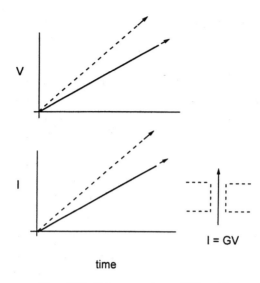

Figure 2.56. Hole, no membrane: *I* follows *V*

Note: In Fig. 2.58 the current *I* through the hole (*left panel*) always follows *V* across the hole, whether positive or negative, but *I* for the membrane alone (*right panel*) is trickier: When *V* is not changing in time (i.e., it is flat), there is no current through the capacitor; when *V* has a positive slope (rises), current is positive; when

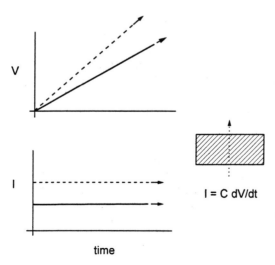

Figure 2.57. Membrane, no hole: *I* follows *dV/dt*

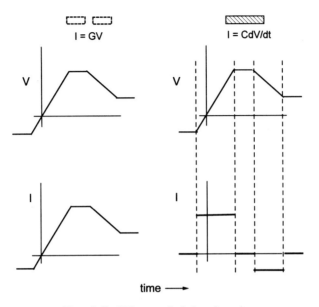

Figure 2.58. $I(V)$ curves for hole and membrane

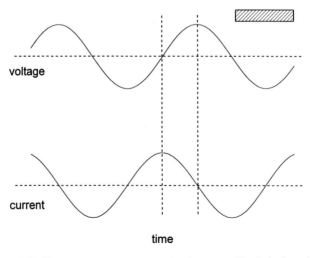

Figure 2.59. Sine waves across a pure capacitor (represented by the horizontal bar).

V has a negative slope (descends), current is negative. The more rapidly *V* rises or descends, the greater the capacitive current level (cf. Fig. 1.26).

Consider a sine wave *V* across a pure capacitor (a membrane without holes); then we have the situation shown in Fig. 2.59. When *V* is at its peak (where it is in fact flat for a brief moment), *I* is zero (for a brief moment); when *V* changes most rapidly (to 0), then *I* is greatest. Positive *V* slopes give positive *I*, as before; however one curve in Fig. 2.59 appears to be *ahead* of (or behind) the other. For this reason we often say that current *lags* voltage. In a sense it does because the maximums and the minimums are out of sync (or out of phase). But this is just a version of Fig. 2.58: There is actually no delay in *generating I* from *V*; when *V* moves, *I* moves too, with a different shape, but always by the same rule. The resistor (the hole) and the capacitor (the membrane) do not really introduce delays (in this sense) when viewed by themselves (when *V* moves, so does *I*; when *I* moves, *V* moves).

We now consider a hole in a membrane, taking into account the interaction between the two parts of this system. The (+)s inside that want to escape are capable of ultimately generating a voltage V_K, but because of the capacity *C* of the membrane, they cannot do it rapidly. Assume the hole is closed at the beginning of the problem, so the Ks want to escape but they cannot. If a gate in the hole opens instantly, and if all the charge escapes instantly, this would generate the full voltage:

$$V_K = \frac{Ne}{C}$$

All the charge that can move before the opposing voltage stops more from moving, that is *Ne*, generates all the possible voltage V_K. But this is not what happens: First some K ions escape, then more escape, etc. When the first (+) ion escapes, there is no voltage across the membrane; the ion moves because of the diffusional potential energy, that is, the gradient (Fig. 2.7). The full *potential energy appears instantly* for the voltage:

$$V_K = -\frac{kT}{e} \ln(K_{in}/K_{out})$$

Only one ion appears in the formula because we show the desire to move as a voltage; however this is really the diffusional potential, i.e., ions want to move because there are *more* inside—concentration, not electricity, and that concentration difference is instantly seen through the open hole. We describe that difference in concentration as $\ln(K_{in}/K_{out})$ and view it as a voltage through the constants (kT/e) (see Fig. 2.10).

When the gate opens, *many* Ks on the inside see the *few* Ks on the outside and try to move instantly; there is no voltage generated until they do move. To obtain V_K, the charge must actually move, so $V_K = -(kT/e)[\ln(K_{in}/K_{out})]$ is the potential to move, expressed as a voltage; $V_K = Ne/C$ is the voltage generated *after* the move.

If the ions never move, there is no voltage; only after the move can we equate the two potential energies to obtain the Nernst equation (p. 59).

After implies time. When one K ion escapes, it is easy; when the next one escapes, it is more difficult because charges accumulate on the membrane surface, it is difficult to find room. Let us consider a point in time when most of those charges have escaped, so a few remain before reaching the maximum value of V_K. Most of the K imbalance across the membrane still remains, that is, $K_{in} \gg K_{out}$. Assume $K_{in}/K_{out} = 10$, then $V_K = -kT/e[\ln(K_{in}/K_{out})] \simeq -60$ mV, and:

$$\frac{Ne}{C} = +\frac{kT}{e}\ln(K_{in}/K_{out}) = +60 \text{ mV} \quad \text{(opposing force)}$$

If $C = 10^{-11}$ F, then:

$$N = \frac{(10^{-11} \text{ F})(60 \text{ mV})}{1.6 \times 10^{-19} \text{ C}} = 38 \times 10^5 \text{ ions}$$

But if $K_{in} = 100$ mM and cell volume is one picoliter (Fig. 2.11):

$$100 \text{ mM} \Rightarrow 100 \times 10^{-3} \times 6 \times 10^{23} \times 10^{-12}$$

$$\Rightarrow 6 \times 10^{10} \text{ ions inside}$$

Thus only a small fraction of the ions actually move:

$$\frac{4 \times 10^6}{6 \times 10^{10}} \cong 7 \times 10^{-5}$$

That is, only 0.007% of the ions.

Nevertheless due to an accumulation of charge on the membrane, it is more difficult for the later ones to escape, and it becomes more difficult as V_K approaches its full value (see Fig. 2.60). Although there is an instant recognition of a K_{in}/K_{out} driving force (the motive), there is a gradual accumulation of (−) charge on the inner membrane surface (the voltage) as the (+) Ks escape.

Consider an equivalent circuit where γ represents hole conductance, V_K represents voltage, $-(kT/e)\ln(K_{in}/K_{out})$ (negative, by convention), and c is the capacitance around that particular channel. When the gate closes and the channel opens at $t = 0$, currents are both ionic and capacitive. The outward single-channel current is:

$$i = \gamma (V - V_K)$$

for whatever V value exists at any moment (remember, V is changing). To emphasize what is changing in time and what is not we write this equation as:

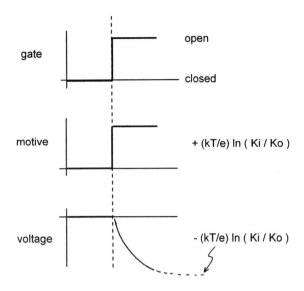

Figure 2.60. Gate, motive, and voltage

$$i(t) = \gamma \left[V(t) - V_K\right]$$

The two currents, ionic and capacitive, are equal at any moment (p. 17):

$$i(t) = c \frac{dV(t)}{dt}$$

These currents must be equal and opposite because this is the only loop (Fig. 2.55). Remember: Whatever charge enters c from the top side ejects a charge on the lower side, so the $c(dV/dt)$ current does not actually consist of ions moving *through* c. At some general time t, we have:

$$\gamma \left(V - V_K\right) = -c \frac{dV}{dt}$$

or

$$c \frac{dV}{dt} + \gamma V = \gamma V_K$$

To emphasize that V_K is the driving force (that appears instantly at $t = 0$), we write this equation as:

$$\frac{c}{\gamma}\frac{dV}{dt} + V = V_K$$

V_K is the parameter that wants to change V. Let us write $V = V(t)$ to remind us of what we are looking for; let the local time constant of the channel be:

$$\tau = \frac{c}{\gamma}$$

Then our equation becomes:

$$\tau\frac{dV}{dt} + V = V_K$$

All three terms have the units of voltage.

Now V_K behaves like a switch: When the gate is closed, there is no V_K; when the gate is open, all of V_K (viewed as a motive) appears at once (Fig. 2.60). We are interested in that very moment and in the following time; all we have to do is solve the equation for $V(t)$. We give the solution, then check that it is correct (cf., Fig. 1.18):

$$V(t) = V_K(1 - e^{-t/\tau})$$

The equation has the well-known shape. Since $V_K \sim -60\,\text{mV}$ for a 10-fold difference in K concentration, voltage across the membrane decreases when the K channel opens (see Fig. 2.60).

So far we considered a single K-selective channel in a lipid bilayer, the selective hole in a membrane. The above equation for $V(t)$ is used in many problems; it is an exponential equation, but instead of increasing (or decreasing) in a simple $e^{-t/\tau}$ way, it moves as $(1 - e^{-t/\tau})$. First we verify that this is a solution using the equation:

$$\tau\frac{dV}{dt} + V = V_K$$

Since V_K is constant, we calculate dV/dt from $V(t)$:

$$\frac{d}{dt}[V_K(1 - e^{-t/\tau})] = V_K\frac{d}{dt}(1 - e^{-t/\tau})$$

One is a constant too, and $d(1)/dt = 0$, so all we have to find is:

$$\frac{d}{dt}(-e^{-t/\tau}) = -\left(-\frac{1}{\tau}e^{-t/\tau}\right)$$

$$= \frac{1}{\tau}e^{-t/\tau}$$

Filling terms in we have:

$$\tau\frac{dV}{dt} = \tau\left(\frac{1}{\tau}e^{-t/\tau}\right) = e^{-t/\tau}$$

Next we substitute:

$$V(t) = V_K(1 - e^{-t/\tau})$$

Therefore:

$$\tau\frac{dV}{dt} + V = e^{-t/\tau} + V_K(1 - e^{-t/\tau}) = V_K$$

This is the original equation, so $V(t)$ is a solution. The solution is valid for the conditions we set, particularly that V_K appears instantly: There is a step function in V_K as soon as the channel opens; that is the condition that gives the solution:

$$V(t) = V_K(1 - e^{-t/\tau})$$

If V_K changes in another way, there is a different result (IMN p. 362). Thus a K-selective channel exits in a lipid bilayer; it opens and the voltage V across the membrane (the lipid surrounding the channel that opened) increases slowly (or decreases slowly) to the Nernst equilibrium potential for K, V_K. What is the value of the flat line before $t = 0$ when the channel opened? We implied that it was zero, that is the initial voltage before $t = 0$ was $V(t) = 0$, but that makes no sense, because if the only channel in the cell were the one we are discussing, and it were closed, then the situation is undefined. That is, since there is no ion-conductive pathway between inside and outside, we cannot define a voltage; it is not zero, it is undefined. The capacitive pathway does not connect inside and outside because no current passes through the capacitor unless voltage is changing.

Let us assume for the moment that the potential before $t = 0$ is $V = 0$. If $V = 0$ is the undefined potential before the channel opens, then when the channel is closed, $V = 0$; when the channel is open, V goes to V_K by $V(t)$. Now consider a number of channels opening and closing—all alike and all K holes. Then the membrane voltage between the inside of the cell and the outside is $V(t)$. In other words the voltage tries to move to V_K (channels open), but when channels close voltage increases to $V = 0$ (our temporary reference). *How fast* voltage increases or decreases depends on how many channels are open. If one channel is present, then the time constant is:

$$\tau = \frac{c}{\gamma}$$

where c is the capacitance that one channel sees. But if there are N_o channels open, then:

$$\tau = \frac{C}{N_o \gamma} = \frac{C}{G}$$

where C is the capacitance that the N_o channels see. But that is *all* the capacitance! To see this consider two cells the same size, then compare one hole with many holes (see Fig. 2.61). Since the holes are small, the lipid membrane area in both cases is actually the same; therefore c in the one-channel cell is the same as C in the entire cell. This means the time constant in the single-channel cell is much larger than the time constant in the many-channel cell. So for many channels that open and close randomly in a membrane, voltage profiles in time resemble Fig. 2.62 for these two cases, where the number of channels open at any time dictates the time constant. Therefore when a K channel opens, it not only moves the potential toward V_K, but it also speeds up the process because N_o increases, and τ decreases.

Remember: N_o, the number of channels open at any time t, is:

$$N_o = pN$$

where p is the open probability. Now we must think of p as changing in time, i.e., since $N_o(t)$ changes in time:

$$p(t) = \frac{N_o(t)}{N}$$

changes in time, too. In the steady-state we think of an average $p(t)$, which is what we usually mean by the symbol p (see p. 107).

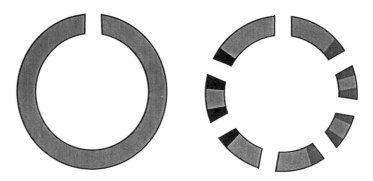

Figure 2.61. One hole versus many

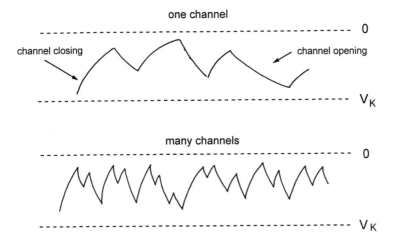

Figure 2.62. How a membrane potential looks when channels open and close: One channel and many channels

There is much to be gained by looking at the problem in real time as in Fig. 2.62. Fluctuation in membrane potential, the role of the capacitance, and how the channel opening influences that channel's ability to change the potential—are at the heart of bioelectricity. For example we will use ideas illustrated in Fig. 2.62 to explain the action potential.

3

Applications

Current

There are two famous equations in membrane biophysics that we must understand; one is for the average current from a population of opening and closing channels, the other is for fluctuations, or noise, around the average current. If we have a population of N channels (the total number without considering status, i.e., whether or not they are open or closed). The N is therefore a constant for all practical purposes, and we do not consider that channels may enter or leave the membrane; we only require N channels to be available to be opened. The average current is

$$I = Nip$$

where i is the current through an open channel and p is the probability that the channel is open. The probability that the channel is open or the probability of a channel being open is not equivalent to the probability of *opening* (see Fig. 2.20 and Fig. 2.21). In the following sections, we explore a common formula for p:

$$p = \frac{1}{1 + e^{-a(V-b)}}$$

This formula expresses the notion that $p = p(V)$: The probability that a channel is open depends on the voltage (called the Boltzmann function). In Fig. 3.1 we replace V by x to show the general structure of the formula and how it depends on parameters a and b. The function is centered on b, which here has the value b = 1. If a becomes very large, the Boltzmann function becomes practically a step function. The limits of $p(V)$ are 1 and 0 at $\pm \infty$. The equation appears to go to 0 at $x = 0$, but this is only true when a is large, as we see by substituting some values. This is one way the probability behaves as a function of voltage if we consider voltage-gated channels

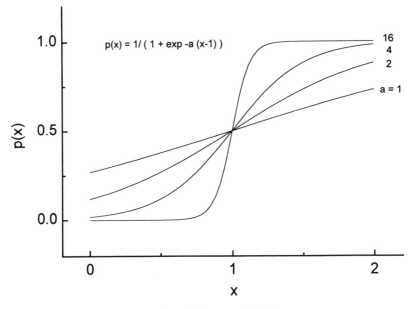

Figure 3.1.   Boltzmann probability

($x = V$) or a chemical controlling the channel; in such a case, x may equal the concentration of that chemical.

Current through an open channel, i, obeys Ohm's law; that is, $V = IR$, but we must change things a bit for voltage-gated channels. We generally use lower case variables for microscopic variables, i.e., i for the microscopic current; therefore $V = iR$ is closer to standard notation. We also like to use conductance, not resistance but because $G = 1/R$ would apply to *macroscopic* current, we need another symbol for microscopic conductance; we use γ. Therefore $V = IR$ becomes $V = i/\gamma$. Note: We did not use a lower case v in the equation $V = i/\gamma$, nor did we write $v = i/\gamma$ because voltage, unlike current or conductance, is the same for one channel as for many channels, since the channels are in parallel in the membrane, next to one another. Thus voltage across one channel is the same as voltage across two channels, etc.

Voltage is also a local parameter (microscopic), but if voltage is the same for all channels, then the membrane voltage never propagates because propagation means voltage changes along the membrane. Nevertheless we often consider a nonpropagating potential, sometimes called a *membrane potential* or a *space clamp*, for which V is a constant everywhere even though current is not. We express this idea as follows:

$$v = V$$

But for space clamp conditions:

$$i \neq I$$

We assume two channels very close to each other (see Fig. 3.2) for this situation.

In a space clamp, voltage remains constant over the membrane area we are considering. This is a simplification; we must still consider channel selectivity. Assume that instead of $V = i/\gamma$ we write:

$$i = \gamma V$$

which is an $i(V)$ curve though the origin, i.e., $V = 0$ implies $i = 0$. The curve is a straight line if γ is constant for all voltages. However we know in an ion-selective channel the zero of current does not occur when $V = 0$ but when $V = E$, where E is the Nernst potential for a selective channel. To show this we write (see Fig. 1.28):

$$i = \gamma(V - E)$$

Now when $V = E$, $i = 0$.

Based on what we have done so far, the final equation for the macroscopic current through a population of N channels is $I = Nip$ or:

$$I = N\gamma(V - E) \frac{1}{1 + e^{-a(V-b)}}$$

Note: We can let $\gamma N = G = $ constant, the maximum conductance of all channels if they were all open; however we need not restrict ourselves to this constant situation: N and γ can both change. Channels come and go in membranes, and the open channel conductance γ can be dependent on voltage, but for now we consider both to be constant. The graphical form for I is the product of two functions that depend on V, namely, $i(V)$ and $p(V)$. Both are sliding functions (see Fig. 1.17); that is they have the *functional form* $i(V - E)$ and $p(V - b)$. Note: ( ) means function here not times; we write $i(V)$ and $p(V)$ to emphasize function of voltage. Exactly where i and p lie on the V-axis depends on E and b, and the slopes of these two functions depend

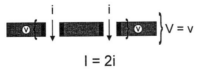

$$I = 2i$$

Figure 3.2. Two channels close to each other

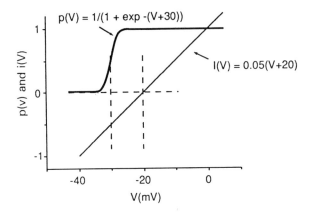

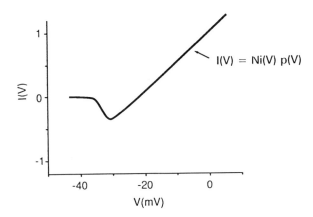

Figure 3.3. *I* as a function of *i* and *p*. Top: $p(V)$ and $i(V)$; Bottom: Product of $p(V)$ and $i(V)$

on γ and a. The total current $I(V)$ is proportional to the product of $i(V)$ and $p(V)$, as illustrated in Fig. 3.3.

So far we have used Ohm's law $V = IR$ and rewritten it as $i = \gamma(V - E)$. Now we ask if ions moving through channels obey Ohm's law? Generally the answer is no. To see this we suppose that ions in a channel obey Nernst–Planck rules instead of Ohm's law; that is, they are subject to both electrical forces *and* diffusion. Then we examine the $i(V)$ results. The flux of an ion ϕ, which has the units of number per unit area per unit time ($\phi \ominus$ #/area · time), obeys the following equation:

$$-\phi = \text{ukT}\frac{dn}{dx} + zenu\frac{dV}{dx}$$

where u represents the mobility of the ion in the channel ukT is the diffusion constant of the ion in the channel; the parameter $n(x)$ is the concentration of the ion at any place along the channel length (x), just as $V(x)$ is the voltage at any place (x). The single-channel current is related to the single-channel flux by the following equation:

$$i = -zea\phi$$

where α is the area of the single-channel, z is the valence, and e is the elementary charge on the ion. We let $i = -zea\phi$ because in standard electrophysiology, we want the inward current to be negative. A different sign convention is possible; however the final equation for the current must agree with the standard convention in biophysics that the inward positive charge flow is a negative current (ICEMb, p. 267). For example if there exist (+) flux into the cell and the spatial sign convention indicates positive flux, the current by convention is negative. That is if dV/dx is negative (goes downhill from left to right, i.e., from a higher, more positive potential to a lower, less positive potential), then (+) ions move from left to right (down the gradient). This voltage gradient may be from 40 to 10 mV, from 0 to -100 mV, or from -20 to -60 mV, etc. In this case the flux ϕ of the (+) ions is positive. Since the charge $e = 1.6 \times 10^{-19}$ C and α = area are both positive quantities (we let z take care of the sign of the charge) and since z is positive in this case, the current i also moves from left to right (down the voltage gradient). So the sign is correct: We obtain negative i for (+) ions moving down a potential gradient (from a higher to a lower potential). Now we write an equation for i based on these two forces.

We write the flux equation as:

$$-\phi = a\frac{dn}{dx} + bn\frac{dV}{dx}$$

The parameters a and b are of course not the a and b in the equation for $p(V)$, but just two parameters that we now define. We then rearrange the equation in the following form (Appendix 2):

$$-\frac{\phi}{a} e^{(b/a)V} dx = d[ne^{(b/a)V}]$$

Now we can integrate the flux equation:

$$-\frac{\phi}{a} \int_1^2 e^{(b/a)V} dx = \int_1^2 d[ne^{(b/a)V}]$$

where 1 and 2 are the two sides of an open channel, outside (1) and inside (2). The integral on the right is immediate (that is why we performed the algebraic manipulation):

$$\int_1^2 d[ne^{(b/a)V}] = n_2 e^{(b/a)V_2} - n_1 e^{(b/a)V_1}$$

The integral on the left cannot be solved without knowing how V depends on x; i.e., how does the voltage V vary with distance across the membrane. Since we do not know that in general, we write

$$\int_1^2 e^{(b/a)V} dx = \ell$$

Note: ℓ = length, which you may think of as the effective length of the channel. It is a barrier to flow that has the units of length that must be overcome to pass through the channel; this length barrier depends on the voltage profile in the channel. With this definition and recalling that $a = ukT$ we can now write:

$$-\phi = \frac{ukT \, [n_2 e^{(b/a)V_2} - n_1 e^{(b/a)V_1}]}{\ell}$$

With this equation we can write an equation for i:

$$i = -ze\alpha\phi = ze ukT \, [n_2 e^{(b/a)V_2} - n_1 e^{(b/a)V_1}] \frac{\alpha}{\ell}$$

The picture starts to become clearer now: α is the open channel area, and ℓ is the channel length. Thus (α/ℓ) is a geometric term that reflects the shape of the channel and the voltage profile in the channel. The terms in brackets describe electrical and diffusional forces. Note:

$$\frac{b}{a} = \frac{ze}{kT}$$

Therefore the equation for single-channel current becomes

$$i = ze ukT \, [n_2 e^{(ze/kT)V_2} - n_1 e^{(ze/kT)V_1}] \frac{\alpha}{\ell} \quad \text{(Nernst–Planck)}$$

We compare this equation with:

$$i = \gamma(V - E) \qquad \text{(Ohm's } law\text{)}$$

where $E = -(kT/ze) \ln(n_2/n_1)$. When $i = 0$, we obtain in both cases:

$$V = -\frac{kT}{ze} \ln(n_2/n_1)$$

Note: In the Nernst–Planck equation for $i(V)$, the concentrations n_2 and n_1, on the inside and outside of the channel do not appear as they do in the Ohm's law; in effect the $i = \gamma(V - E)$ form with γ as a constant ignores diffusional force.

We equate the two equations to see what γ in Ohm's law means in terms of the Nernst–Planck version. We use the equation (IMN, p. 71):

$$R = \frac{\rho L}{A}$$

where ρ is the resistivity of the resistor material that we consider in units ohm $\cdot$ cm, and A and L are the area and length of the resistor, respectively; therefore:

$$G = \frac{A}{\rho L}$$

These equations for R and G are written on the macroscopic scale; on a microscopic scale, we write

$$\gamma = \frac{\sigma \alpha}{\ell}$$

where σ is the conductivity (1 divided by the resistivity ρ) and α/ℓ is the area: length ratio of the conductor, that is, the single channel. You can now write an expression for σ to point out the difference between the two formulas for $i(V)$.

Boltzmann Equation

Where does the Boltzmann equation for $p(V)$ come from? The idea behind diffusion is contained in the following equation (see Figs. 2.4–2.9):

$$PE = kT \ln N$$

which means that the potential energy for a particle (in a set of N particles) to leave the group is proportional to $\ln(N)$, the constant of proportionality is kT. We owe this equation, which takes many forms, to Boltzmann.

As a shorthand, we let μ = PE. If we consider two separated groups within N, say, N_1 and N_2, both consisting of the same kind of particles but in different proportions, then:

$$\mu_1 = kT \ln N_1$$

$$\mu_2 = kT \ln N_2$$

As far as diffusion is concerned, we know that if $N_2 > N_1$, then the particles move on average from Region 2 to Region 1. If we combine these two equations, by subtracting μ_1 from μ_2, then:

$$\mu_2 - \mu_1 = kT \ln\left(\frac{N_2}{N_1}\right)$$

And:

$$\frac{N_2}{N_1} = \exp[(\mu_2 - \mu_1)/kT]$$

which is also called the Boltzmann equation; this is another way of describing diffusion. This equation says that the ratio of particles in Regions 2 and 1 depend on the potential energies of particles in the two regions. Therefore, if $\mu_2 = \mu_1$, then $N_2 = N_1$, etc. Energy μ is proportional to the particle number through $\ln N$, and the particle number is proportional to the energy through $\exp(\mu/kT)$.

The usefulness of the new form for N_2/N_1 permits us to write the actual ratio of the number of particles in two volumes, say, 1000 and 100; then $N_2/N_1 = 10$ and:

$$10 = \exp[(\mu_2 - \mu_1)/kT]$$

or $\mu_2 - \mu_1 = kT \ln 10 = 2.3$ kT. Since kT = 0.4 vJ (let v = vento = 10^{-20}) (p. 54), the difference in energy is less than 1 vJ. We can also think of the ratio as a concentration ratio if we include the volumes. Thus if there are 1000 particles per μm^3 (cubic microns) and 100 particles per μm^3, then we obtain the same answer except that now 1000 means 1000 per μm^3, etc.; in other words 1000 is not a pure number. However, if we have 10 times the volume where 1000 N_2 particles are located, then the concentration ratio is:

$$\frac{1000/10 \, \mu m^3}{100/1 \, \mu m^2} = 1$$

Even though the number of particles is greater where N_2 particles reside, concentrations are equal in the two volumes, and there is no net desire for the particles to

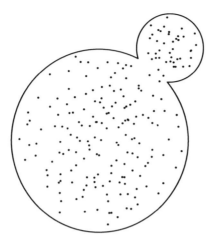

Figure 3.4. Boltzmann idea

move. Figure 3.4 shows how particles balance even though there are more in one place than another. We must not only consider how many particles there are, i.e., the actual number, but how many per unit volume. We must also think about the concentration of channels, that is the density (number divided by area) as well as the absolute number of channels—not one or the other. Looking at the balance in Fig. 3.4, we see that we can also write:

$$\frac{n_2}{n_1} = \exp[(\mu_2 - \mu_1)/kT]$$

where the ns represent concentration in the two regions. We now recognize that the term $(\mu_2 - \mu_1)$ can represent any energy difference, not just the diffusional potential energy that we began with—it could be gravitational, electrical, or anything that drives particles to move (see Fig. 2.9 and Fig. 2.10).

Concentration can also refer to the concentration of a particular state in a multistate channel model. Consider a two-state model in which a channel can be open or closed (IMN, p. 296):

$$C \Leftrightarrow 0$$

If there are N total channels, and N_o and N_c represent the momentary number in each state, then $N = N_o + N_c$; that is, no channels are created or destroyed. At any moment then:

$$\frac{N_o}{N} = \text{Fraction of open channels}$$

$$\frac{N_c}{N} = \text{Fraction of closed channels}$$

If we consider a steady-state when the average number in O or C is constant, then:

$$p = \frac{N_o}{N} = \text{Probability of being in an open state}$$

$$q = \frac{N_c}{N} = \text{Probability of being in a closed state}$$

Assume we are in state O; what are the chances of staying there? The first question we ask is, where do we go when we leave O? A reasonable point of reference is C, because that transition goes to the open state, which is the state that we measure (i.e., current passes through the open state, and we measure current). That may not always be true (perhaps we can measure the closed state in some situations, for example, blocking a channel), but we usually measure from the open state. So the concentration of open channels is N_o/N, and the concentration of closed channels is N_c/N; therefore the ratio is:

$$\frac{N_o}{N_c} = \exp[(\mu_2 - \mu_1)/kT]$$

The Ns in the numerator and denominator on the left-hand side cancel, but we could also write:

$$\frac{p}{q} = \exp[(\mu_2 - \mu_1)/kT]$$

The term $(\mu_2 - \mu_1)$ now means the difference of energy between the open and closed states, thus $(\mu_o - \mu_c)$. According to the above equation, the ratio of open to closed channels equals e^x (the ratio of closed to open probabilities equals e^{-x}). Note:

$$\frac{N_o}{N_c} = \frac{N_o}{N - N_o}$$

and:

$$\frac{p}{q} = \frac{p}{1-p}$$

This is true because no channels appear or disappear; N is a constant number (this may not always be the case, but it is for now. We can now write:

$$\frac{p}{1-p} = \exp[(\mu_2 - \mu_1)/kT]$$

therefore:

$$p = (1-p)\exp[(\mu_2 - \mu_1)/kT]$$

This is a new form of the Boltzmann equation. It says that the probability of being open is proportional to the probability of being closed $(1 - p)$, which is logical, since we cannot reach O without leaving C. Solving the equation for p:

$$p + pe^x = e^x$$

$$p(1 + e^x) = e^x$$

(where for brevity $x = (\mu_2 - \mu_1)/kT$) or finally:

$$p = \frac{e^x}{(1 + e^x)}$$

which is a form of the Boltzmann equation that gives the probability of a channel being open in terms of the energy difference between open and closed states $(\mu_o - \mu_c)$. For example if $\mu_o = \mu_c$, then we have:

$$p = \frac{e^o}{1 + e^o} = \frac{1}{2}$$

A simpler way of writing the equation depends on observing that:

$$\frac{e^x}{1 + e^x} = \frac{1}{1 + e^{-x}}$$

(multiply numerator and denominator by e^{-x}). Then we can write:

$$p = \frac{1}{1 + e^{-(\mu_o - \mu_c)/kT}}$$

Now we see where the formula $p(V)$ comes from:

$$p = \frac{1}{1 + e^{-a(V-b)}}$$

(see p. 123). In this equation a and b were simply parameters without a particular meaning; now they have meaning. To achieve the latter form, we relied on a simple idea about how energy is related to voltage and made the correspondence:

$$\frac{(\mu_o - \mu_c)}{kT} = aV$$

Note: b in $a(V - b)$ is a way of shifting the expression $p(V)$ along the V axis (Fig. 3.1). If we imagine that the electrical energy capable of driving the channel from the closed to the open state is qV, where q is a charge on a gate within the channel that senses the voltage, then:

$$qV = (\mu_o - \mu_c)$$

and:

$$a = \frac{q}{kT}$$

The b in $(V - b)$ is often written as:

$$b = V_{1/2}$$

because it is the voltage at which $p(V)$ has half its maximum value. Recall: $V = V_2 - V_1$, and we consider $V_1 = 0$ (reference potential). By this convention the expression for current through N channels that are selective for certain ions concentrated on the inside (n_2) and on the outside (n_1) is $I = Nip$ or:

$$I = N\{zeukT(\alpha/\ell)[n_2 e^{(ze/kT)V} - n_1]\}\left\{\frac{1}{[1 + e^{-q/kT(V - V_{1/2})}]}\right\}$$

Note: ze in the ze/kT term in the first set of brackets is the charge *on the ion* moving through the open channel, whereas q in the q/kT term in the second set of brackets is the charge *on the channel gate* controlling open and closed states. The voltage V appears in both sets of brackets.

Fluctuations in Current

Suppose voltage is fixed, but probability changes with time; a classic example is an Na channel that inactivates with time after opening at positive voltages (ICEMb, p. 80). Current is always given by:

$$I(t) = Nip(t)$$

where we suppress everything except the time dependence of $p(t)$ because voltage is fixed. Current I is the mean current about which fluctuations occur, and the variance σ^2 measures these fluctuations (for a discussion of the variance and the mean see IMN, p. 94 and ICEMb, p. 322). The second most famous equation in membrane biophysics is:

$$\sigma^2 = Ni^2p(1 - p)$$

where σ^2 is the variance of fluctuations in current (σ is the standard deviation.) The equation (derived in IMN, p. 318) states that current fluctuations are proportional to the open probability p times the closed probability $(1 - p)$. This makes sense because the current is maximally noisy, as measured by σ^2 when half the channels are open or half are closed (and not noisy when all are open or all are closed). The largest value that $p(1 - p)$ can assume is 1/4. Note: Even though the variance is measured in current squared (i^2), the equation uses N, not N^2. The equation for variance is valid even when probability is changing over time; thus we can eliminate p in the above equations:

$$\sigma^2 = Ni^2 \left(\frac{I}{Ni}\right)\left[1 - \frac{I}{Ni}\right]$$

or:

$$\sigma^2 = iI - \frac{I^2}{N}$$

Thus if we can measure the mean current and the fluctuations we can deduce the single-channel current i without having seen it. We plot σ^2 against I (the two properties we measure), then fit the data. This plot was made popular by Fred Sigworth. From the same plot, we estimate the number of channels N available to open. Furthermore once we solve for i and N, we can use $I = Nip$ to find p. This formulation holds because voltage is fixed and we measure the current, but we may use the same reasoning and measure voltage. That is we plot the variance of voltage fluctuations against the mean voltage, then deduce the elementary voltage event. The equations are more complicated (see IMN, p. 375). This was first done in 1971 by Katz and Miledi (*J. Physiol.* **224**:665) to measure elementary voltage produced by the interaction of ACh with a nicotinic ACh receptor (ICEMb, p. 159).

PROBLEM. We have considered the Bernoulli distribution when discussing channels opening and closing randomly:

$$B_N(N_o) = \frac{N!}{N_o!(N - N_o)!} \, p^{N_o}(1 - p)^{N - N_o}$$

where $B_N(N_o)$ is the probability of finding exactly N_o channels open in a population of N channels. Show that if the ratio of the two probabilities (no-channels open/one-channel open) is R_{01}, then:

$$N = \frac{1}{(r - R_{01})}$$

where $r = i/I$ and $R_{01} = \sigma^2/I^2$.

Double-Sided Boltzmann Equation

The simple form of the one-sided Boltzmann equation is (let b = 0):

$$p(V) = \frac{p_o}{1 + e^{-aV}}$$

In the previous discussion, we let $p_o = 1$; i.e., the maximum probability is 1. But that need not be the case: The maximum probability is less than 1 if all channels cannot open at even the most permissive voltage. We consider this case, given the preceding conditions. Think of this function as $p(V)$, i.e., p as a function of V. Recall Fig. 1.17: Given $p(V)$, $p(V - b)$ means slide $p(V)$ to the right by b. Thus if we substitute $V - b$ in the function for V, then $p(V - b)$ looks just like $p(V)$, but it has shifted. We may write $p(V - b)$ although we usually write $p(V)$:

$$p(V - b) = \frac{p_o}{1 + e^{-a(V - b)}}$$

The center of this function lies at $V = b$ (Fig. 3.1), which we can think of as a characteristic point that slides left and right as b becomes smaller and larger. Now the function is limited in height by the value of p_o, and it increases as V becomes larger. It is easy to make $p(V)$ decrease by reversing the sign of the argument of the exponential; thus the Boltzmann equation would decrease as V becomes larger instead of increasing:

$$p(V) = \frac{p_o}{1 + e^{a(V-b)}}$$

We can also think of b as being negative. To obtain a double-sided Boltzmann equation, that is, an equation that both increases and decreases, we can *restrict* the positive-a function to the V-positive region, and the negative-a function to the V-negative region (a is always positive, so −a is negative); see Fig. 3.5, where the +a function is on the right and the −a function is on the left. Note: This is not handy because we must have a different equation for each domain; also strange effects can occur at zero where the two functions meet.

We know that b slides the function left and right (think of the one-sided function, i.e., the function on either side of $V = 0$), while a makes the rise (or fall) steeper: the larger a, the steeper the rise (or fall). We explored this in Fig. 3.1, although we now also consider a decreasing Boltzmann function. We plot two decreasing Boltzmann functions for different a, keeping b constant, and we take extreme values of the steepness factor (a) in Fig. 3.6. For these extremes the Boltzmann function practically becomes a step or a line in a certain value range. Note: At $V = b$ the curves coincide because we keep b = 10 in Fig. 3.6, the same for the functions with different a. This means that for small a, there is almost no flat part before the function starts to decrease; thus for a double-sided Boltzmann

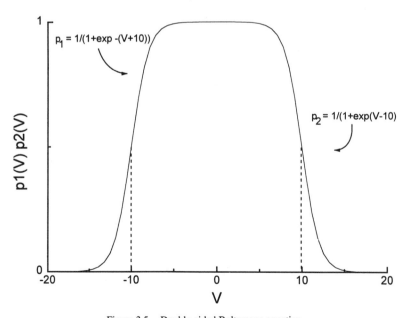

Figure 3.5. Double-sided Boltzmann equation

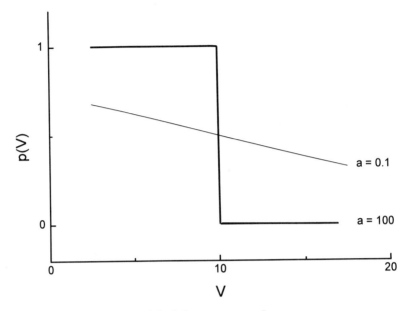

Figure 3.6.   Boltzmann steepness factor

equation generated by truncating the two equations and letting each apply only to one domain, there is a peak at the center of the graph if a is small (see Fig. 3.7). Dotted lines show the two functions (with −a and +a) on the other side (even though we agreed to ignore them); the solid lines in Fig. 3.7 show the functions (−a and +a) that we actually consider. If we adhere to this view, the total function made from

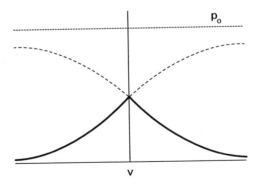

Figure 3.7.   Truncating the Boltzmann equation

the ascending and descending truncated functions (*solid lines*) have a discontinuous peak at the center, and it is below the maximum value of p_o. The discontinuity occurs if we consider the total (*left and right*) function as two separate equations. The double-sided Boltzmann equation is controlled by b (where increases and decreases are located on the V-axis) and a (slope of the increases and decreases); a has the additional power to change the shape of the total function from one with no sharp discontinuities to one with discontinuities because we cut off the −a Boltzmann equation and the +a Boltzmann equation at the $V = 0$ axis.

Let us adopt one function for both sides that has no sharp corners, namely:

$$p(V) = \frac{p_o}{1 + e^{a(V-b)}} \frac{p_o}{1 + e^{-a(V+b)}}$$

which we can think of as two probabilities p_1 and p_2, multiplied. In fact there is no need to have the a and b the same on both sides or p_0; thus:

$$p = p_1 p_2$$

where:

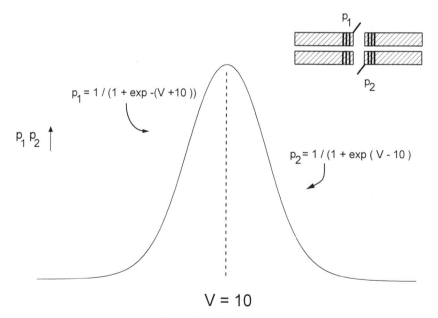

$p_1 = 1 / (1 + \exp{-(V + 10)})$

$p_2 = 1 / (1 + \exp{(V - 10)})$

$V = 10$

Figure 3.8. Gap junction

$$p_1 = \frac{p_o}{1 + e^{a_1(V - b_1)}}$$

$$p_2 = \frac{p_o}{1 + e^{a_2(V - b_2)}}$$

We can also think of the p_os as different. The function $p(V) = p_1 p_2$, does not have sharp discontinuities; it may apply for example to the open probability of the gap junction formed between two cells as a means of electrical communication. Think of the gap junction as two channels in series (ICEMb, pp. 232, 257). If each half of the functional gap junction complex is the same except that they are opposed to one another, then we have the situation in Fig. 3.8, where we selected arbitrary values for the functions to show how the composite equation looks. The formula $p = p_1 p_2$ states that the open gap junction channel (both halves must be open) depends on each half being open. Since it is a simple product, the equation also says the two halves are independent. Thus the Boltzmann function for probabilities (Fig. 3.1) can also apply to a case where probability increases and decreases as voltage changes.

Boltzmann Distribution: Some Channels always Open

Assume that channels can be open (p) or closed (q) but some channels are always open (p_o). Note: We let p_o previously represent the maximum probability of being open; here we let the same symbol represent the minimum probability. Let open channels be derived only from closed channels *than can open* according to the usual Boltzmann equation:

$$p = qe^{-x}$$

where x can represent the diffusional potential, the electrical potential, pressure, etc. (x is used for convenience).

We know that all possible channel states are related by:

$$p + q + p_o = 1$$

therefore:

$$q = 1 - p - p_o$$

so

$$p = (1 - p - p_o)e^{-x}$$

Rearranging this equation yields

$$p + pe^{-x} = (1 - p_o)e^{-x}$$

or:

$$p = \frac{(1 - p_o)e^{-x}}{(1 + e^{-x})}$$

When we measure current through the open state, we are dealing with $p + p_o$ channels, where p may change but p_o does not; thus we are interested in $p + p_o$:

$$p + p_o = \frac{(1 - p_o)e^{-x}}{1 + e^{-x}} + p_o$$

$$= \frac{(1 - p_o)e^{-x} + p_o(1 + e^{-x})}{1 + e^{-x}}$$

$$= \frac{p_o + e^{-x}}{1 + e^{-x}}$$

which is the Boltzmann distribution when some channels are always open (see Fig. 3.9).

In Fig. 3.9 $(p + p_o)$ is plotted as a function of voltage (x represents voltage). The function $(p + p_o)$ declines with V to a fixed value p_o. Note: Instead of $p = qe^{-x}$, we could begin with any distribution, not necessarily the Boltzmann distribution. There are other ways of generalizing the result in Fig. 3.9; e.g., if we consider $x = a(V - b)$, then:

$$p + p_o = \frac{p_o + e^{-x}}{1 + e^{-x}}$$

becomes

$$p + p_o = \frac{p_o + e^{-a(V-b)}}{1 + e^{-a(V-b)}}$$

We can also write the increasing expression (e^x instead of e^{-x}) and we can change the rule to any function of x, not just $p = qe^{-x}$ for another result. We can also apply this idea to gap junctions. Derive a formula for gap junctions, like the one used in Fig. 3.8, but where a fixed fraction of the channels are always open. For more fun

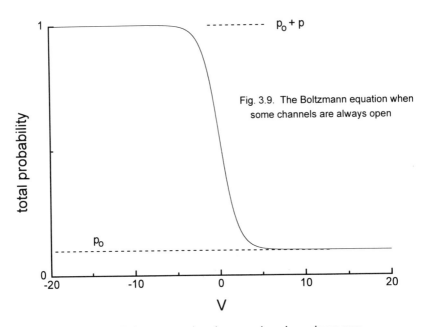

Fig. 3.9. The Boltzmann equation when some channels are always open

Figure 3.9.   Boltzmann equation when some channels are always open.

derive an expression for the case when total probability is less than 1; i.e., a certain number of channels are always closed.

Gating Currents

How does voltage open a channel? To answer that question we must see what gating currents are, then see if we can describe them fairly well mathematically (ICEMb, p. 56). First we must consider ionic currents.

The basis of bioelectricity is the random opening and closing of channels in the membrane. Hodgkin and Huxley suggested that a translocation of charge within membrane molecules accompanied voltage-gated currents and these were the gates for ion movement. After all that is really the only way to create a voltage-sensitive molecule, which must have a charge to respond to voltage. It is difficult to imagine a voltage sensor without movement; i.e., the charge feels the voltage, it moves, and the protein channel opens (or closes). Where do these ideas take us as far as current goes?

As a channel opens or closes, a charge moves in the membrane; we draw this complicated situation as a gating current in the membrane, that is, a current

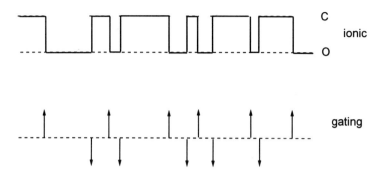

Figure 3.10. Gating currents. Top: Ion channel currents; Bottom: Gating currents for channel closings (C) and openings (O).

associated with the movement of charge. In Fig. 3.10 we represent this as a sharp arrow (cf. Fig. 1.15). Think of *Na* current a few milliseconds after changing the voltage, say, from −70 mV to +10 mV. The *Na* channel, more or less closed at −70 mV, now opens and closes, with more openings during the first moments just after voltage changes (we confine our discussion to these initial events). A small blip of gating current occurs, arrow up (channel open) and arrow down (channel closed) each time the channel undergoes a transition. In fact the gating current occurs just prior to the channel transition and causes the transition. We must consider the gating current, which we have drawn as a delta function, in more detail.

What we imagine is that some charged portion of the membrane protein moves within the membrane—not across the membrane (as ions do) but *within* the membrane (ICEMb, p. 441). Let us draw a functioning channel to see what the principles are (Fig. 3.11). As a charge in the Na channel protein moves up (toward the outside of the membrane), it generates a small outward current (*upward arrow* in Figs 3.10 and 3.11). The basic idea of the gating current is that the charge does not move away but stays in the membrane. Note: It has to have a shape, not just a sharp spike, but some feasible form, i.e., it is quick, but not a true delta function. The area under the current blip (the charge) must be the same in the increasing and decreasing directions, but it does not have to have the identical shape (even though it is in Figs. 3.10 and 3.12). The gating current is like a capacitive current; i.e., the gating current occurs only during a *change*. When the channel has been closed for a while, there is no gating current; however when the voltage changed from −70 to +10 mV it tends to open the channel (on average), so there is a gating current. Note: The channel transition coincides with the gating current, not the step in voltage. At +10 mV the Na channel is more likely to open. If the *gate* does open (as shown in Fig. 3.11), there is a gating current, and ionic current follows.

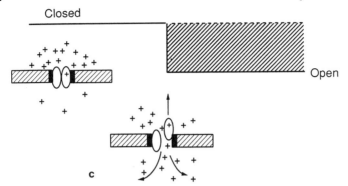

Figure 3.11.   Charge moves in the membrane: (a) Channel opening; state of the channel in the (b) closed and (c) open positions.

Therefore the gating current is very similar to a capacitive current (see Fig. 1.7). Consider again a true capacitor that could for example represent the lipid bilayer (see Fig. 3.12). In Fig. 3.12 the voltage $V(t)$ is stepped across the capacitor, and a current $I(t)$ results. The arrow represents a very sharp current and ideally it is a delta function (see Fig. 1.33) because we imagine that the voltage $V(t)$ changes infinitely fast. In the ideal capacitor:

$$I(t) = C \frac{dV(t)}{dt}$$

Thus $I(t)$ changes proportional to dV/dt, and the slope is infinite in this ideal case. Nothing at all happens if V does not change. How does this relate to the gating charge? When voltage changes the charge in the protein moves. Note: It does not have to move at that instant, but the probability that it will move increases. However

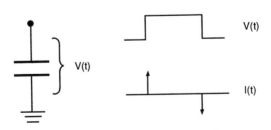

Figure 3.12.   Capacitor current. Left: Voltage applied across a capacitor; Right: A step change in voltage (top) and the accompanying capacitative currents (bottom).

the gating current is *not* necessarily proportional to the slope of the voltage change (as is the capacitor); i.e., gating current does not have to obey *CdV/dt*. Gating current may have a more complex dependence on the change in voltage, and the gating current stops only because it is *physically* constrained within the membrane. Thus in the end there is not really much of an analogy between gating currents and capacitive currents; there is only qualitative similarity. We cannot know much about gating currents until we know more about how the channel protein is actually built, but we can still make some calculations.

How large is a typical gating current? Let us call the gating current i_g; if the charge that moves is one electron equivalent e and the charge moves completely within 1 μsec, then:

$$i_g \sim \frac{1.6 \times 10^{-19} \, C}{1 \times 10^{-6} \, \text{sec}} \sim 0.2 \, \text{pA}$$

This is a large current for a single electronic charge, because we said that it moved rapidly. This indicates that a small charge need not result in a small current. Note: We did not say how far the charge moved in the membrane, although it would be nice to know. Only how much charge moved in a certain time matters. However let us assume the charge moves only a few angstroms, say, 10, which would be a lot. Then the average velocity must be about:

$$\frac{10 \times 10^{-8} \, \text{cm}}{1 \times 10^{-6} \, \text{sec}} = 0.1 \, \text{cm/sec}$$

Even if the gating charge moved only 1 Å, the velocity would be far from infinite; thus a gating current is far from a delta function, even though it is often convenient to think of it as such.

Gap Junction Model

Now that we have an idea how voltage controls channel opening, we consider a more complicated model of gap junctions. Many internal components in a channel may have to move so that it can open, thus a series of gating current arrows could precede an opening, not just one. This is true for voltage-gated channels like the Na channel and gap junctions. We assume the gap junction is composed of two abutting structures, each containing six integral membrane proteins. For convenience we shall call each of the six proteins a particle and designate the junction by the following diagram:

$$C \mid C$$
$$C \mid C$$
$$C \mid C$$
$$C \mid C$$
$$C \mid C$$
$$C \mid C$$

In this diagram C stands for the closed state of one particle; that is each of the 12 particles can undergo the reaction:

$$C \underset{\beta}{\overset{\alpha}{\Leftrightarrow}} O$$

where O is its open state and α and β are the familiar rate constants that govern transitions between closed and open states. We assume that α and β are voltage dependent.

The six-gap junction (12 paired particles) is more realistic, but the combinations are enormous. To understand the structure of the problem, we consider a reduced model, namely a two junction:

$$C \mid C$$
$$C \mid C$$

Note: We named the junction by the number of pairs; thus each half of the total gap junction (for now) is made up of two particles. We assume that a fraction of the gap junction is open when two *aligned* particles are open, e.g.:

$$O \mid O$$
$$C \mid C$$

The OO represents an opening through the gap junction, and the CC is closed. In this model we do not allow a cross opening, i.e., the following does not form an open state:

$$O \mid C$$
$$C \mid O$$

The particles must be aligned for conductance to occur. This simple two-pair system has a probability diagram that we now formulate. First consider the following:

$$\text{C} \mid \text{C} \qquad \begin{array}{c} \alpha \\ \text{C} \Leftrightarrow \text{O} \\ \beta \end{array} \qquad \begin{array}{c} \text{O} \mid \text{C} \\ \text{C} \mid \text{C} \\ \\ \text{C} \mid \text{O} \\ \text{C} \mid \text{C} \\ \\ \text{C} \mid \text{C} \\ \text{O} \mid \text{C} \\ \\ \text{C} \mid \text{C} \\ \text{C} \mid \text{O} \end{array}$$

None of the four states on the right-hand side are open through the gap (O and C do not align); they are possibilities that we are considering to make a point. The four-closed particles (on the left in the above diagram) can go in four ways to the one open particle. If the rate of C → O is α, then the rate of going from all four closed to any one open is 4α. Once we are in any one of the one-open-particle states, however there is only one way to return; hence the reverse reaction rate is just β. Note: The situation would be similar if we were considering, say, K channel gates.

For the two-pair system, we can write the reaction scheme in Fig. 3.13, where the bottom row of numbers, 0–4, represents the number of open particles regardless of position; for example in the middle column, 2 means either:

$$\begin{array}{c} \text{O} \mid \text{C} \\ \\ \text{C} \mid \text{C} \end{array} \quad \begin{array}{c} \alpha \\ \rightarrow \\ \cdot \end{array} \quad \begin{array}{c} \text{O} \mid \text{C} \\ \\ \text{O} \mid \text{C} \end{array} \qquad \text{(still closed)}$$

or:

$$\begin{array}{c} \text{O} \mid \text{C} \\ \\ \text{C} \mid \text{C} \end{array} \quad \begin{array}{c} \alpha \\ \rightarrow \end{array} \quad \begin{array}{c} \text{O} \mid \text{C} \\ \\ \text{C} \mid \text{O} \end{array} \qquad \text{(still closed)}$$

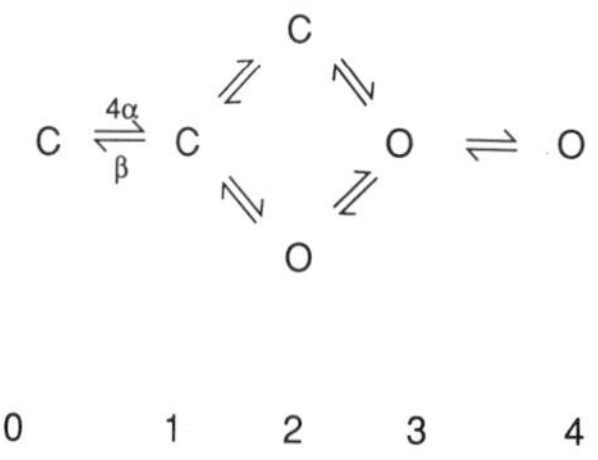

Figure 3.13. Gap junction for two pairs

That means the rate is 2α to these particular two-open-particle (but still closed) states; because there are four states with one open particle, the rate to all closed states with two open particles is 8α. Note: Only four are distinct. This gives the top C in the center column in Fig. 3.13, and there should be an 8α over the arrow leading to that state. Likewise if we look at the bottom state in Column 2, which is an open state, then:

$$O \mid C \qquad \xrightarrow{\quad\alpha\quad} \qquad O \mid O \qquad \text{(open)}$$
$$C \mid C \qquad\qquad\qquad\qquad C \mid C$$

This is the only way the open transition can happen; and that is true for any one of the four states. The rate to the open state in Column 2 is thus 4α. Diagram other states and fill in the α and the β factors on the respective arrows in Fig. 3.13.

Note: For the two-pair system, we can have a double-open situation. Thus we identify open states with a subscript (1 or 2) to indicate that it is a singly open state or a doubly open state; the latter is just this:

$$O \mid O$$
$$O \mid O$$

Therefore in the two-pair gap junction, we have three possible open conditions: O_1, O_1, and O_2. There are two O_1s because there are two ways of obtaining this condition, top or bottom (fill in the 1s and the 2s on the open states in the diagram in Fig. 3.13). To be specific we assume that one of the four individual particles in the two-pair system can have a conductance of 80 pS. Then the conductances of these three states, O_1, O_1, O_2, are respectively, 40 pS, 40 pS, and 80 pS. Two equal conductances in series have *half* the value of one of the conductances (just the opposite of resistors); thus:

$$80 \mid 80 = 40$$
$$0 \mid 0$$

and:

$$0 \mid 0$$
$$80 \mid 80 = 40$$

But two conductances in parallel add; therefore if all four of the particles (the hemichannels) are in the open state, they add up to:

$$80 \mid 80 \qquad\qquad 40$$
$$\Rightarrow \qquad\qquad \Rightarrow \quad 80$$
$$80 \mid 80 \qquad\qquad 40$$

In this case the final 80 pS value for the double open state results because two 80s in series give 40, and two of these 40s in parallel give 80.

To discuss ion channels or gap junctions further, we must understand how α and β depend on voltage. We let $\alpha(V)$ and $\beta(V)$ mean that α and β depend on voltage and nothing else that we are considering explicitly. If we have only an open state and a closed state, these must feed into one another; i.e., one can grow only at the expense of the other, as the following diagram shows:

$$\overset{\alpha}{\underset{\beta}{C \Leftrightarrow O}}$$

If we assume the Boltzmann condition:

$$O = Ce^{a(V-b)}$$

Note: As before (see p. 132) the exponent is positive because we want the O:C ratio to grow as V becomes positive. No matter what else is going on, the open state, O, is always proportional to the closed state, C, and to some function of voltage. We assume that this function is $e^{a(V-b)}$, where a is some constant, but in general it could be any function $f(V)$. For now let $b = 0$; if there are 100 particles in the C state at $V = 0$ ($e^{aV} = 1$), then $100/e \sim 37$ open at $V = 1/a$ (of course we mean 37 open in the steady state: We change V from 0 to $1/a$, then wait; when everything settles down, we see we have on average only 37 open out of an original 100). We could let O represent the *number* of open particles or the probability of being open; for example there may be 1000 total particles, so 100 represents 10%, or 0.1 probability. Then 37 represents 0.037 probability. As before p = probability of being open (steady state, for now); then we write:

$$p = (1-p)e^{a(V-b)}$$

since the probability of being closed plus the probability of being open is 1. Solving this equation for p leads to the familiar Boltzmann equation (see Fig. 3.1).

Let us look at the problem again from a different point of view. If we consider single particles in either a channel or a gap junction, then:

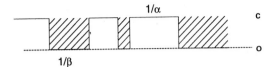

Figure 3.14.   Mean open time and mean closed time

$$C \underset{\beta}{\overset{\alpha}{\Rightarrow}} O$$

We now also see that in the steady state:

$$p = \frac{\alpha}{\alpha + \beta}$$

This is because $1/\beta$ is the mean open time and $1/\alpha$ is the mean closed time of a single gate going back and forth between C and O (SCRa, p. 142); see Fig. 3.14. The following ratio is therefore the mean open time over the total time for an average cycle, i.e., the probability of being open:

$$\frac{1/\beta}{1/\alpha + 1/\beta} = \frac{\alpha}{\alpha + \beta}$$

This probability is written for one particle, and the former probability (from the Boltzmann equation) was written for many particles, but they have the exact same meaning; i.e., if we increase voltage from 0 to 1/a, as in the first example, then the sample channel open time (averaged of course) increases from 10% open to 3.7% open (or from $p = 0.1$ to $p = 0.037$).

Since these ps are the same, we can equate them; therefore:

$$p(V) = \frac{1}{1 + e^{-a(V-b)}} = \frac{\alpha(V)}{\alpha(V) + \beta(V)}$$

where we now write αs and βs explicitly as functions of V, so we can solve for one in terms of the other. First we do this generally in terms of $p(V)$:

$$(\alpha + \beta)p = \alpha$$

$$cv\alpha p - \alpha = -\beta p$$

$$\alpha = \left(\frac{p}{1-p}\right)\beta$$

If $p = 1$, then $\alpha \to \infty$, which means that $1/\alpha \to 0$; i.e., the channel is always open (Fig. 3.14). If $p = 0$, then $\alpha = 0$ and $1/\alpha \to \infty$, which means the channel is always closed. Note: The range of $p/(1-p)$:

$$0 < \left(\frac{p}{1-p}\right) < \infty$$

Therefore α can be greater than β (if $p/(1-p) > 1$) or less than β (if $p/(1-p) < 1$). Everything has a positive value. If we now include the functional dependence on V:

$$\alpha(V) = \left[\frac{p(V)}{1-p(V)}\right]\beta(V)$$

Thus if we know the macroscopic behavior of a population of particles $p(V)$ and the microscopic behavior of one particle $\beta(V)$ = inverse mean open time, then we can find $\alpha(V)$. It is easy to measure the mean open time from single-channel records $1/\beta$ when there is a very low closed probability, but it is difficult to measure $1/\alpha$ in that case. Thus we can combine a microscopic and a macroscopic measurement to obtain both microscopic parameters α and β.

In the gap junction model, there must be *two* particles in series to have an open condition; therefore O–C is not open, but O–O is. If p is the probability that one particle is in the open state, the probability that both particles begin at the same time is p^2. This is the old rule: If we have two coins and the chance of heads is one-half on one coin, then the chance of heads on both coins is one-fourth. This means that an open time for two particles is not $1/\beta$ but $1/2\beta$. For three pairs of six particles to be open at once:

$$\alpha(V) = \left[\frac{p^{1/6}(V)}{1-p^{1/6}(V)}\right]\beta(V)$$

In the six-pair gap junction, the probability that all 12 particles are in the open state at the same time is $p^{12}(V)$; this corresponds to the maximum conductance state, which we obtain from a macroscopic measurement. If we can estimate $\beta(V)$ from looking at simple openings, then we know both $\alpha(V)$ and $\beta(V)$.

Coupled Model of Gap Junctions

The independent gate model assumes that each gate is a simple open–close switch and gate conductances add independently; thus we assume the situation Fig. 3.15. Although we stated that six gates make up a *single* gap junction complex, nothing in the theory so far changes if the six pairs are physically separated from one another. Because these simple models do not completely describe the data, we consider ways of extending the model, which also serve as an example of coupling between gates that may apply to channels and how coupling influences their gating. Let us assume that all six pairs (each pair is a gate) must be open for the gap junction to be fully open (we considered partially open gap junctions previously). If p is the probability that one particle (which is called one *connexin* unit) is in the open state, then p^2 is the probability that one *gate* is open, and p^{12} is the probability that one gap junction is fully open. This is a simple form of cooperativity between particles that form gates; channels have it too; for example in the simplest form of the Hodgkin–Huxley model viewed in channel terms, the K channel has four particles that must all be open to form an open gate (n^4 kinetics).

Experimentally for gap junctions we see a maximal conductance of 240 pS about 10% of the time; thus $p^{12} = 0.1$ and $p \sim 0.8$. Under this extreme form of interaction between states, we see only the 240 pS state; however if we imagine something similar for five gates, and four, etc., then from one gap junction, we see:

$$p^2, p^4, p^6, p^8, p^{10}, p^{12}$$

which for $p = 0.8$ gives:

$$0.64, 0.51 \ldots 0.1$$

This form of interaction does not work because this is not the observed distribution.

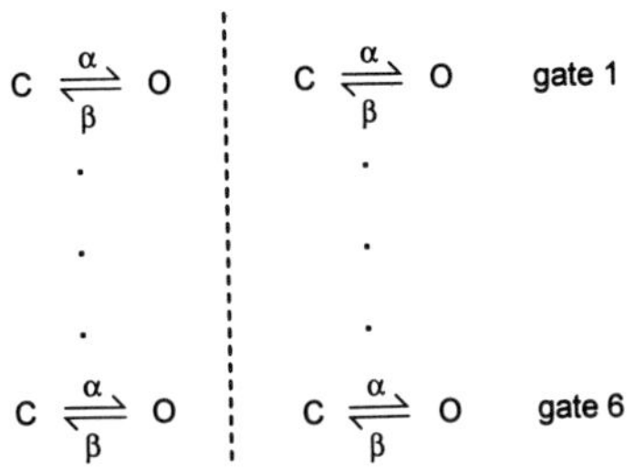

Figure 3.15. Independent gate model

As an exercise, let us assume that when one connexin opens, it influences another to open, and when one gate opens, it similarly influences another gate to open. For the moment, we consider only adjacent gates. We number the connexins in each pair, 1–6. If we assume that Connexin 2 being open can influence closed Connexin 1 through a term $\xi O_2(1 - O_1)$ and if we assume the six pairs form a ring so that Connexin 1 is adjacent to Connexin 6, then this equation describes the kinetics of Connexin 1:

$$\frac{dO_1}{dt} = \alpha(1 - O_1) - \beta O_1 + \xi O_2(1 - O_1) + \xi O_6(1 - O_1)$$

and the kinetics of its neighbor O_2 is given by:

$$\frac{dO_2}{dt} = \alpha(1 - O_2) - \beta O_2 + \xi O_1(1 - O_2) + \xi O_3(1 - O_2)$$

In this cooperative model, we let the constant ξ be the same for all paired interactions. Thus the number of connexins O_2 in the open state grow *not only* in proportion to the number of O_2s in the closed state $1 - O_2$, but also in proportion to the number of connexins in neighboring gates that are *in the open state*. To see what is going on consider, the following diagram:

$$C_1 | C_1$$
$$C_2 | C_2$$
$$C_3 | C_3$$
$$C_4 | C_4$$
$$C_5 | C_5$$
$$C_6 | C_6$$

Thus when C_1 changes to O_1, for example, it increases the probability that C_2 and C_6 (which is next to C_1 if we consider this to be a circle) opens. Likewise when C_2 opens, it changes the probability that C_1 and C_3 open, etc. This coupled model gives a different amplitude histogram of the possible open states compared with the independent model: The shift is toward the higher conductance states, which mean that it is less likely to find one pair open alone and more likely to find the 240-pS states. We may also assume that the coupling constant is a function of temperature, thus:

$$\xi = \xi(T)$$

where T is the absolute temperature. Let us assume that as T increases, the coupling constant ξ increases. If this were true, as we cool the gap junction, we would see less and less of the 240-pS states. The cooperative model (nearest neighbor) looks like this:

$$C_1 \mid C_1 \quad \alpha(1 - O_1) - \beta O_1 + \xi(O_2 + O_6)(1 - O_1)$$
$$C_2 \mid C_2 \quad \alpha(1 - O_2) - \beta O_2 + \xi(O_1 + O_3)(1 - O_2)$$
$$C_3 \mid C_3 \quad \alpha(1 - O_3) - \beta O_3 + \xi(O_2 + O_4)(1 - O_3)$$
$$C_4 \mid C_4 \quad \alpha(1 - O_4) - \beta O_4 + \xi(O_3 + O_5)(1 - O_4)$$
$$C_5 \mid C_5 \quad \alpha(1 - O_5) - \beta O_5 + \xi(O_4 + O_6)(1 - O_5)$$
$$C_6 \mid C_6 \quad \alpha(1 - O_6) - \beta O_6 + \xi(O_1 + O_5)(1 - O_6)$$

where C_1 and C_6 are next to each. For comparison the uncoupled model looks like this:

$$C_1 \mid C_1 \quad \alpha(1 - O_1) - \beta O_1$$
$$C_2 \mid C_2 \quad \alpha(1 - O_2) - \beta O_2$$
$$C_3 \mid C_3 \quad \alpha(1 - O_3) - \beta O_3$$
$$C_4 \mid C_4 \quad \alpha(1 - O_4) - \beta O_4$$
$$C_5 \mid C_5 \quad \alpha(1 - O_5) - \beta O_5$$
$$C_6 \mid C_6 \quad \alpha(1 - O_6) - \beta O_6$$

All of this is speculative as far as gap junctions go, and we present it mainly to see how to approach the problem of cooperativity. Before leaving the topic, let us consider the real gap junction. The first gap junction protein and cDNA was isolated from the liver; it is called CX32 (connexin). Altogether about a dozen CXs have been cloned, and each has four membrane-spanning domains. Six connexins form one hemichannel (one particle in the former discussion). Thus CX# refers to connexin, the four membrane-spanning domain protein, and *connexon* refers to the hemichannel composed of six connexins; these are illustrated in Fig. 3.16, which shows only one connexin on either side of the gap junction (we must imagine that six of these on each side form the entire junctional complex). The figure also illustrates that the conductance of the gap junction (G), the conductance from one cytoplasmic compartment to the other, depends on the *transjunctional* voltage (voltage between one cytoplasmic compartment and the other). The curve $G(V)$ is qualitative, but in Fig. 3.8 we saw how to develop a theory of $G(V)$. In general $G(V)$ need not be symmetric, and in some cells it is not. In Fig. 3.16 V represents voltage *across the double membrane* (in this sense the gap junction is topologically similar to the abutting membranes of mitochondria). Thus if two adjacent cells have the same potential, then $V = 0$ and conductance between the two cells is greatest. However when voltage between the cells is different (in either direction), gap

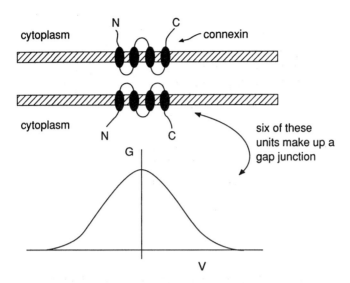

Figure 3.16.   Conductance of the gap junction depends on the voltage across it; six of these units make up a gap junction.

junction conductance decreases. How would this affect the propagation of an action potential in a tissue composed of cells connected in this way?

Voltage-Gated Ion Channels

The gap junction is a voltage-gated channel, as are many other channels, even some channels that are gated by ligands; but this term usually refers to the Na, K, and Ca channels that underlie excitability. The Na channel was the first ion channel of any kind to be cloned; it was followed by a large family of voltage-gated K and Ca channels (ICEMb, p. 253). One of the reasons that Na was first is that organs in the electric eel use numerous Na channels to generate a shock, and this facilitated purification. The K and Ca channels are structurally similar to Na channels, and in particular areas of the proteins making up these channels the amino acids are highly conserved. Sequence conservation in ion channels tends to be more prominent in hydrophobic (membrane-spanning) regions.

The Na and Ca channels are markedly different from K channels in one regard: These channels (omitting from the discussion associated subunits that make up the native channels) consist of one gene product. The Na channel has four homologous domains, each of which has six true hydrophobic regions. The region called S4 has positively charged amino acids, and it is believed to form part of a voltage-sensing apparatus (see Fig. 3.11); the region called S5 is believed to form the ion-conducting

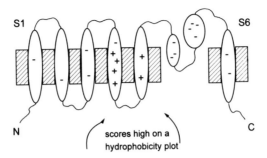

Figure 3.17.   K-channel unit

pore. The basic unit of a K channel resembles *one* of the four homologous domains in a Na channel; one of these domains is illustrated in Fig. 3.17. Note: Sections of the protein with high hydrophobicity may also contain charged residues. Four of the separate K-channel gene products aggregate into a tetramere to form the complete channel. In an Na (or Ca) channel, the four units are contained in one gene product, as illustrated in Fig. 3.18. Note: In this figure we omitted the internal and external loops but emphasize that the four units form a single protein.

It is difficult to reconcile these complex structures with the simple open–closed kinetics of ion channels. An interesting exercise involves comparing cartoons of ion channels from 1984 to 1995 (ICEMa, p. 63 and ICEMb, p. 66). One way of approaching this problem is to consider two energy levels representing open and closed states of the protein; at physiological voltages these two levels are close to one another so that the channel can change spontaneously between the two states. We can change the distribution of these levels however by adding energy to the system. One way of doing this is to add electrical energy to the system, since we are speaking about voltage-gated ion channels.

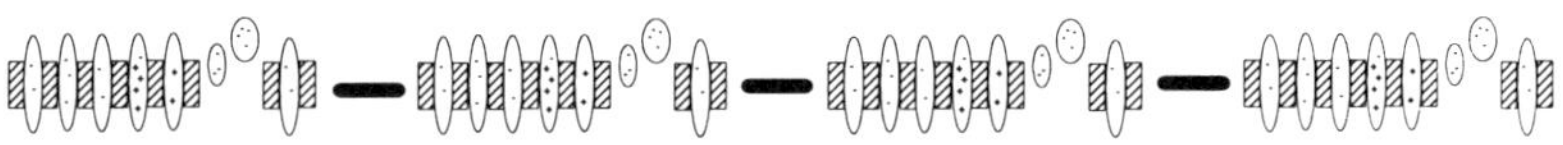

Figure 3.18.   Na-channel unit

Electrical energy is defined by:

$$E_{elec} = qV$$

where q is the charge sensing the voltage V (see the discussion on p. 132 and ICEMb, p. 55). For example let us consider a channel closed 70% of the time and open 30% of the time; this is described as an energy profile (ICEMb, p. 311). If we change the voltage, we can change this distribution, say, to 50% and 50%, as illustrated in Fig. 3.19. In analyzing channel proteins, we want to find the molecular charge that senses voltage. Since only the charge within the electrical field itself can sense the field, we mean the place where the voltage has a gradient. In the cytoplasm and extracellular space, there is no voltage gradient, so there is no field, but in the membrane there is a voltage gradient, so that is where the field-sensing charges must reside. It is possible of course that a charged portion of the channel in the cytoplasm is part of the gate mechanism; in that case the voltage gradient near the membrane is important. Consider that the hydrophobicity plots tell where transmembrane segments lie; we expect these regions to be uncharged, yet that is precisely where the field-sensing charge must be. Thus regions of the protein (S4 in Fig. 3.17) have significant charge but are in the membrane, so we look for sensors there. Only a few well-placed amino acid residues are responsible for the voltage-gated mechanism. The following table lists charged amino acids at physiological pH.

Positive	Negative
Lysine: K^+	Aspartic acid: D^-
Arginine: R^+	Glutamic acid: E^-
Histidine: H^+	

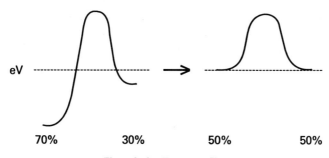

Figure 3.19. Energy profile

How Action Potentials Arise from Single-Channel Currents

In free-running membranes, voltage changes not only during action potentials but also when the membrane is at rest. When channels open or close, they affect the local voltage. Other channels sense this new voltage, change their kinetics, and open or close accordingly. The extent to which channels are able to sense other channels depends on channel density, i.e., interchannel distance, lipid bilayer capacitance, and intracellular and extracellular resistivity. In this section we treat the relatively simple problem of a space-clamped membrane in which the potential is the same everywhere.

The usual approach is to first describe ionic currents under voltage clamp; for purposes of discussion, we consider only Na and K currents, following these steps:

1. Apply voltages to a space-clamped axon under conditions that separate currents so only one type of current is being measured.
2. Apply a series of voltage steps that span the normal range of the action potential and record the currents at each step.
3. Build a model describing the time-variant, voltage-dependent kinetics of the particular current being measured.
4. Repeat the process for each current underlying the action potential.

With a model for each current, we can combine the currents in their natural proportions, then construct the action potential; we can also calculate the time course of each current during the action potential. The currents during an action potential are called the action currents.

We now demonstrate a method of finding action currents that relies on single-channel data obtained during the action potential. Channel currents are measured from a small patch of membrane (see Appendix 1). We assume that the membrane outside the patch experiences uniform potential, so one of the critical limitations is knowing the voltage at the patch, a version of the space clamp problem. We are in a better position however to separate currents because at the single-channel level, we exclude by inspection patches containing more than one kind of channel; however the possibility of small unresolved channels always exists. No voltage protocols are necessary because voltage is driven by the cell, and no model is needed because the average behavior over many action potentials automatically includes open-channel currents, channel kinetics, and dynamic open–close probabilities, however complicated they may be. Repeating measurements for each channel category contributing to the voltage is essential, and we assume all channels of a type to be identical; there should be enough repetitions to represent their average properties.

Consider one Na channel in a cell-attached patch (Appendix 1) on a spontaneously beating heart cell. The Na channel density in most cells makes the presence of only one Na channel in a typical patch highly unlikely, but extending the argument to more channels is straightforward. The average Na current in the patch $<i_{Na}(t)>$ is the miniature version of the Na action current through corresponding Na channels outside the patch. The time integral of the Na action current, scaled by channel density and membrane capacity, is the contribution of Na current to the action potential.

Not only ionic current but capacitive currents and nonspecific leak currents also flow through the patch. In the case of Na, subtracting the capacitive current is crucial because the Na action current and the capacitive transient overlap. Removing these background currents in the patch involves the equation:

$$c\left[\frac{dV(t)}{dt}\right] + gV(t) + i_o$$

where c is capacitive current for the patch; g is a passive, linear leak of the patch, and i_o is a steady offset leak current. By fitting these terms to a region of the action potential that does not include the Na current and by extrapolating the results back to the Na domain, we can separate the Na current from the background current. In the following discussion, we assume that capacitive and leak currents were subtracted.

We assume that for a space-clamped cell:

$$C\left(\frac{dV}{dt}\right) + \Sigma I_i(t) = 0$$

where C is the capacitive current through the cell and ΣI is the sum of all the ionic currents. This equation must be true because all currents leaving a cell must equal the currents entering the cell (see Fig. 2.34). In the above equation, $V(t)$ is the cell action potential; we assume that the equation holds for example in small, spontaneously beating heart cells isolated in tissue culture. Since we consider only Na and K currents, the equation becomes:

$$dV = -(I_{Na}/C)dt - (I_K/C)dt$$

If other currents are present, they are added to the preceding expression. The macroscopic currents I depend on voltage and change with time. They are composed of individual ionic currents according to $I = Nip$, but now the equation becomes a little more complicated because the voltage and probabilities are changing in time (SCRa, p. 292):

$$I[V(t)] = N \times i[V(t)] \times p[V(t),t]$$

where square brackets define the functional dependence of the current and the probability. This equation holds for each type of channel, where N is the number of channels. This equation essentially defines excitability. On the time scale we are interested in, N is a constant, the open-channel current i depends on voltage (and varies with time because the voltage does), the open-channel probability p explicitly depends on time as well as on voltage. Note: $p = p(V, t)$, and not $p = p(V)$ because $p = p(V)$ applies only to the steady state when t $\rightarrow \infty$; it is the average probability at long times after a change in voltage. In the free-running membrane problem we are considering, voltage is changing moment to moment. We introduced this idea in Figs. 2.23–2.25, but now it becomes more explicit. Thus the form $p = p(V, t)$ arises because p obeys a differential equation in time. For example in $I_K = N_K i_K p_K$ for Hodgkin–Huxley potassium channels, we can think of I_K functionally as a time-varying current:

$$I_K (V, t) = N_K i_K(V) p_K(V, t)$$

where $i_K (V) = \gamma_K (V - E_K)$ does not depend on time; however the following equation does depend on time:

$$p_K = n^4 \text{ and } n = \frac{\alpha(V)}{\alpha(V) + \beta(V)} \{ 1 - e^{-[\alpha(V) + \beta(V)]t} \}$$

The $\alpha(V)$s and $\beta(V)$s determine the response of I_K to voltage, and the $\exp[-(\alpha + \beta)t]$ determines the time evolution of $I_K (V, t)$; see Fig. 1.31 and SCRa, p. 324. The N and i are usually considered independently of time; however if the concentration of K ions changes as K current flows, then E_K changes and i_K is a function of time. This happens in cells, but we do not consider it here.

For our purposes we consider only the average value of i *times* p over many action potentials, thus:

$$\text{avg}\{ i[V(t)] \times p[V(t), t] \} = <i>$$

Therefore:

$$I = N<i>$$

where $<i>$ is the measured average current through a particular kind of channel. Using this notation for average current and integrating the equation for dV on p. 159 gives an equation for the action potential $V(t)$ in terms of individual currents:

$$V(t) = -\left(\frac{N_{Na}}{C}\right) \int_0^t < i_{Na}(u) > du - \left(\frac{N_K}{C}\right) \int_0^t < i_K(u) > du$$

where u is a dummy variable of integration; u stands for time in the integrand, but we integrate over u, so u disappears; t in $V(t)$ is the limit of the integral $\int_0^t$ (see p. 34

and Fig. 1.33). We set the constant of integration $V(0)$ to zero. We rewrite the equation to define the contribution of each ion pathway to the potential as:

$$V(t) = V_{Na}(t) + V_K(t)$$

where V_K is the part due to K, V_{Na} is the part due to Na, etc.; thus:

$$V_{Na}(t) = -\left(\frac{N_{Na}}{C}\right)\int_0^t < i_{Na}(u) > du$$

$$V_K(t) = -\left(\frac{N_K}{C}\right)\int_0^t < i_K(u) > du$$

The point is not only to see the relationship between the voltage and underlying currents in a new way: The integrands are also measurable quantities. These equations determine the relative proportion of Na and K to the action potential through the constant scaling factors N_{Na}/C and N_K/C, which represent channel densities in the membrane.

Action Potentials Composed of Ion Channel Currents

So far we have considered the action potential as if it were a voltage protocol. If ion conductances were strictly voltage-dependent, currents from spontaneously beating cells and action-potential-driven cells would be identical. In simple cases we expect exact correspondence, but if factors besides voltage regulate channels, there may be only a qualitative relationship between voltage clamp currents and derived action currents. As an example consider a highly simplified squid axon membrane that contains one K channel and one Na channel. We also add a leak channel L, which is not time variant. The leak current is always on; this situation is illustrated in Fig. 3.20 (compare Fig. 3.20 with SCRa, pp. 337, 339). At $t = 0$ the K channel has been in the open state for a long time, and voltage is given by the solution to the equation (see SCRa, p. 336):

$$C\left(\frac{dV}{dt}\right) + \gamma_L V + \gamma_K(V - E_K) = 0$$

which evaluated at $t = 0$ gives:

$$V = \frac{\gamma_K E_K}{(\gamma_L + \gamma_K)}$$

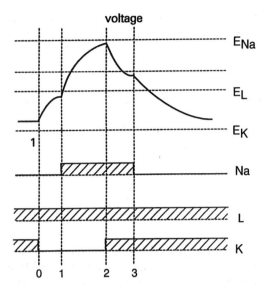

Figure 3.20.   Three-channel action potential

Solving similar equations for the various states of the two channels gives the following results (leak always open): At $t = 0$ the K channel closes, and voltage moves toward V_L according to:

$$V(t) = E_L[1 - \exp(-\gamma_L t/C)]$$

At $t = 1$ the Na channel opens, and the voltage moves toward E_{Na} according to:

$$V = \frac{E_{Na}\gamma_{Na} + E_L\gamma_L}{(\gamma_L + \gamma_{Na})}$$

with time constant:

$$\tau = \frac{C}{(\gamma_L + \gamma_{Na})}$$

At $t = 2$ the K channel opens, and the voltage decays toward a new potential that involves all three of the channel's equilibrium potentials and conductances. The time constant of the decent is:

$$\tau = \frac{C}{(\gamma_L + \gamma_K + \gamma_{Na})}$$

At $t = 3$ the Na channel closes, and voltage moves toward its original value. The voltage thus generated is a primitive action potential composed of one Na, one K opening and closing; and one leak channel; Fig. 3.20 shows a qualitative description of what is going on. Using a model with many channels, we can make such calculations accurately on a computer (see Fig. 3.21). Figure 3.21a shows an excitable membrane from a probabilistic interpretation of the HH equations; 500 Na channels and 50 K channels are placed in $10 \mu m^2$ of membrane, then allowed to run free. These calculations, which were done in a reduced Hodgkin–Huxley model, where Na kinetics are mh (not m^3h) and K kinetics are n (not n^4), result in a spontaneously active membrane (firing automatically without stimulation). The diastolic depolarization phase that precedes the action potentials represents random openings of Na channels that on reaching a critical value cause the precipitous opening of Na and K channels that generate action potentials. Since the number of channels is still relatively small, the action potentials are stochastic in shape: No two are alike. Fig. 3.21b shows the same calculation for 1 cm^2 of membrane containing many more channels. The action potentials all have the same shape.

Although we are not restricted to the Hodgkin–Huxley model, it is instructive to consider this model in detail to make the correspondence between macroscopic and microscopic descriptions explicit. The general HH model (a reduced model is used in Fig. 3.21) is a stochastic single-channel simulation program (MCHAN DeFelice, Goolsby, and Mazzanti, 1989, *Ann. N.Y. Acad. Sci.* **558**:174–184). This program (available from the author on request) may be used in free-run mode where membrane voltage is described by:

$$\frac{C_M dV}{dt} + \bar{g}_K n^4(V - E_K) + \bar{g}_{Na} m^3 h(V - E_{Na}) + \bar{g}_L(V - E)_L = 0$$

where C_M and V are membrane capacitance and membrane potential, respectively; E_K, E_{Na} and E_L are equilibrium Nernst potentials for sodium, potassium, and leakage ionic currents, respectively; $\bar{g}_K$, $\bar{g}_{Na}$, and $\bar{g}_L$ are fully activated conductances for the respective ions; and n, m, and h are first-order voltage- and time-dependent conductance parameters; $p_K = n^4$ and $p_{Na} = m^3 h$ represent the proportion of single channels in the conducting state; p is modeled in MCHAN as a stochastic function. The HH gating variable equation is:

$$\frac{dx}{dt} = -[\alpha_x(V) + \beta_x(V)]x + \alpha_x(V)$$

where x is h, m, or n; the equation represents the behavior of large numbers of stochastic channels. The K channels have five discrete states (CCCCO) with α_n and β_n controlling state occupancy. The equations are ($V \ominus mV$ and αs and $\beta s \ominus$ msec^{-1}):

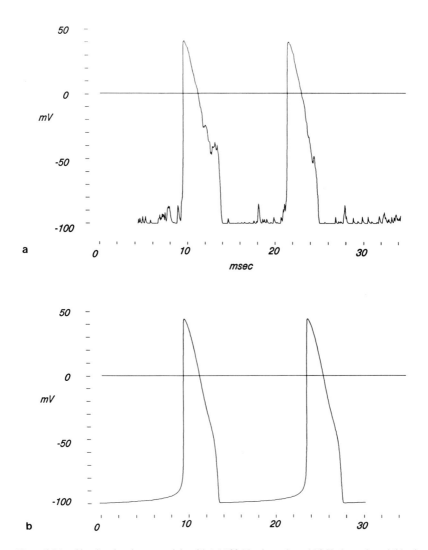

Figure 3.21.   Simulated action potentials with (a) 500-Na channels and 50 K channels and (b) a large number of Na and K channels

$$\alpha_n(V) = \frac{0.01(V+50)}{\{1 - \exp[-0.1(V+50)]\}}$$

$$\beta_n(V) = 0.125 \exp[-(V+60)/80]$$

Sodium channels have eight discrete states controlled by α_m, β_m, α_h, and β_h:

$$\alpha_m(V) = \frac{0.1(V+35)}{\{1 - \exp[-0.1(V+35)]\}}$$

$$\beta_m(V) = 4\exp[-(V+60)/18]$$

$$\alpha_h(V) = 0.07\exp[-(V+60)/20]$$

$$\beta_h(V) = 1/\{\exp[-(V+30)/10 + 1]\}$$

Leak channels have a single state with constant conductance (selected to give 0.3 mS/cm^2). Single-channel conductances, cell capacitance, and equilibrium potential are:

$$\gamma_K = 4 \text{ pS}$$

$$\gamma_{Na} = 6 \text{ pS}$$

$$C_M = 1 \ \mu\text{F/cm}^2$$

$$E_K = -72 \text{ mV}$$

$$E_{Na} = +55 \text{ mV}$$

$$E_L = -50 \text{ mV}$$

Single-channel conductances were selected for consistency with classical conductances from original HH equations. They are lower than modern values.

Figure 3.22a shows a measured cardiac action potential from spontaneously beating a 7-day chick ventricle cell isolated in tissue culture; Fig. 3.22b shows the measured Na action current (p. 158) on an expanded time scale. In this experiment the dynamic reversal potential for the Na current was ~10 mV, which gives an outward component of the Na current following the upstroke of the action potential. Figure 3.22c shows the expected Na action current from a Hodgkin–Huxley-like model adapted for cardiac cells; a substantial outward Na current occurs during the initial phase of the cardiac action potential in agreement with experiment. The

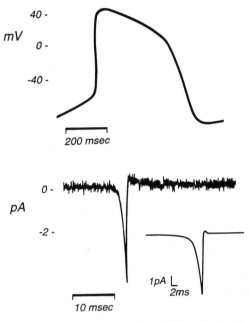

Figure 3.22. The Na action current during a heart beat. (a) Recorded cardiac action potential; (b) Recorded Na action current compared to a theoretical model (c).

integral of the measured Na action current $<i_{Na}(t)>$ multiplied by a scaling factor N_{Na}/C gives the voltage the Na current contributes to the action potential:

$$V_{Na}(t) = -\left(\frac{N_{Na}}{C}\right)\int_0^t <i_{Na}(u)> du$$

Compare this equation with Fig. 3.22.

Figure 3.23a shows another measured action potential from a spontaneously beating 7-day chick ventricle cell isolated in tissue culture (it is not identical to the action potential in Fig. 3.22 because cells at this development stage are different). The measured K action current (leak and capacitive current subtracted) is shown in Fig. 3.23b on the same time scale. In this experiment the dynamic reversal potential for the K current was −75 mV. Although voltage during the action potential dips below this value, there is virtually no inward current through this pathway because the open-channel probability is essentially zero at these times. Figure 3.23c shows the expected K action current from the Hodgkin–Huxley-like model adapted for cardiac cells, with the K reversal potential at −75 mV. The integral of the K action

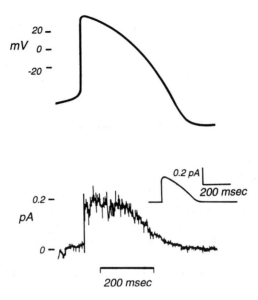

Figure 3.23. The K action current during a heart beat. (a) Recorded cardiac action potential; (b) Recorded K action current compared to a theoretical model (c).

current $<i_K(t)>$ multiplied by a scaling factor N_K/C is the voltage the K current (in this case the delayed rectifier) contributes to the action potential:

$$V_K(t) = -\left(\frac{N_K}{C}\right)\int_0^t <i_K(u)>du$$

Compare this equation with Fig. 3.23. Because a negative sign precedes the equation for $V_{Na}(t)$ and because the Na current is inward (i.e., negative), its contribution to the potential is positive. The K current is outward, so its contribution to the action potential is negative. Integrals $V_{Na}(t)$ and $V_K(t)$ are shown in Fig. 2.34, where the two expressions plotted show the *shapes* that measured Na and K action currents contribute to the action potential, but not their absolute contributions:

$$V_{Na}(t) \sim -\int_0^t <i_{Na}(u)> du$$

$$V_K(t) \sim -\int_0^t <i_K(u)> du$$

To know the absolute contributions, we must know the densities of Na and K channels:

$$\left(\frac{N_{Na}}{C}\right) = \text{Na channel density} \div 1 \ \mu F/cm^2$$

$$\left(\frac{N_K}{C}\right) = \text{K channel density} \div 1 \ \mu F/cm^2$$

Normally there are many more Na channels in an excitable membrane than K channels. Even without these scaling factors however, we can make the following generalizations for cardiac cells: The Na current depolarizes heart cells but because of the outward component unexpectedly contributes to the fast *repolarization* phase following the upstroke; the delayed-rectifier K current begins repolarizing heart cells immediately after the upstroke at its maximum rate. To obtain the true action potential, we must add not only the wave forms in Fig. 3.24 but also those of other currents, such as Ca current, all scaled for channel density and membrane capacitance.

In this section we showed how to reconstruct excitability from single-channel data obtained during action potentials. The relationship underlying this reconstruction is:

$$V(t) = -\left(\frac{1}{C}\right) \Sigma_i N_i \int_0^t <i(u)> \, dt$$

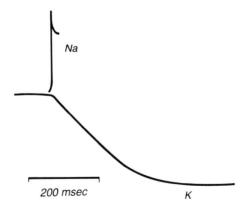

Figure 3.24.   Time integrals of the Na and K action currents

This equation, which is little more than an identity, has practical value, since we can measure $<i(u)>$ directly. Although we may not know channel densities (and are unable to scale the currents), we can extract information about individual currents and how they contribute to excitability. Ultimately however we must relax the assumption of uniform channel density and space clamp to consider propagating potentials. We attack propagation by considering saltatory conduction between channels, where patches of channels may be separated by regions of low channel density; however that subject is beyond the scope of this book.

Logistic Equation

In the preceding discussion on the relationship between ion channel currents and action potentials, we assumed that channels interact through voltage. In a free-running membrane when channels open, voltage changes, which changes the probability that channels open. If voltage is constant, as in a voltage clamp experiment, this interaction vanishes. Voltage matters, but all channels see the same voltage. We now consider a situation where voltage is constant, but channels can interact (coupling) even so. We introduced this concept in the discussion on pp. 152–154 (gap junction), but we do it here again in another way with voltage-gated channels in mind.

Consider a coupling term that works this way: A closed channel encounters an open channel, and as a result its likelihood of opening is increased. Note: We can also think of these as two gates in one channel instead of two separate channels. Thus in addition to a spontaneous change from the C state to the O state (whether or not another O is present), there is an additional spontaneous change from C to O if another O is encountered. This may be written as $\gamma N_c N_o$, where γ is the frequency of the encounter between C and O (in the gap junction we used the symbol ξ as the coupling constant). This γ is *not* conductance. Because $N_c = N - N_o$, the differential equation governing O becomes in this case:

$$\frac{dN_o}{dt} = \alpha(N - N_o) - \beta N_o + \gamma(N - N_o)N_o$$

or:

$$\frac{d}{dt}(N_o/N) = \alpha(1 - N_o/N) - \beta(N_o/N) + \gamma(1 - N_o/N)N_o$$

Let $p = N_o/N$ be the probability of opening; then:

$$\frac{dp}{dt} = \alpha(1 - p) - \beta p + \gamma(1 - p)N_o$$

Since $N_o = pN$:

$$\frac{dp}{dt} = \alpha + p[\gamma N - (\alpha + \beta)] - p^2 \gamma N$$

where we can simplify the equation with the definitions:

$$\frac{dp}{dt} = \alpha + \text{ap}\left(1 - \frac{p}{k}\right)$$

$$a = \gamma N - (\alpha + \beta)$$

$$k = \frac{a}{\gamma N} = 1 - \frac{\alpha + \beta}{\gamma N}$$

The preceding equation for dp/dt is a standard form of the logistic equation, but the equation may also be written in the form:

$$-\frac{dp}{dt} = bp^2 - \text{ap} - \alpha$$

where $b = \gamma N$. When γ goes to zero (no coupling between channels), we return to the familiar equation. We are interested in the logistic equation (which involves a term in p^2, making it nonlinear) because it is a nonlinear equation that can be solved analytically. We now proceed to solve it. Rearranging the preceding equation leads to:

$$\frac{dp}{bp^2 - \text{ap} - \alpha} = -dt$$

Now let $bp^2 - \text{ap} - \alpha = (p - p_1)(p - p_2)$, where p_1 and p_2 are roots of the quadratic equation. Then:

$$\frac{dp/b}{(p - p_1)(p - p_2)} = -dt$$

In general:

$$\frac{1}{(p - p_1)(p - p_2)} = \frac{A}{p - p_1} + \frac{B}{p - p_2}$$

$$= \frac{A(p - p_2) + B(p - p_1)}{(p - p_1)(p - p_2)}$$

where $A(p - p_2) + B(p - p_1) = 1$. For $p = p_1$,

$$A = \frac{1}{p_1 - p_2}$$

For $p = p_2$:

$$B = \frac{1}{p_2 - p_1} = -\frac{1}{p_1 - p_2}$$

Therefore:

$$\left(\frac{1/b}{p_1 - p_2}\right)\left(\frac{dp}{p - p_1} - \frac{dp}{p - p_2}\right) = -dt$$

The equation to be solved becomes:

$$\frac{dp}{p - p_1} - \frac{dp}{p - p_2} = b(p_2 - p_1)dt$$

Integrating term by term leads to:

$$\int_{p(o)}^{p(t)} \frac{dp}{p - p_1} - \int_{p(o)}^{p(t)} \frac{dp}{p - p_2} = b(p_2 - p_1)t$$

or:

$$\ln\left[\frac{p(t) - p_1}{p(o) - p_1}\right] - \ln\left[\frac{p(t) - p_2}{p(o) - p_2}\right] = b(p_2 - p_1)t$$

Rearranging terms gives:

$$\ln\left\{\frac{[p(t) - p_1]}{[p(o) - p_1]} \frac{[p(o) - p_2]}{[p(t) - p_2]}\right\} = b(p_2 - p_1)t$$

or

$$\frac{p(t) - p_1}{p(t) - p_2} = \frac{p(o) - p_1}{p(o) - p_2} e^{b(p_2 - p_1)t}$$

Solve this equation for $p(t)$:

$$p(t) - p_1 = [p(t) - p_2]\left[\frac{p(o) - p_1}{p(o) - p_2}\right]e^{b(p_2 - p_1)t}$$

or

$$p(t)\left[1 - \frac{p(\text{o}) - p_1}{p(\text{o}) - p_2}\right] e^{b(p_2 - p_1)t} = -p_2 \left[\frac{p(\text{o}) - p_1}{p(\text{o}) - p_2}\right] e^{b(p_2 - p_1)t} + p_1$$

Finally

$$p(t) = \frac{p_1 - p_2 \left[p(\text{o}) - p_1/p(\text{o}) - p_2\right] e^{b(p_2 - p_1)t}}{1 - \left[p(\text{o}) - p_1/p(\text{o}) - p_2\right] e^{b(p_2 - p_1)t}}$$

or

$$p(t) = \frac{p_1[p(\text{o}) - p_2] - p_2[p(\text{o}) - p_1] e^{b(p_2 - p_1)t}}{p(\text{o}) - p_2 - [p(\text{o}) - p_1] e^{b(p_2 - p_1)t}}$$

This is the solution to the problem. Recall that p_1 and p_2 are roots of the quadratic equation $bp^2 - ap - \alpha = (p - p_1)(p - p_2)$ and in principal are known; $p(\text{o})$ is an initial value. To give a more specific answer, consider the case that $p(\text{o}) = 0$. Then:

$$p(t) = \frac{p_1 p_2[1 - e^{b(p_2 - p_1)t}]}{p_2 - p_1 e^{b(p_2 - p_1)t}}$$

To find p_1 and p_2, set $bp^2 - ap - \alpha = 0$; then:

$$p_1 = \frac{a + (a^2 + 4b\alpha)^{1/2}}{2b} \quad p_1 p_2 = -\frac{\alpha}{b}$$

$$p_2 = \frac{a - (a^2 + 4b\alpha)^{1/2}}{2b} \quad p_2 - p_1 = -\frac{(a^2 + 4b\alpha)^{1/2}}{b}$$

Note: $a = b - (\alpha + \beta)$; therefore:

$$a^2 + 4b\alpha = b^2 + (\alpha + \beta)^2 - 2b(\alpha + \beta) + 4b\alpha$$

$$a^2 + 4b\alpha = b^2 + 2b(\alpha - \beta) + (\alpha + \beta)^2$$

where $b = \gamma N$. As p_1 and p_2 are defined:

$$p_1 > p_2$$

Therefore $p_2 - p_1 < 0$. As $t \to \infty$, $p(t) \to p_1$. Therefore $p_1 = p_\infty$ is also the steady-state value of $p(t)$.

Then:

$$p_\infty = \frac{\gamma N - (\alpha + \beta) + [\gamma^2 N^2 + 2\gamma N(\alpha - \beta) + (\alpha + \beta)^2]^{1/2}}{2\gamma N}$$

The solution of the standard uncoupled model gave: $p_\infty = \alpha/(\alpha + \beta)$. If we let $\gamma = 0$ and attempt to recover the simpler formula, the answer is 0/0, which is undefined. There are ways of handling this situation, but here we merely accept the solution to the simpler differential equation as the proof.

We now have a fairly complete solution of the original coupling problem defined by:

$$\frac{dN_o}{dt} = \alpha(N - N_o) - \beta N_o + \gamma(N - N_o)N_o$$

The solution predicts how the probability behaves if channels (or gates in channels) communicate by this means. We compare the logistic solution:

$$p(t) = \frac{p_1[p(o) - p_2] - p_2[p(o) - p_1] e^{b(p_2 - p_1)t}}{p(o) - p_2 - [p(o) - p_1] e^{b(p_2 - p_1)t}}$$

To $p(t)$ without coupling ($\gamma = 0$):

$$p(t) = p(o) + p_\infty(1 - e^{-t/\tau})$$

Let $p(o) = 0$, $\tau = 1$, $p_\infty = 1$, $p_1 = -1$, and $p_2 = -2$. Compare the logistic solution to the standard solution $1 - e^{-t}$, then compare the logistic solution to $(1 - e^{-t})^2$ and $(1 - e^{-t})^3$, etc., to represent multiple gates. These are two different ways of introducing nonlinearity into the gating problem. In the logistic approach, each gate obeys a nonlinear equation; in the standard treatment of channels, we introduce multiple linear gates. An interesting example of the logistic equation approach comes from quantum mechanics; Planck quantized energy because it took two different theories to describe the radiation spectrum from hot objects—one formula worked at the low end of the spectrum, the other worked at the high end. The objective was to find one physical explanation for the entire spectrum, which involved the analytic solution to a logistic equation (see Max Born, *Quantum Mechanics*, pp. 78–79).

Transporters

We have considered gap junctions and voltage-gated ion channels; another category of protein that moves ions and substrates across membranes is transporters. Perhaps the simplest way of approaching the problem of transporters is to ask what elementary transporter event looks like. Transport is a molecular event that moves ions across membranes, but what should we draw for the event akin to what we draw for channels?

The answer is unclear in transporter terms. Let us start with the idea that transporters are like channels and obey the equation:

$$I = Nip$$

As with channels, N is the total number of transporters in the membrane, whether they are transporting or not; i represents current through an open transporter; and p is the probability that the transporter is open; however, we do not usually think of a transporter as open. We will attempt to describe stoichiometric transport from a quasi-channel point of view; first we consider the transporter in Fig. 3.25, where a substrate S approaches the transporter T from the outside (o), binds to it, and then is somehow moved to the other side where it enters the inside (i); S can be a single molecule, like sugar, or a group of molecules, like GABA, Na, and Cl, that must act together for anything to happen. There are primary transporters (pumps) that use chemical energy (or other energy sources, such as light) to move substrates across membranes, and there are secondary transporters that use the existing gradient of one substrate to move another substrate (EIP, p. 4). These gradients are maintained by pumps, like Na/K ATPase (EIP, p. 168). Here we consider cotransporters—secondary processes that use existing gradients to move other molecules. How do we model this? Let us look at Fig. 3.26, where the transporter is a wagon carrying S to the other side (a carrier model). In this case we imagine that S is charged (+), which can be the charge on one molecule or the net charge on a group of molecules traveling together. In Fig. 3.26, the wagon cannot leave the platform. The net S complex has one (+) charge; S enters, the wagon carries the charge, then S escapes. To transport again, the empty wagon must return to where it came. Evidently the flux of transported molecules, which we call ϕ, is the same as the flux of the wagon if we are in a steady state, and current generated by this shuttling is proportional to the flux. To bind S to T, we must consider the percentage of loaded

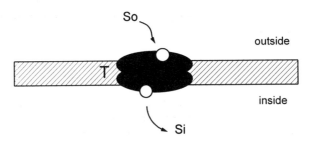

Figure 3.25.   Transporter model

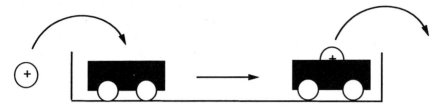

Figure 3.26. Wagon theory

transporters, i.e., the ratio of loaded transporters to total transporters (loaded and unloaded). If we let T represent the empty transporter and TS represent the bound transporter, that ratio is given by:

$$\frac{TS}{T + TS}$$

We can also think of this ratio as the probability that S binds to T; thus it represents the entering (or escaping) process. We do not know the values of TS or T in the membrane, i.e., transporter concentrations in these two states, but we do know S, the concentration(s) of the substrate(s) in the solution. Therefore we define another parameter that relates T and TS to the concentration of S. If we define the disassociation constant K as free divided by bound, then:

$$K = \frac{T \cdot S}{TS}$$

We let $T = [T]$, $S = [S]$, and $TS = [TS]$ stand for the concentrations; however, they have different units: T and TS are measured in #/cm^2, but S is measured in #/cm^2. The dot stands for the product. It is easy to show from the definition of K that:

$$\frac{TS}{T + TS} = \frac{S}{K + S}$$

This is a convenient expression, because K is a characteristic number for the binding process, and S is often known. We can think of $S/(K + S)$ as the probability p that the binding reaction occurs (on one side or the other):

$$p = \frac{S}{K + S}$$

So far the transporter current consists of three stages: enter, cross, and escape. Each transporter generates a current; to determine total current, as with channels we multiply by N, the number of transporters.

We now describe a specific model of steady-state γ-aminobutyric acid (GABA) transport based on these ideas, then determine the relationship between GABA-induced current through the transporter, GABA concentration, cotransported ion concentration, and membrane voltage. The GABA transporter is modeled by the cyclic scheme:

$$T_o \Leftrightarrow ST_o \Leftrightarrow ST_i \Leftrightarrow T_i \Leftrightarrow T_o$$

where:

$$T_i \Leftrightarrow T_o$$

is the empty transporter shuttle. Subscripts indicate the outside (o) or inside (i). Note: To write compact equations, we introduced the following notation: T represents the concentration of empty GABA transporters [T] in the membrane. In our representation T is measured in surface density units ($T \oplus$ #/cm^2). Let S stand for the substrate GABA and the cotransported ions Na and Cl. We assume that the fully loaded transporter on either side of the membrane, designated as ST_o or ST_i, has the fixed stoichiometry Na$_2$:Cl:GABA:T. The disassociation constant is defined as the ratio of free to bound reactants, is given by:

$$K = \frac{[Na]^2[Cl][GABA][T]}{[Na_2:Cl:GABA:T]}$$

To simplify the notation further, we could let [Na] = N, [Cl] = C, and [GABA] = G be the bulk concentrations of the ions and the substrate in the solution adjacent to the membrane; these are measured in units of volume concentration (#/cm^3). Thus $N_o = [Na]_o$ stands for the concentration of Na in the external bulk solution, which we assume is the concentration adjacent to the membrane that is ready to react with the transporter. Note: In this notation, ST_o represents the density of loaded transporters on the external surface, but S_oT_o represents the *product* of free ion and substrate concentrations (S_o) and free transporters (T_o) in the bulk solution. Thus we need not write $S_o \cdot T_o$ because the dot is implied; also order does not matter, that is, $S_oT_o = T_oS_o$ and $ST_o = TS_o$, etc. Using this shorthand, the equilibrium constants of dissociation are

$$K_o = \frac{S_oT_o}{ST_o}$$

$$K_i = \frac{S_iT_i}{ST_i}$$

where K represents the total reaction between all ions and substrates with the transporter; In this example, K is measured in $(\#/cm^3)^4$, a composite disassociation constant for the entire reaction. The model assumes that no partial reactions result in the *transport* of any ion or substrate; for example such bound states as NaT or Na_2T do not transport Na. Furthermore free ions and substrates are excluded from traversing the membrane by this pathway; thus the only way to move is by TS combinations. The model assumes however that *transporters* can cross the membrane unloaded. Indeed for net transport to occur, empty transporters must return to the other side, where they are free to load ions and substrates for another cycle. We can summarize these assumptions by the statement that only the transition $ST_i \Leftrightarrow ST_o$ transports ions and substrates through the membrane.

Assume the total number of transporters is constant and equal to $N = T + ST$ at any position in the membrane. Let Φ represent the flux of N transporters. Now in the steady state, the flux (per unit area) of loaded transporters and the flux of the empty transporters are equal and opposite, thus:

$$\Phi_{ST} = -\Phi_T$$

If we allow for the possibility that not only ions and substrates (S) but also the transporter (T) can be charged, then total current through the membrane of area A is given by:

$$I = (z_{ST}e\Phi_{ST} + z_Te\Phi_T)A$$

where z is the valence of the charge carrier and e is the elementary charge. If $Q_{ST} = z_{ST}e$ and $Q_T = z_Te$ represent the net charge on the loaded and unloaded transporter, respectively, then:

$$I = (Q_{ST} - Q_T)\Phi_{ST}A = q\Phi_{ST}A$$

where $q = Q_{ST} - Q_T$ is the net charge on all transported substrates (S) bound to T. The net current across the membrane is the *transported* charge, since the current that a charged transporter contributes cancels because it goes back and forth. Note: The flux of ST can exist in both directions—$ST_o \Leftrightarrow ST_i$; i.e., current may flow inward via TS, or outward.

If we had considered an ion channel obeying Nernst–Planck, then current through a single channel is:

$$i = zeukT[n_2e^{(ze/kT)V_2} - n_1e^{(ze/kT)V_1}]\left(\frac{\alpha}{\ell}\right) \quad \text{(Nernst–Planck)}$$

In this expression $D = ukT$ is the diffusion constant of the ion in the channel, ze is the charge on the ion, and (α/ℓ) is a geometric factor for the channel that involves the profile of the electric field (see the discussion on p. 128); n represents concentrations of mobile ions on the two sides of the membrane ($\#/cm^3$). Thus if we were speaking of a K channel, n_2 would be the concentration of K ions on the inside of the cell. Verify that this equation for i has the correct units of current. We often lump parameters together, then define a permeability p for the channel:

$$i = p\,[n_2 e^{(ze/kT)V_2} - n_1 e^{(ze/kT)V_1}]$$

$$p = ze D\left(\frac{\alpha}{\ell}\right)$$

Do not confuse this p with the probability.

As we saw, transporters (possibly charged) transporting substrates (possibly charged) across a membrane generate a current:

$$I = (z_{ST} - z_T)e\Phi_{ST}A$$

where $(z_{ST} - z_T)e$ is the net charge on all bound transported substrates. How does this equation compare to $I = Nip$ for channels? When we write $I = Nip$ we are considering the total number of channels, whatever the area, so A is not written. If we are considering the number of transporters per unit area, A appears. Thus $\Phi_{ST} = N\phi_{ST}$, where ϕ_{ST} represents single-transporter flux. A more serious problem concerns the probability: Where is p in the transporter formula $I = (z_{ST} - z_T)e\Phi_{ST}A$? It is not there because we have assumed that when the transporter is loaded, it transports! That is, once the TS state is formed, transport is obligatory. Note: In ion channels, once we attain permissive voltage (analogous to loading the transporter), it is not certain that the channel will open, only more likely; in fact the channel may close even though the voltage remains (ICEMa, p. 64). Using probability in channel currents seems a reasonable position to take, so we ask: What is the elementary flux for transporters, and how can we introduce probability?

It is convenient to define the fraction of transporters loaded on each side of the membrane:

$$n_o = \frac{ST_o}{N}$$

$$n_i = \frac{ST_i}{N}$$

With these definitions it is possible to write a steady-state current associated with loaded transporters and governed by electrodiffusion as:

$$I = q\Phi_{ST}A = Nqr[n_i \exp(Q_{ST}V/kT) - n_o]A$$

In the above equation, q is the net transported charge and r is the rate of transport. Examine the units $n_i \ominus$ #/cm^2—the number of loaded transporters per unit area of membrane. The first term in the equation, $n_i \exp(Q_{ST}V/kT)$, describes the pressure on TS_i to move outward; pressure refers to diffusional pressure due to the presence of TS_i and electrical pressure due to the charge on TS_i; this is the familiar Nernst–Planck idea. Likewise n_o is the pressure of TS_o to move inward. Note: Although the inward and outward terms may appear asymmetric in form, they are actually symmetric in their dependence on voltage. The equivalent symmetric equation is:

$$I = Nqr[n_i \exp(Q_{ST}V_i/kT) - n_o \exp(Q_{ST}V_o/kT)]$$

This reduces to the former equation if $V_o = 0$ and $V = V_i - V_o$. It is easy to show that r has the units of rate, i.e., $r \ominus 1/\text{sec}$. The factor Nqr points out the difference between the equation for channels and the usual equation for transporters:

$$I = Nip \qquad \text{Channels}$$

$$I = Nqr \qquad \text{Transporters}$$

We typically think of transporters as having a turnover rate r and transporting a charge q each time it turns over. But now we have multiplied by the factor Nqr ($n_i \exp[Q_{ST}V/kT] - n_o$) to account for the presence of a certain number of charged loaded transporters. To make this clear, suppose $V = 0$; then:

$$I = qr (TS_i - TS_o)$$

We are in the steady state, so there are always a fixed number of loaded transporters on either side. Since the reaction $TS_i \Leftrightarrow TS_o$ can go either way, it is reasonable to find that the net current is proportional to the difference in the number of loaded transporters on either side; if there is a voltage, V pushes (or pulls) as well. Thus if we consider diffusional and electrical forces that act on mobile loaded transporters, we have a reasonable equation; if we allow the analogy between channels and transporters, it is easy to show that $r = D/\delta \ell$, where D is the diffusion constant of ST in the membrane; δ is the thickness of the membrane, and ℓ is the integral $\int \exp[Q_{ST}V(x)/kT]dx$ across the membrane (p. 128 and Appendix 2).

Thus far we have considered current due to loaded transporters when the probability for transport equals 1 if they are loaded, but we have not considered the probability that the transporters *are* loaded on both sides of the membrane, which is the only way for transport to occur. To do that we must multiply the equation for *I* just given by a factor *p* that describes these reactions. Consider the reactions that occur on each side and recall that:

$$p_o = \frac{S_o}{(K_o + S_o)}$$

$$p_i = \frac{S_i}{(K_i + S_i)}$$

where we identify p_o and p_i with the probabilities that the reactions occur. These equations follow from the definition of K: $K = S \cdot T/ST$. If we assume for the moment that these chemical reactions are independent of one another, then the probability that both reactions occur is given by $p = p_o p_i$; however the transporters available to undergo these reactions are limited in number. To account for this restriction, we take into consideration the number:

$$N = T_o + ST_o + T_i + ST_i$$

Thus values of p_o and p_i depend on the actual distribution of transporters in these four states, and this depends on reaction rates between the states. With this assumption an expression for the current through the membrane is

$$I = Nqr\,[n_i \exp(Q_{ST}V/kT) - n_o]p_o p_i$$

This equation allows for the contribution by the charge associated with the transporter itself. We can reduce this equation to its more familiar form by assuming that the transporter has no inherent charge and there is no zero-current asymmetric distribution of the transporter within the membrane. For the GABA transporter we assumed that:

$$q = (z_G + 2z_{Na} + z_{Cl})e = e$$

and therefore:

$$I = Nqr[n_i \exp(eV/kT) - n_o]p_o p_i$$

This heuristic formula can be compared with the more complete treatment given in EIP, p. 73. In this model the steady-state current is given by:

$$I = Nq\left[\frac{S_o}{(K_o + S_o)}\right]\left[\frac{S_i}{(K_i + S_i)}\right]\left[\frac{(aq - bp)}{(a + b + p + q)}\right]$$

where we use our notation for charge, substrates, and disassociation constants. The term $[S_o/(K_o + S_o)][S_i/(K_i + S_i)]$ is equivalent to our term $p_i p_o$. The quantities a and b are voltage-dependent rate constants in an equivalent two-state model of the four-state model we assumed, and p and q are the voltage-independent rate constants. If we equate the two expressions for I given above, the turnover rate r becomes:

$$r = \frac{1}{[\mathcal{A}\exp(qV/kT) - \mathcal{B}]}$$

where $\mathcal{A}$ and $\mathcal{B}$ are constants depending on voltage and the concentration of loaded and empty transporters. Thus $r \neq$ constant as we assumed in the heuristic treatment, but it is a complex function of the voltage and the rate constants in the reaction scheme:

$$T_o \Leftrightarrow ST_o \Leftrightarrow ST_i \Leftrightarrow T_i \Leftrightarrow T_o$$

Indeed it is these terms in $r(V)$ that lead to current saturation at extreme voltages in coupled cotransport. Note: In experiments on transporters transfected into host cells, we have clamped the voltage across the norepinephrine (NE) transporter (returns NE into the presynaptic terminal after it is released into the cleft) and varied the NE concentration on the outside. In this case the NE-induced current saturates according to the familiar rule:

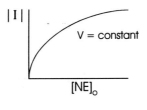

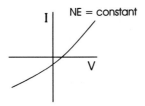

Figure 3.27. Transporter current as a function of NE concentration (top) and voltage (bottom)

$$I \propto \frac{[NE]}{K + [NE]}$$

This is shown in Fig. 3.27, where we plot the absolute value of the NE-induced current; however if we hold the [NE] constant and vary the voltage, the current does not saturate. This need not be true for all transporters, but it is true for NE transporters; thus we can think of NE as a ligand that opens pores for NE and its cotransported ions. Because there are only so many transporters in the membrane, eventually (at constant voltage) the NE-induced current becomes saturated; however if a certain number of pores are open (at a constant NE concentration), voltage drives current through the transporters just as it does through open ion channels (Fig. 3.27).

Proteins as Capacitors

Lipids can act as a capacitor, and internal charge in a voltage-gated ion channel can act like a capacitor. Let us consider how a capacitor works, then see if we can make one with a protein, not in the sense of internal charge moving but in the sense of ions jumping on and off proteins, as they do in transporters.

We know that a true capacitor does not really conduct ionic current through the membrane: (+) and (−) charges move up to the barrier, whatever it is, and *other* charges escape on the other side of the barrier, as in Fig. 3.28. It is not the same charge that enters on the left and leaves on the right; that is the basic idea for a capacitor. In an open channel, that may also be true, e.g., in Fig. 3.29 a charge jumps to a binding site on the left, and it eliminates a charge at a site on the right (ICEMb, p. 311); again it is not the same ion that moved up when another charge escaped (see Fig. 3.29). Eventually the left (+) is able to pass through. The first encounter

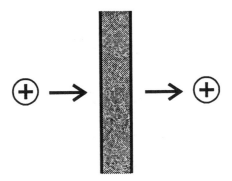

Figure 3.28.   Capacitor current

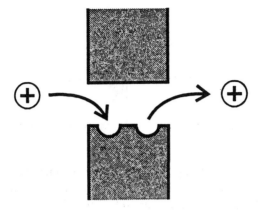

Figure 3.29. Knock-on channel current

of the ion with the binding site (knock-on) is *C*-like, so every chain reaction of this type has a capacitive property. Can we make a *C* with a membrane protein? Looking at the transporter in Fig 3.25, we note that there is no hole (as there is in Fig. 3.29) but instead a charge jumps on and a charge jumps off (Fig. 3.30). For the sake of argument, we assume that the right-hand (+) is *always* different from left-hand (+) in the process shown in Fig. 3.30; (+) charges may be transferred by some other means, but that is not the problem here. The protein *T* removes charge on the inside,

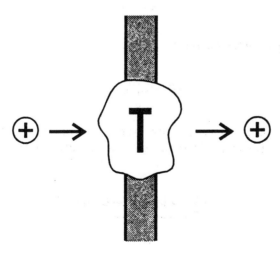

Figure 3.30. Transporter as a capacitor

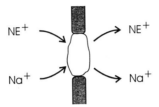

Figure 3.31.   Hypothetical transporter reaction: Wrong

say, when the voltage is changed, just like a true capacitor. Each transporter may have many different sites; some of these sites may be for the transmitter, no-repinephrine (NE⁺), say, and its cotransported ions, Na⁺ and Cl⁻.

Let us follow a hypothetical reaction for transporters, considering only one cotransported ion, Na (see Fig. 3.31); would work as a transporter because it is removing NE on the outside by binding it and releasing NE on the inside. But this is not how transporters work; it is presented to illustrate a different possibility for capacitor-like currents. Ions and substrates really do move through transporters, just as they do through channels; however if a protein worked as in Fig. 3.31, it would for all intents and purposes be a capacitor.

Since a true capacitor C conducts current only in response to a changing voltage V, is the same true for proteins that act like capacitors? A true capacitor works as shown in Fig. 3.32, where current through the capacitor is:

$$I_C = C\frac{dV}{dt}$$

Solving this equation for V changing in time:

$$V_C(t) = \frac{1}{C}\int_0^t I_C(u)\,du$$

where u is a dummy variable for t. We could have written t for u, but then there would have been two kinds of t on the right-hand side of the equation. Since the ts

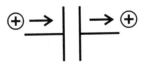

Figure 3.32.   True capacitor

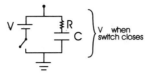

Figure 3.33. Equivalent circuit

in the integrand are eventually replaced by the limits, we substitute them with another symbol called a dummy variable. The t in $V(t)$ refers to the t in the limit. Maybe we can build a "capacitor" in another way that would still allow both a transient current and a steady current to occur.

Let us look at an equivalent circuit for a protein in a membrane; it is not the traditional RC circuit with R and C in parallel, but rather as in Fig. 3.33, where R and C are in series. If we close the switch, there is a current surge through R and C, and then eventually nothing, because C stops all the steady current. Let's look at the situation when we do have current. At some early time:

$$i_R = i_C$$

Now V occurs across R and C in series, so:

$$V = V_R + V_C = i_R R + \frac{1}{C} \int_0^t i_C(u)\, du$$

Therefore:

$$i_R = \frac{V}{R} - \frac{1}{RC} \int_0^t i_C(u)\, du$$

This is an integral equation in i_C, because $i_C = i_R$ and:

$$i_C(t) + \frac{1}{RC} \int_0^t i_C(u)\, du = \frac{V}{R}$$

Since R and C are in series, $i_R = i_C$, but we cannot solve for $i_C(t)$ by using $i_R = i_C$ equation because:

$$i_R - i_C = \frac{V - V_C}{R} - C \frac{dV_C}{dt} = 0$$

In the resistive capacitor composed of a true R and a true C in series, another equation for "capacitor" current replaces the simple CdV/dt equation. Thus capacitance has an interpretation beyond the lipid capacitor and the dumbbell dielectric (see Fig. 1.6).

Na/Glucose Cotransporter

Cotransporters use an existing gradient for a particular molecule to drive another molecule against its gradient. For example an Na gradient exists across most cell membranes, with more Na outside than inside; if a protein in the membrane insists such that glucose and Na travel together, then this Na gradient can drive glucose into cells: As Na moves down its gradient, it drags glucose with it. This is a property of a specialized protein called the Na/glucose cotransporter. We assume the Na gradient is always maintained by some other means, namely, Na/K ATPase. Thus cotransporters do not use ATP directly, but they use energy stored in the Na gradient, which is maintained by ATP (EIP p. 168).

At the molecular level, the Na/glucose transporter is a macromolecule that can bind Na and sugar with a certain stoichiometry, in this case two Na ions and one sugar molecule. If the cotransporter faces outward to begin with (i.e., the first reaction occurs on the outside), consider the possibility that the macromolecule itself has a charge. Although the charge is distributed in some complex manner, we think of it as arising from point charges represented by the two (−) signs in Fig. 3.34. In this case when the cotransporter is fully loaded, it has a neutral charge, but this need not be the case, and in general the bound complex is not neutral.

When the cotransporter turns over, the Na and sugar escape. The transporter itself does not actually revolve, but we think of a certain turnover rate r of Na and sugar transport from the outside to the inside. Therefore as the cotransporter goes through its cycle facing out, binding 2 Na and 1 S then facing in, we have the net movement of Na and sugar into the cell; the Na is just moving down its concentration gradient, dragging along sugar. We can think of this as a Na-sugar-selective pore because sugar cannot move without Na, and the Na cannot move without sugar; we can also think of this as a way of moving Na into a cell using sugar.

Since Na moves into the cell in a directed manner, it generates a Na current; it is as much an Na current as if it were moving through an Na-selective ion channel. The difference however is that Na channels move tens of thousands of ions per cycle, i.e., per open-close sequence, whereas a classical cotransporter moves only a few ions per cycle—two in this case. Other transporters, such as transporters for GABA and NE, are channel-like and thus move many more ions than predicted by the stoichiometry (see Fig. 3.27). Although Na ions move temporarily in the neutral environment illustrated in Fig. 3.34, charges eventually pass through; negative charges on the transporter remain in the membrane, and net movement is two Na

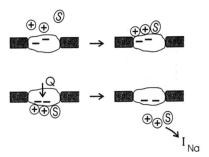

Figure 3.34. Na/glucose transporter. Top: One sugar and two Na ions bind to the transporter; Bottom: The transporter relocates to the other side of the membrane, and the sugar and Na ions unbind.

ions. As the two Na ions moved from the outside to the inside, as did one sugar molecule, two negative charges on the transporter also translocated within the membrane. Each of these charges, 2 Na ions and Q (Q represents the inherent charge on the cotransporter itself), generate a current, therefore total current equals:

$$I_{Na} + I_Q$$

As with channels these are the ionic current and the gating current; we expect these two currents to have different kinetics. For example suppose we apply a step change in voltage across the cotransporter in the absence of any substrates, i.e., no Na and no sugar; then we have a transient current due to the movement of Q alone. This would occur for example if we make the interior of the cell (-80 mV) change to $+20$ mV. We can think of the -80 mV as keeping the two ($-$) Qs facing outward, and the $+20$ mV as drawing them inward (see Fig. 3.11 for channels). This illustrates how to obtain an I_Q without net out-to-in movement of Na or sugar.

This I_Q current *must be* transient—there can be no steady-state current because the cotransporter is bound to the membrane and its two ($-$) Qs (assumed for illustration) can move only so far. Even though we continue to keep applying the steady $+20$ mV, I_Q is soon over. This is familiar from our discussion of capacitors: We make a step change in voltage across the membrane, and we obtain a transient change in the current. Let us consider the direction of the current. An arrow pointing up indicates the current in the circuit in Fig. 3.35, in this case an outward current. This is correct because a ($-$) movement *inward* is current *outward*. This situation is exactly like a capacitance current, and it is similar to what happens in channels (see Fig. 3.11). Since this I_Q is what we expect from an ordinary capacitor, it can be modeled as a capacitor current (see Fig. 3.35).

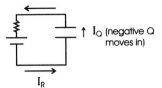

Figure 3.35.   Transporter equivalent; I_Q indicates that negative Q moves in (down).

How is this electrical circuit superimposed on the membrane? The capacitor in Fig. 3.35 is the transporter in this equivalent (we are considering only I_Q), the resistor is the rest of the cell, and the battery is internal voltage from the cell. Current through the capacitor must flow back through the rest of the cell. What happens when the cotransporter is fully loaded, as in Fig. 3.36? At this particular moment and in the special case that Q on the transporter exactly balances the net ion and substrate charge, we have already seen that:

$$I_{Na} + I_Q = 0$$

By this strict two-for-two condition, we do not need return current through the rest of the cell until Na ions *actually jump off*; if we consider what happens at the molecular level, the question of timing becomes critical. One of the most interesting facts about classical transporters (strictly coupled) is that the ionic current and the gating current are about the same size; when Na ions are bound to the transporter, (not necessarily neutral as in Fig. 3.36) they are in a sense part of the gating current. When Na-channel-gating currents were first observed, the objection was raised that some of the gating charge (measured in the absence of Na) was actually due to Na ions located in the channel. The idea was to measure pure charge movement on the Na channel protein itself. However some researchers felt that the protocols never exclude all Na, so that some of the gating charge was due to a cloud of Na ions within the channel. This idea persists even in recent literature, but there is not much

Figure 3.36.   Fully-loaded transporter. Left: One sugar and two Na ions bind to the transporter; Right: Net movement of charge within the membrane is zero.

evidence for it. In transporters a very similar idea is an accepted feature of the standard model.

CFTR Cl Channel

Recently defects in ion channels have been identified as major causes of disease. The first and most famous example is a defect in a Cl channel associated with cystic fibrosis (CF), a lethal autosomal recessive disease. One person in 25 carries a defective gene, and two genes are necessary to have the disease, which affects one in every 5000. For over 10 years we have known that CF involves a defect in Cl conductance; the name cystic fibrous transmembrane conductance regulator (CFTR) reveals something about the early thinking. When the gene was first cloned 8 years ago, it was thought to produce a protein that acted as a channel regulator but was not clearly a channel. The CFTR protein is now considered as a relatively low-conductance, Cl-selective, ohmic channel that responds to cAMP-dependent protein kinase A (PKA) and ATP (ICEMb, p. 218). If the CFTR protein (~ 1500 residues) lacks one phenylalanine at position 508, it fails to reach the apical membrane of the airway epithelium; this is the most common mutation responsible for more than 70% of all CF cases (there are more than 35,000 in the United States). In another form of the disease, CFTR mutants reach the correct place, but they fail to function; the absence of functional Cl channels in specific tissues causes CF. One critical location of CFTR is the pulmonary epithelium, where it is involved in water transport: Air passages of CF patients have a thick mucus caused by dehydration. Since water movement and Cl movement are linked, CFTR is manifested as debilitating congestion.

In order to function, CFTR must bind ATP, but it remains unclear whether CFTR must hydrolyze the ATP. In one model ATP activation occurs in two steps: ATP binds to two membrane domains, then PKA phosphorylates a cytoplasmic loop called the R domain; however we still have little knowledge of how ATP interacts with these nucleotide-binding regions. Presumably the R domain plugs the pore that conducts Cl. Phosphorylation may add a negative charge to the R domain, which leads to conformational changes that open the channel. Thus the R-domain, part of the CFTR protein, regulates the Cl channel action, and Cl channel blockers rapidly block single-channel events but only in the hyperpolarized direction. These Cl blockers, like fluformic acid, work better at lower Cl concentration where they actually compete with the Cl ion.

A number of questions arise: If R is the plug that closes the channel, what does phosphorylation do? Can we compare the R domain of CFTR to the ball and chain on the Shaker K channel (ICEMb, p. 437)? Is activated PKA a prerequisite to ATP regulation? For example in PKA-activated channels in the presence of ATP, the channel may stay open longer; alternatively channel conductance may increase or channel closures may decrease. Mutations that produce mild forms of CF create Cl channels with abnormally low conductance; thus the normal action of ATP may involve some combination of these effects. Furthermore more than one kind of anion can occupy the CFTR pore: In 154-mM Cl channel conductance is 7 pS, and in 150-mM thiocyanate (SCN) and 4-mM Cl, it is 10 pS. Curiously CFTR conductance is lower when both types are present: In 144-mM SCN and 10-mM Cl, CFTR conductance is only 2 pS; thus CFTR becomes an ideal channel for studying multi ion pore behavior and mole fraction effects.

The biophysical studies may offer direction for ion channel intervention to help CF patients; strategies are being developed based on these studies. For example one of the side effects of CFTR abnormality is an increase in the uptake of Na ions. Since Na cotransport seems to contribute to the dehydration of air passages, blocking Na channels is suggested as a therapy; learning how to open nonconducting mutants is another obvious direction. Ultimately the hope is to find a rational approach to intervention; these questions suggest that basic channel biophysics can show how CFTR works and what the defect actually does.

Researchers are beginning to draw parallels between CFTR Cl channels and other channels and transporters that govern substrate movement through membranes. Many of these proteins belong to a group called the ATP Binding Cassette (ABC) superfamily, associated not by the usual amino acid homology but rather by their similar structural motifs within the membrane. The proposed structure of the ABC superfamily has six membrane-spanning domains, usually consisting of two such units linked together. This view allows comparisons between molecules as different as P-glycoprotein and the L-type Ca channels. Another feature of CFTR channels is the critical role of Cl ions: Although Cl channels are late comers to the voltage-gated ion channel field, Cl conductance figures in a wide range of physiological mechanisms (ICEMb, p. 136).

With this introduction, let us look at the CFTR protein in epithelial cells lining air passages in the lungs (see Fig. 3.37). Cells normally secrete a certain amount of water, which is essential to keeping mucus also secreted by these cells at a certain level of fluidity. For the water to move however, Cl ions must also move. Since Cl is carried by the CFTR Cl channel, if Cl cannot move, then water is not transported normally, and mucus becomes less fluid. This leads to gradual suffocation and bacterial buildup. The CFTR brings up the interesting problem of water movement in membranes; let us see what rules govern this.

Obligatory Water Loss

Now we consider the movement of water and what it means to a cell, particularly to cell volume. Consider a cell in osmotic balance with as many osmotically active particles inside as outside. For convenience we think of (•) as the osmolite,

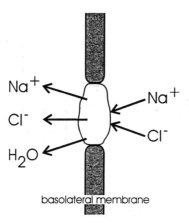

Figure 3.37.   CFTR

which is uncharged. In Fig. 3.38 the dashed-line box represents an external volume (solutes in water), equal in size to the cell, and the solid-line box is the cell. Because we have two particles (or two trillion particles) on the inside and two (trillion) particles outside, we have balance. Let us add the exact volume of water equal to the original volume of the external water plus the cell—with no osmolites—to the outside, as shown in Fig. 3.39.

In most cases the cell swells to the correct size to achieve osmotic balance (see Fig. 3.39); i.e., a volume of water equal to the original volume of the cell moves into the cell. Figure 3.39 shows only a snapshot because solutes and cells readjust, as shown in Fig. 3.40, where osmotic balance is reestablished. We now have half the concentration of particles we started with because we added two volumes of

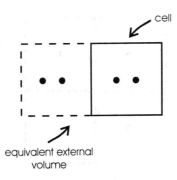

Figure 3.38.   Osmotic balance

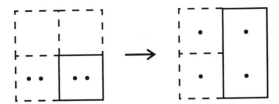

Figure 3.39.   Adding water to the bath (left) causes the cell to swell to maintain balance (right).

water. After a few minutes most real cells undergo exactly this process in regulatory volume decrease (RVD). As we see from Figs. 3.39 (right) and Fig. 3.40, one of the osmolites (•) had to cross the membrane for RVD to occur. Now assume that the solutes are charged. Normally this obligatory loss of water involves the movement of Cl ions (and possibly other ions, like K) through the membrane. One of the channels involved in regulation volume through water movement is a channel-inducing protein (CHIP); it can be thought of as a water channel. The CHIP is a 28-kDa protein about 40% homologous with another protein, called major intrinsic protein (MIP), discovered more than 10 years ago. The CHIP exists in a nonglycosylated form and a higher molecular weight glycosylated form; it is a tetramere rarely found in any other state *in vivo*. However only one (or maybe two) of the members of the foursome are glycosylated. In a red blood cell, there are 250,000 copies of CHIP per cell.

If the CHIP protein is expressed in frog oocytes that normally do not have it, they swell and burst (appropriately called the *exploding oocyte* assay). A typical experiment shifts CHIP-CRNA injected cells to a solution in which they swell and

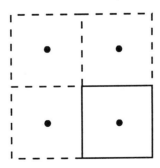

Figure 3.40.   Cell readjustment

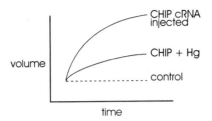

Figure 3.41.   CHIP volume regulator

burst; Fig. 3.41 illustrates an experiment that uses Hg to block these CHIP H_2O channels. (Hg is also a diuretic, probably for the same reason.) In Fig. 3.41 we add Hg to the CHIP-cRNA injected oocytes to reduce the effect of CHIP on volume. The current theory is that CHIP forms a channel (a four-barreled channel) in analogy with the porin molecule. This idea is based in part on the notion that each subunit has an external loop in 180° symmetry; i.e., each subunit contains a reverse repeat within the six transmembrane (TM) domains. Loops between TMs fold inward to form a channel in the membrane; these *funnel tunnels*, as they are called, are fairly common motifs for ion channels, e.g., the external mouth of the Na channel; however the unusual 180° reverse symmetry makes CHIP special.

The number of water molecules that move through one CHIP molecule is estimated to be 3×10^9/sec. If water had a net charge, this would represent a current of about 500 pA—which is one way of seeing that this is a rather large movement; this is why we do not view CHIP as a transporter. As we have seen, the distinction between transporters and channels is blurred; transporters may have channel-like properties, and some channels may have transporter properties. Since water has no net charge, we cannot measure water current. Based on the biophysical ideas that we have presented, can you think of how to use the patch clamp technique to look at the movement of water through CHIP?

Protein Transport

If there are channels for water, there may be channels for other unexpected molecules. What about channels that conduct proteins? Protein synthesis occurs in the cytosol, yet 90% of the proteins are targeted to membrane-bound organelles or to the plasma membrane. Once they reach their destination, how do the proteins pass through the organelle membrane? How are they integrated into the organelle membrane or into the plasma membrane? (Some protein synthesis does occur in mitochondria and chloroplasts; no one has demonstrated synthesis in the nucleus. At any rate most proteins must traverse a membrane at some stage.)

A protein signal sequence is necessary and sufficient for membrane transport, but is it valid to think of proteins moving through membranes as if in a protein-conducting channel? An experiment that supports this idea places vesicles from the pancreatic reticulum in the *cis* side of a chamber separated by a lipid bilayer membrane. Before adding the reticular vesicles, the synthetic lipid bilayer has a very high resistance (a low conductance) to the passage of anything. Adding monosomes to the *cis* side increases the membrane conductance separating the two compartments of the chamber; thus the reticular vesicles are thought to contain channels that are incorporated into the bilayer. In a ribosome for rough endoplasmic reticulum, the protein-to-lipid ratio is about 1:1; in the experiment just described, only about one vesicle in 1000 binds to the membrane. The implication is that there are very few channels with respect to the number of ribosomes. Puromycin is commonly used to study protein transport in such systems; Fig. 3.42 shows what happens. The signal peptide is thought to gate a channel that opens: It first lets ions

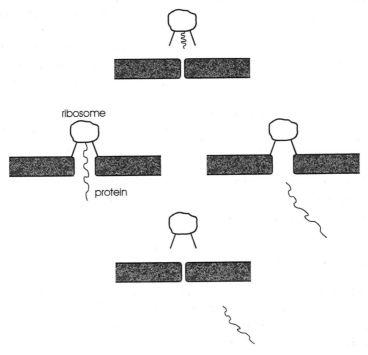

Figure 3.42. Protein channels: A ribosome approaches the membrane (top) and opens a pore through which the protein translocates (middle), whereupon the ribosome detaches and the pore closes (bottom).

flow through, then translates the protein through an open channel. Channel conductance is large, about 200 pS; a signal sequence can be placed on virtually *any* protein, and the protein will be transported in similar fashion.

The multidrug resistance (MDR) protein P-glycoprotein (see p. 190) may also have channel-like behavior. Certain drugs used in chemotherapy accumulate in cells, where they are toxic; thus there appear to exist drug-induced pumps in cells. In tumor cells accumulated concentration of toxic drugs used in chemotherapy is much higher than in healthy cells, thereby destroying tumor cells. In healthy and in some tumor cells, the toxin is expelled by MDR proteins like P-glycoprotein. How does this work? Not much is known, but there are some hints: Ninety percent of the drugs used for chemotherapy are basic, although some, like colchicine, are exceptions. The basic nature of the drugs alters their effectiveness, indicating that intracellular pH is involved. If we load cells with a pH-sensitive dye, the following reaction occurs

$$CO_2 + H_2O \Leftrightarrow HCO_3^- + H^+$$

Therefore accumulation can easily be followed as a function of pCO_2. In this way the accumulation of chemotheraputic drugs has been shown to correlate with an elevation of internal pH. Some drug accumulation occurs on a short time scale, independent of cell division; thus division alone does not account for the difference between healthy and tumor cells. Another property of a tumor cell is the high metabolic rate and the high internal pH that distinguish tumor cells from healthy cells. In the broadest sense this parallels fertilization: Immediately after sperm–egg fusion, internal pH (and earlier internal Ca) increase dramatically in the egg, and the metabolic rate of the zygote rises well above its prefertilization rate; the consequence is cell division.

In the last few sections we have expanded the concept of a channel considerably from the original voltage-gated ion channels, which arose from the HH theory of membrane excitably. Channels exist not only for ions but for water, sugar, neurotransmitters, and large proteins; bioelectricity certainly plays a role in these transport mechanisms. Now we consider the largest channel of all, the nuclear pore, which has some rather singular features.

Transport across the Nuclear Pore

By definition eukaryotic cells contain a nucleus, a roughly spherical body inside cells that encloses well-known molecules and organelles. The nucleus is defined by a thin nuclear envelope that transports macromolecules; transport is highly regulated, and it changes dramatically for example during the cell cycle and the cell's morphological or developmental stages. The majority of books describe the nuclear envelope as freely permeable to small molecules, such as Na, K, Ca, and Cl ion

The consensus seems to be that at least with regard to small ions, the nucleus is merely a sieve with large aqueous pores. However according to a minority of researchers, the nuclear envelope can restrict the movement of small molecules, including peptides, amino acids, and sugars. Furthermore some experiments support the idea that ions like Ca and Na can accumulate in (or be excluded from) the nucleus under certain conditions. Ion selectivity is supported by experiments showing that the nucleus maintains an electrical potential with respect to the cytoplasm and it can swell or shrink in response to osmotic forces. These electrochemical phenomena could come from the selective absorption of ions by the nucleoplasm or from a selective property of the nuclear envelope.

The idea that the state of the internal matrix—and not the membrane—is responsible for selectivity began with the plasma membrane. Gilbert Ling stressed that the gel-like interior of cells is responsible for membrane potential rather than the selective permeability of the membrane surrounding the cell (*A Physical Theory of the Living State*, p. 283). Ling, one of the inventors of the glass microelectrode to measure cell potentials, argued that cytoplasm's ion-selective properties are most important for generating and propagating electrical potentials. Although the membrane clearly does not separate two purely aqueous phases, it remains unclear what role the cell matrix plays in maintaining and regulating cell potentials. Curiously a story related to this point is emerging for secretory granules and synaptic vesicles: It appears likely that secretory structure interiors contain a gel with ion exchange properties and this gel plays an important regulatory role in secretion. Thus the relationship between the fusion of vesicles with plasma membranes and the subsequent release of secretions (ICEMb, p. 95) is far more complex than previously thought.

We explore the idea that not only the interior matrix of the nucleus but also the nuclear envelope has selective properties for small ions. These properties resemble those of a semipermeable plasma membrane, and they can maintain electrochemical gradients between the cytoplasm and nucleoplasm. The main conduit or channel between the cytosol and the nucleoplasm is the nuclear pore, a complex structure made up of over 100 gene products with a total molecular weight of more than 100 MDa. The nuclear pore sits in a double membrane, as shown in Fig. 3.43. The pore in the double membrane consists of eight symmetrical units that define a large central opening that may contain a plug whose significance is unknown: The plug may move within the pore and thus regulate transport through the pore. So far there is little evidence, and some researchers regard the plug as a protein trapped in transient. Certainly the nuclear pore governs the movement of nucleic acids and large-molecular-weight proteins into and out of the nucleus: RNA must leave the nucleus for cytosol translation; certain proteins, like nucleic acid polymerization enzymes, must enter the nucleus from the cytosol, and DNA-binding proteins must enter for transcription and gene regulation. However the nucleus excludes the majority of cytosolic proteins from its domain, and selection of certain nuclear

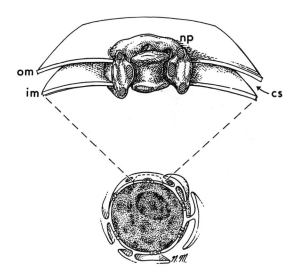

Figure 3.43. Nuclear envelope: om (outer membrane), im (inner membrane), np (nuclear pore), cs (cistern).

proteins is exact. *In vitro* transport of macromolecules across the nuclear envelope can require GTP or ATP. Let us now ask how the nuclear pore shown in more detail in Fig. 3.44 be like a channel.

For the moment let us forget that the nuclear envelope is a double membrane and that pores traverse the cisterns in some complex fashion. Instead we model the nucleus as a cell within a cell and define four cellular domains as in Fig. 3.45. The nucleus is represented by a rectangle, and the nuclear pore connects Space 2 (cytoplasm) and Space 4 (nucleoplasm). Applying what we know about the plasma membrane to the nuclear envelope we regard the double membrane as a semipermeable membrane spanned by nuclear pores. The flux of any substrate in terms of electric and osmotic forces is (Appendix 2):

$$-\phi = \mathrm{u}kT\left(\frac{du}{dx}\right) + ze\mathrm{nu}\left(\frac{dV}{dx}\right)$$

Note: Because flux flows down a negative gradient (i.e., downhill) there is a minus sign on the left. The symbol ϕ represents the flux of any material, i.e., the number of molecules that move per unit area per unit time ($\varnothing$ #/cm^2 sec); $n(x)$ is the substrate concentration ($\varnothing$ #/cm^3) at position x, $V(x)$ is the voltage (mV) at position x, u is the mobility of the substrate through the barrier ($\varnothing$ velocity/force), k is the Boltzmann constant, T is the absolute temperature in degrees Kelvin, z is the valence, and e is the electronic charge. These quantities appear as the ratio:

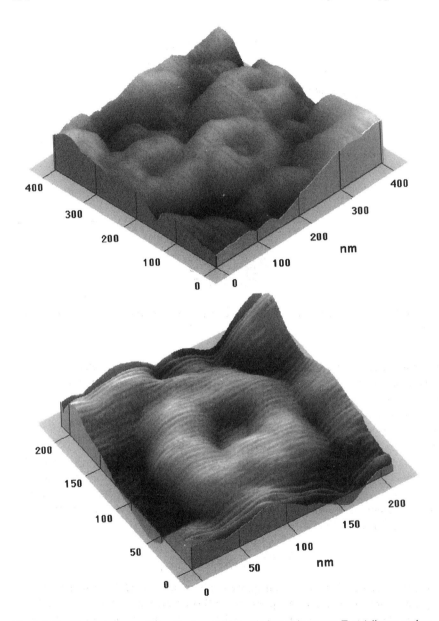

Figure 3.44.   The nuclear pore: Reconstructions from atomic force microscopy. Top: Adjacent nuclear pore complexes located in the nuclear envelope; Bottom: The dimple in the doughnut is the nuclear pore. (This image was kindly provided by Carmen Perez.)

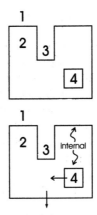

Figure 3.45.   Sign conventions for intracellular membranes

$$a = \frac{ze}{kT} = \frac{zF}{RT} = \frac{z}{25 \text{ mV}} \quad \text{at } 23 \text{ °C}$$

Considering the convention in Fig. 3.45 and integrating the flux equation between the nucleoplasm ($nu = 4$) and the cytosol ($cy = 2$), the expression for the flux becomes the familiar (Appendix 2):

$$-\phi = ukT \frac{n_{nu}e^{-aV\text{nu}} - n_{cy}e^{-aV\text{nu}}}{\int e^{aV(x)}dx}$$

This assumes that u is constant and flux is in a steady state (no accumulation or depletion of substrate; thus ϕ is constant). Recall that $D = ukT$, where D is the diffusion constant of the substrate in the barrier. In deriving this equation, no assumption was made about the spatial form of the voltage or concentration gradients $V(x)$ or $n(x)$; only values of n and V far from the envelope come into play. To integrate the denominator $V(x)$ must be known, the actual shape of the voltage gradient across the barrier. $V(x)$ is never known and may not be constant. If we assume $V(x)$ to be a linear function of x, the Nernst–Planck equation leads to the Goldman equation (see Appendix 2). Rather than assume a particular $V(x)$, we leave the integral undetermined and replace it by the symbol ℓ:

$$\ell = \int e^{aV(x)}dx$$

where $\ell \ominus$ length (cm) and $ukT/l = D/\ell$ is measured in units of velocity ($\ominus$ cm/sec); we call this ratio the permeability p (cm/sec), and for the flux of any substrate, we write:

$$-\phi = p \left(n_{nu} e^{-aVnu} - n_{cy} e^{-aVcy} \right)$$

In this case p is the permeability of the nuclear pore to the transported material. Could this theory apply to the transport of macromolecules across the nuclear envelope? Let us assume we are dealing with K ions that cannot pass through the envelope unless they combine with the nuclear pore complex and eight (or a multiple of eight) K ions must interact with the pore before their transport can occur. Note: We selected eight as the stoichiometry because of the structure of the nuclear pore; thus we might reasonably expect eight K interactions between the nuclear pore and ions. Under this assumption:

$$8\,K + P \Leftrightarrow K_8 P$$

$$K_{kp} = [K]^8 \, [P]/[K_8 P]$$

where P stands for the nuclear pore complex and K_{kp} is the disassociation constant for the reaction (see the discussion on p. 175). Consider a charged macromolecule *M* that undergoes a similar interaction with *P*, but one molecule at a time:

$$M + P \Leftrightarrow MP$$

$$K_{mp} = [M] \, [P]/[MP]$$

where K_{mp} is the disassociation constant for the reaction. Assume that $K_8 P$ and MP can move across the envelope, but that K, M, and P by themselves cannot. Now consider two fluxes: the flux of $K_8 P$ bound to the pore:

$$-\phi_{kp} = p_{kp} ([K_8 P]_{nu} e^{-aVnu} - [K_8 P]_{cy} e^{-aVcy})$$

and the flux of MP bound to the pore:

$$-\phi_{mp} = p_{mp} ([MP]_{nu} e^{-aVnu} - [MP]_{cy} e^{-aVcy})$$

where p_{kp} is the permeability of $K_8 P$, and p_{mp} is the permeability of MP through the envelope. If we consider the transport of macromolecules and the transport of ions to be coupled, then the steady-state condition reduces to:

$$\phi_{kp} = \phi_{mp}$$

This equation treats the nuclear pore as a transporter, and it assumes that ion and macromolecule flux are coupled. The equation means that if a certain number of these pores in the kp state flux in one direction, then an equivalent number in the mp state flux to the other. Under these assumptions, we can solve for the flux of

MP. Note: We do not know in molecular terms what "face" and "fluxes" actually mean; here they merely represent transport process. The disassociation constants K_{kp} and K_{mp} describe probabilities of interactions of macromolecules, M, and the ions K, attached to the nuclear pore, P; as in the case of transporters, we want to formulate these in terms of substrate concentrations [K] and [M], and the pore concentration, [P].

$$[K_8P] = \frac{[K]^8[P]}{K_{kp}}$$

$$[MP] = \frac{[M][P]}{K_{mp}}$$

where K_{kp}, K_{mp}, and of course substrate concentrations may differ on each side of the nuclear envelope. The equations are constrained because the total number of pores is fixed; thus we can write macromolecular flux in terms of $[K]_{cy}$, $[K]_{nu}$, $[M]_{cy}$, and $[M]_{nu}$. This completes the Nernst–Planck approach to the coupled transport of ions and macromolecules across the nuclear envelope.

Let us now assume if that the nuclear pore consists of eight channels for ions and one channel for charged macromolecules, then the fluxes of ions and macromolecules are coupled through their electric charge without an additional assumption about cotransport. We write the flux equations:

$$-\phi_k = p_k([K]_{nu}e^{-aVnu} - [K]_{cy}e^{-aVcy})$$

$$-\phi_m = p_m([M]_{nu}e^{-aVnu} - [M]_{cy}e^{-aVcy})$$

where we dropped the p in the subscript kp, etc., to distinguish the channel model from the cotransport model. In the channel model, the steady-state condition reduces to:

$$8\phi_k + z_m\phi_m = 0$$

Here, z_m is the valence of the macromolecules. This too leads to an expression for macromolecular flux in terms of substrate concentrations. Because the flux of a charged molecule, whatever that molecule may be, is an electric current and the relationship between flux through N nuclear pores, then $\Phi = N\phi$ (ϕ #/cm^2 sec), and the fluxes lead to a current. Either the cotransport model or the channel model requires a balance of fluxes or currents. For example, if the charged macromolecule were RNA, then we would have:

$$I_K + I_{RNA} = 0$$

It may be strange to think of RNA movement as a current, but it is perfectly valid; a similar equation, like a microelectrophoresis of RNA and proteins, applies to charged proteins. If we assume that 10^9 RNA molecules move across the nuclear envelope per minute and one unit charge per base and 10^4 bases per RNA molecule, then I_{RNA} is on the order of 10 nA for a typical nucleus and less than 1 pA for an individual nuclear pore. Thus for a charged macromolecule to move, it must be accompanied by a countercurrent to maintain charge neutrality. Large molecules are charged, and in so far as they move across a barrier, the same laws apply.

Sign Conventions for Intracellular Membranes

The sign convention for the plasma membrane is "inside minus outside" (in the original Hodgkin–Huxley papers, it was the reverse). One wrinkle occurred for the gap junction (see Fig. 3.16), where V referred to cell "cytoplasm to cell cytoplasm" cell. But generally we agree that:

$$V = V_{in} - .V_{out}$$

We take V_{out} as zero (ground), so that $V = V_{in}$; for example, $V = -60$ mV means -60 mV with respect to the outside (set arbitrarily to zero). What is the sign convention for intracellular membranes, like the ones we have been discussing?

Consider first something like the endoplasmic reticulum, which is an extension of the outer membrane of the nuclear envelope (see Fig. 3.43). The endoplasmic reticulum is a separate membrane-bound space inside cells, which can also be represented by Region 4 in Fig. 3.45. Note: Region 1 refers to extracellular space, which we see can penetrate the cell (as with the T tubules in muscle cells); then Region 2 refers to the cytoplasm, and Region 4 refers to an intracellular volume, viewed here in a two-dimensional world. In Fig. 3.45 notation, $V = V_2 - V_1$. What sign convention should we adopt for the membrane-bounding Region 4 notation? For the membrane around Region 4 in the diagram, Berti *et al.* (*Science* **258**: 873, 1992) suggest $V = V_2 - V_4$, because the side of the membrane around Region 4 that contacts the cytoplasm is developmentally like the inside of the plasma membrane (*internal* in Fig. 3.45). Then if for example current flowed *out* of Region 4 into the cytoplasm, current would be *inward* using this notation.

Assume we have a K channel in the plasma membrane and the same one in the intracellular organelle 4; these K channels are oriented in the same way with respect to the membrane (see Fig. 3.46). Then the inside face of each channel points toward the inside of the cell. If we place patch electrodes on each channel (represented by triangles in Fig. 3.46), then measure the $i(V)$ curve of each one, the $i(V)$ curves look the same if we adopt the preceding convention. When $V_2 - V_1$ is positive, current is positive and outward (i.e., out of the cell); when $V_2 - V_4$ is positive, current is

Figure 3.46.   Membrane asymmetry

positive and outward (i.e., out of the organelle). This means that we must define the Nernst potential so that it is consistent with this idea; namely:

$$E_K = -\frac{kT}{e} \ln \frac{K_{in} \text{ (cytosol)}}{K_{out} \text{ (extracellular)}}$$

This works for the plasma membrane, e.g.,

$$E_K = -\frac{kT}{e} \ln \frac{150}{5}$$

which is a negative number. Then we adopt

$$E_K = -\frac{kT}{e} \ln \frac{K_{in} \text{ (cytosol)}}{K_{out} \text{(lumen of SR)}}$$

We call Region 4 the lumen of the SR to make the example explicit, but it could be any membrane-bound organelle inside a cell. It does not matter what the sign of E_K (the lumen) is, i.e., K_{in} (cytosol) does not *have* to be larger than K_{out} (lumen), but the *sign* of E_K, whatever it is, must be preserved in this way. Although we are used to letting $V_1 = 0$, we usually cannot think of the voltage V_4 in this same way; however, we can set $V_1 = 0$, as usual. If the lumen electrode is inside the SR, then according to this convention, we define the voltage measured as in Fig. 3.47: Therefore, $V = (V_2 - V_1) - (V_2 - V_4) = V_4 - V_1$. Note: If we move the electrode from inside to outside, we obtain $V = V_1 - V_4$. Remember: The nucleus is surrounded by membrane-bound lumens, called cisterns, that are continuous with the endoplasmic reticulum. Cisterns (cs in Fig. 3.43) surround a separate space, the nucleoplasm (Region 4). It is tempting to equate Region 4 with Region 2, that is consider nuclear pores as communication pores; however the cytoplasm and the nucleoplasm may not be in perfect electrical communication, so the question of what sign combination to use for the nucleus is more complex. (A similar problem exists for mitochondria and chloroplasts; however in these organelles, there is less bias about the communication between the interior of a mitochondria, e.g., and the cytoplasm.)

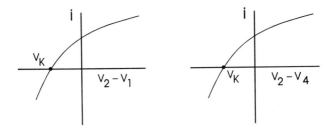

Figure 3.47.   The convention works: A K channel in the membrane (left) has the same $I(V)$ curve as a K channel in an internal organelle (right).

Acetylcholine (ACh) Receptor-Channel Complexes

So far we have not discussed auxiliary proteins accompanying almost all ion channels. Auxiliary proteins may not be involved in pore formation, but they can modify pores; examples are Na and Ca channels (ICEMb, p. 251). In other cases several proteins are required to form the native pore; an example is the K channel. The classical example of subunits actually forming the pore is the nicotinic ACh receptor channel complex (AChRs; ICEMb, pp. 237, 254). Five subunits make up the channel, and two of these are identical; together they form the $\alpha_2\beta\gamma\delta$ complex illustrated in Fig. 3.48.

In this model, the β subunit sits between the two alphas. Since the sequences of the four different gene products are 40% identical, they are thought to fold in the membrane in similar ways; therefore they must each have a symmetry compatible with pentagonal structure. There can never be complete symmetry. The 5-HT receptor is a similar receptor channel complex; GABA, glycine, and other receptors also have a similar structure. Figure 3.49 shows a topological map of the α subunit of the ACh complex.

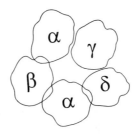

Figure 3.48.   Looking down on the ACh receptor channel complex

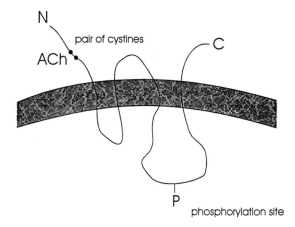

Figure 3.49.   Structure of one subunit: The α subunit binds ACh.

Note the location of ACh binding sites (external) and the phosphorylation site (P) on the cytoplasmic face. The ACh molecule (which is positively charged) seems to bind on a noncharged region of the α structure; binding sites form an aromatic group. The π electron system of aromatic groups is thought to generate a dipole interaction with the quaterionic aromatic group. If we reduce one of these sites, we inevitably inhibit the receptor (e.g., with DTT causing S $\rightarrow$ SH). When S sites are protonated (reduced) they can be bound with a 9-Å locker and an N^+ group; that is the basis of the search for a negatively charged 9-Å S-S at the binding site. In reconstruction experiments, channel activity is usually not found without at least three subunits, but there are some exceptions with different α clones. However ACh can bind to these trimere constructs; surprisingly α cannot form a binding site for ACh when expressed by itself.

If there are similar sequences and nearly identical three-dimensional structure, then the pentamere symmetry is 360/5 = 72°. What about the pore in the center? Cystine is highly reactive, and it has been methodically mutated in the putative channel region of the pentamere. The idea is to mutate cystine in order to bind cystine with small molecules that tend to block the channel; the reaction is:

$$CH_3S-\overset{\displaystyle O}{\underset{\displaystyle O}{\overset{\displaystyle \|}{\underset{\displaystyle \|}{S}}}}CH_2\text{-----}X \quad X = N + \text{sulfhydrol reagents}$$

Cystine mutagenesis has been explored extensively in the M2 region of the subunits because M2 is known to be involved in both selectivity and conductivity. This example illustrates that channels can be composed of many proteins and that these proteins can be manipulated to reveal function.

Are voltage-gated ion channels fundamentally different from ligand-gated channels, like the ACh-receptor-channel complex in Fig. 3.48? In principle they are not; once the pore is formed, it obeys the usual rules; in fact there are specific similarities between voltage-gated ion channels and ligand-gated ion channels. Muscle AChRs are comprised of more than 10 different subunit clones, and these can form various $\alpha_{2-8}\beta_{2-4}$ complexes. In some cases α subunits can form channels by themselves. In neuronal AChRs there is a distinct genetic type: $\alpha_2\beta_1\delta\varepsilon$.

Muscle AChR conducts mainly Na and K; in pure Ca solutions however, the muscle AChR can also conduct Ca. But in neuronal AChRs, Ca is a regular carrier of the current, along with Na and K. In Ca conduction there are some similarities between the neuronal AChR and the L-type channel; Fig. 3.50 compares the two. The Ca channel presumably has two Ca (•) binding sites, which (regardless of number) have a higher affinity for Ca than the single Ca site in the neuronal AChR channel. The number of binding sites, a complex property of the channel per se, is usually determined from a well model, with the measured parameter being the ratio of Ca and Na permeabilities. For neuronal AChRs this ratio is independent of concentration; for L-type Ca channels, it is not. This result suggests two binding sites for Ca channels. Experiments show that less than 10% of the current through a neuronal AChR is carried by Ca; this result comes from measuring Ca directly with Ca-sensitive dyes and by integrating the pure Ca current. In muscle AChRs Ca current is less than 2% of the total, but any percentage is significant considering the potency of Ca as a regulator. Neuronal channels demonstrate a type of modu-

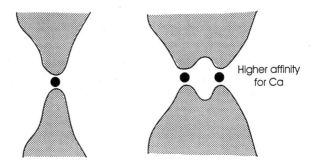

Figure 3.50. Neuronal receptor channel complex: (a) neuronal ACh channel; (b) L-type Ca channel with a higher affinity for Ca.

lation unique to neurons and absent in muscle AChRs: As Ca increases, the probability of opening a Ca channel, p_{Ca}, increases. Synapses are regulated by this modulatory process, and miniature synaptic potentials are longer in higher Ca. The Ca concentration can change drastically in a restricted space by merely turning off neuronal AChRs; this does not occur in muscle. Comparing different ways that ions like Ca cross cell membranes plays an important role in membrane biophysics, and we sometimes discover that one mechanism applies equally well to another channel type.

Ion Channels in Sperm

Channels are everywhere! We turn our attention to a new study of the role of ion channels in sperm development. *Caenorhabditis elegans* sperm are out of the ordinary, and rather unlike the whip-tail mammalian sperm; however because *C. elegans* constitute a powerful genetic model, their sperm are useful in studying spermatogenesis and the role ion channels may play during development. Four spermatids derive from one spermatocyte and intracellular organelles localize specifically to spermatids as they bud off from an anuclear residual body (see Fig. 3.51). Most of the electrophysiology so far has been done on spermatocytes and spermatids. In these worms sperm are shaped more or less like an ice cream cone.

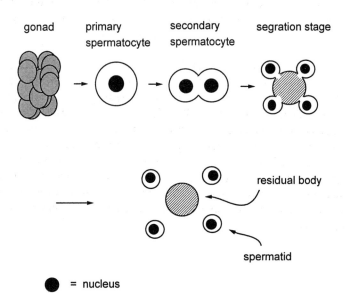

Figure 3.51. A spermatocyte becomes a residual body and four spermatids.

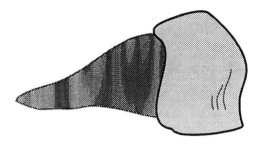

Figure 3.52.   Worm sperm: No tubulin, no organelles except mitochondria.

There is no flagellum in *C. elegans* sperm, only a foot (the cone), which sperm use the foot to crawl onto oocytes in amoebae fashion. Even stranger, after the testis make sperm it becomes an ovary and makes eggs; then these gametes can fertilize each other. There are hermaphrodites *and* males, but there are no females. Sperm from males are preferred to the hermaphrodite sperm, suggesting a sperm hierarchy. Curiously nearly every oocyte is fertilized by every sperm, which is a far cry from the situation in mammals or invertebrates such as the sea urchin, where only a minority of sperm ever succeed. In *C. elegans* gametes are more or less matched in number, and they meet in the spermatheca. During the development of spermatocytes to spermatozoa, the spermatocyte deposits all its ribosomes and other organelles into the residual body, which takes about 15 minutes. Thus no protein synthesis can occur in spermatids, and none is required for their evolution into sperm. Only Cl channels are found in these spermatids (about 5 um in diameter) and only a few per cell.

Apparently the numerous ion channels in the spermatocyte membrane isolate themselves to either the residual body or spermatids; although several different types of voltage-gated ion channels exist in spermatocytes, only a single channel type can be detected in spermatids. The channel in spermatids is an inward-rectifying Cl channel, as indicated by Cl-dependent shifts in current-voltage relationships and sensitivity to Cl channel blockers. They are not perfect Cl channels (see Appendix 2), but they are selective to Cl over cations by a good margin. The amazing fact is that treating spermatids with Cl channel blockers induce their differentiation into spermatozoa. No one knows why this occurs, but this is a startling example of an ion channel is intimately involved in one of life's fundamental processes.

Appendix 1

Operational Amplifiers

Figure A.1 shows a model of an operational amplifier. The input is $(e - e')$ and the output is $(V - V') = A(e - e')$. R_i is the input resistance and R_o is the output resistance. In the ideal operational amplifier, there is no connection between the input circuit and the output circuit. The operational amplifier also has an infinite input resistance $(R_i \rightarrow \infty)$, infinite gain $(A \rightarrow \infty)$, and zero output resistance $(R_o = 0)$.

Figure A.2 shows the symbol for an operational amplifier, where e is the negative input and e' is the positive input. We show only one output line because V' is connected to ground (reference), which is always considered as zero.

Buffer

The buffer is an impedance matcher that moves a signal (E) from one circuit to another circuit without distortion regardless of the output resistance of the signal source or the input resistance of the signal destination. To make a buffer, we connect the output of the operational amplifier to its negative input through a feedback resistance R_f (negative feedback; see Fig. A.3). To analyze this circuit, we redraw Fig. A.1 with the new conditions of Fig. A.3; this is shown in Fig. A.4; where a feedback resistor connects the output (V) to the negative input (e); a signal (E) goes into the positive input (e'), and V' is connected to ground.

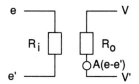

Figure A.1. Operational amplifier: A model of the input circuit (left) and the output circuit (right) of an op-amp.

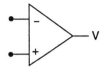

Figure A.2. Symbol for an operational amplifier

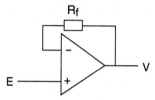

Figure A.3. Buffer

Simplifying further we can redraw the circuit as in Fig. A.5. Using the cross-multiplication rule of circuit analysis (IMN, p. 87):

$$V = \frac{ER_o + A(e - E)(R_f + R_i)}{R_o + R_f + R_i}$$

From the constancy of current in a branch (IMN, p. 87):

$$\frac{V - E}{R_f + R_i} = \frac{e - E}{R_i} \quad \text{or} \quad e - E = \frac{R_i}{R_f + R_i}(V - E)$$

Substituting $(e - E)$ into the previous equation:

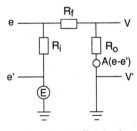

Figure A.4. Buffer circuit

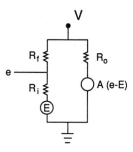

Figure A.5. Buffer analysis

$$V = \frac{ER_o + AR_i(V - E)}{R_o + R_f + R_i}$$

If $R_o = 0$:

$$V = \frac{AR_i(V - E)}{R_f + R_i} = \frac{A(V - E)}{(R_f/R_i + 1)}$$

If $R_i \to \infty$:

$$V = A(V - E)$$

or

$$V - \frac{V}{A} = E$$

If $A \to \infty$:

$$V = E$$

The output of the buffer (V) equals its input (E). An ideal buffer does not distort beecause its input resistance is infinite and its output resistance is zero. The input resistance of the buffer is the resistance to ground seen by E, which from Fig. A.5 is buffer input resistance = $R_i + R_f + R_o \to \infty$ as $R_i \to \infty$. The output resistance of the buffer is the resistance seen by V, which from Fig. A.5 is:

$$\frac{R_o(R_f + R_i)}{R_o + R_f + R_i} = \frac{R_o[(R_f/R_i + 1)]}{(R_o/R_i) + (R_f/R_i) + 1}$$

$$= 0 \quad \text{as } R_o \to 0 \text{ and } R_i \to \infty$$

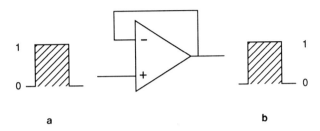

Figure A.6. Buffer with $R_f = 0$: (a) from any circuit, regardless of output resistance; (b) to any circuit, regardless of input resistance.

Because buffer input resistance is infinite, the buffer draws no current from the source of E, and the voltage E passes undisturbed to the output V. Because buffer output resistance is zero, the buffer, viewed as the source of V, does not load the circuit it is attached to. In the buffer equations, R_f disappears.

PROBLEM: R_f can have any value. Rework the buffer example with $R_f = 0$, i.e., solve the circuit in Fig. A.6, which shows the usual configuration for a buffer.

Voltage Amplifier

The voltage amplifier is similar to the buffer except that input voltage is changed by a fixed amount at the output. To make a voltage amplifier, we connect the output of an operational amplifier to its negative input through a feedback resistor R_f, as in Fig. A.3. In the voltage amplifier however, we apply the signal E to the negative input through resistor R, and we connect the positive input to ground (see Fig. A.7).

Following the procedure of Fig. A.4 and Fig. A.5, the circuit in Fig. A.7 is equivalent to the amplifier circuit in Fig. A.8. To save work, we let $R_i \rightarrow \infty$ initially.

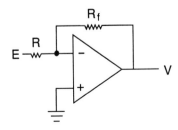

Figure A.7. Voltage amplifier

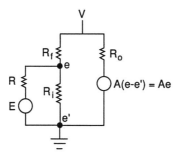

Figure A.8. Amplifier circuit

The circuit in Fig. A.8 reduces to the schematic in Fig. A.9. Using the cross-multiplication rule:

$$V = \frac{ER_o + Ae(R_f + R)}{R_o + R_f + R}$$

From the constancy of current in a branch:

$$\frac{V - e}{R_f} = \frac{e - E}{R} \quad \text{or} \quad e = \frac{RV + R_f E}{R + R_f}$$

Substituting e into the above equation:

$$V = \frac{ER_o + A(RV + R_f E)}{R_o + R_f + R}$$

If $R_o = 0$:

$$V = \frac{A(RV + R_f E)}{R_f + R}$$

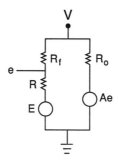

Figure A.9. Analysis of an amplifier

Solving for V:

$$V = \frac{A R_f E}{R_f + R - AR} = \frac{R_f E}{[(R_f + R)/A] - R}$$

If $A \to \infty$:

$$V = -\frac{R_f}{R} E$$

The output of the voltage amplifier (V) is negative (R_f/R) times the input (E). Unlike the buffer, the input resistance of the voltage amplifier is not infinite. The input resistance is the resistance to ground seen by E looking into the voltage amplifier circuit; even if $R_o = 0$, this is:

$$R + R_f + R_o = R + R_f$$

However, output resistance of the voltage amplifier is still the resistance seen by V; if $R_o = 0$, from Fig. A.9, this is:

$$\frac{R_o(R_f + R)}{R_o + R_f + R} = 0$$

Since the voltage amplifier input resistance is finite and it depends on values of R and R_f, for the voltage amplifier the resistance of the source of signal E matters. For example if the source of E has an output resistance of 50 Ω, then ($R + R_f$) must be much greater than 50 Ω to prevent loading. The output resistance of the voltage amplifier has the ideal value of zero. Practically it must be much smaller than the input resistor in the device *it* is connected to.

We derived the two equations:

$$e = \frac{RV + R_f E}{R + R_f}$$

$$V = -\left(\frac{R_f}{R}\right) E$$

Therefore $e = 0$! Connecting the *positive* input to ground in effect holds the *negative* input at zero. This is called virtual ground. The solid dot in Fig. A.7 is this circuit's virtual ground. Using the concept of virtual ground makes analysis simple and direct; from Fig. A.7:

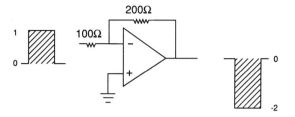

Figure A.10. Amplifier with 2× gain: The input voltage (left) is amplified and inverted at the output (right).

$$\frac{E-0}{R} = \frac{0-V}{R_f} \quad \text{or} \quad V = -\frac{R_f}{R} E$$

PROBLEM. Assuming the output resistance of the source of signal E is zero, the voltage amplifier increases by R_f/R and inverts. Figure A.10 shows an amplifier with a gain of 2. This seems less than ideal because the output is inverted. Design an amplifier to correct for this.

PROBLEM: Suppose the source of E has an output resistance of 50 Ω. What is V? What values of R and R_f give a 1% error in V assuming a gain of 2 is desired?

We connect the positive input to a battery rather than directly to ground. In Fig. A.11 since E_2 is also an input to the circuit, we labeled the two inputs 1 and 2. Following the usual procedure, the preceding circuit is equivalent to the circuit in Fig. A.12. To let $R_i \to \infty$ simply erase it, as we did before. Now however e' [the positive input to the operational amplifier] is equal to E_2, not to zero. This is the only effect of connecting the positive input to a battery rather than to ground. Using the cross-multiplication rule:

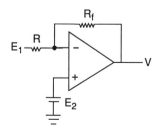

Figure A.11. Positive battery input

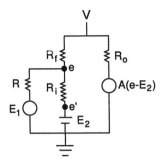

Figure A.12. Circuit for battery at positive input

$$V = \frac{E_1 R_o + A(e - E_2)(R_f + R)}{R_o + R_f + R}$$

From the constancy of current in a branch:

$$\frac{V - e}{R_f} = \frac{e - E_1}{R} \quad \text{or} \quad e = \frac{RV + R_f E_1}{R + R_f}$$

Substituting:

$$V = \frac{E_1 R_o + A(RV + R_f E_1) - A E_2(R_f + R)}{R_o + R_f + R}$$

If $R_o = 0$:

$$V = \frac{A(RV + R_f E_1) - A E_2(R_f + R)}{R_f + R}$$

Solving for V:

$$V = \frac{A R_f E_1 - A E_2(R_f + R)}{R_f + R - AR}$$

$$= \frac{R_f E_1 - E_2(R_f + R)}{[(R_f + R)/A] - R}$$

If $A \rightarrow \infty$:

$$V = -\left(\frac{R_f}{R}\right)E_1 + \left(\frac{R_f + R}{R}\right)E_2$$

or

$$V = -\frac{R_f}{R}(E_1 - E_2) + E_2$$

The output of the voltage amplifier connected to ground through a battery is a negative R_f/R times the difference between the voltages at the negative and positive inputs ($E_1 - E_2$); this voltage is offset by E_2. The input and output resistance are the same as when the voltage amplifier is connected directly to ground.

We will now show that battery E_2 in Fig. A.11 applied to the positive input appears at the negative input. We saw this before when e' was zero; now we will see that it is generally true. We derived two equations for Fig. A.11:

$$e = \frac{RV + R_f E_1}{R + R_f}$$

$$V = -(R_f/R)E_1 + \left(\frac{R_f + R}{R}\right)E_2$$

Substituting the expression for V into the expression for e gives:

$$e = E_2$$

Now that we have proved this, simply letting $e = E_2$ in Fig. A.11 simplifies the analysis; the dot in Fig. A.11 is at virtual E_2. From Fig. A.11:

$$\frac{E_1 - E_2}{R} = \frac{E_2 - V}{R_f}$$

or as before:

$$V = -\frac{R_f}{R}(E_1 - E_2) + E_2$$

We refer to virtual potentials in Figs. A.7 and A.11 because the dot is not directly connected to the voltage source at the positive input (zero or in general any voltage); however it acts as if it were. This is the consequence of infinite gain ($A \rightarrow \infty$) in the fundamental model in Fig. A.1.

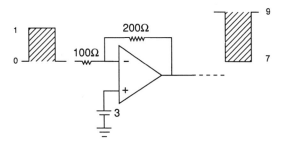

Figure A.13. Amplifier with offset: The input voltage (left) is amplified, inverted, and offset at the output (right).

PROBLEM. Assume the output resistance of the *sources* of E_1 and E_2 are zero. Show that the diagram of input and output in Fig. A.13 is correct.

Current-to-Voltage Converter

To measure current as we do in a patch clamp experiment (ICEMb, p. 89), we use the configuration of an operational amplifier in Fig. A.14 (see SCRa, p. 4). Note the similarity between the Figs. A.7 and A.14. To analyze Fig. A.14, we use rules already derived to write directly (the dot is virtual ground):

$$\frac{0-V}{R_f} = I \quad \text{or} \quad V = -IR_f$$

Remember: The voltage at the negative input is zero because the infinite gain ($A \rightarrow \infty$) of the op-amp forces the potential at the negative input to equal the potential at the positive input. Therefore the voltage drops across R_f is $(0 - V)$, and current through R_f is $(0 - V)/R_f$. The current through R_f must equal I, the current flowing into the amplifier, because the input resistance of the op-amp is infinite ($R_i \rightarrow \infty$)

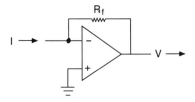

Figure A.14. Current-to-voltage converter

and current I cannot flow elsewhere. (To see where I goes after it arrives at V, analyze the complete circuit that is built from the op-amp model, as we did in Fig. A.8.)

If the positive input in Fig. A.14 were connected to a battery E_2, as in Fig. A.11, then the equation for the circuit would be

$$\frac{(E_2 - V)}{R_f} = I \quad \text{or} \quad V = -IR_f + E_2$$

Thus current I is measured as a voltage drop across R_f, while *the input connection* (the dot in Fig. A.14) *is held at constant voltage E_2*. There is a small dissatisfaction with this simple circuit the offset, but this is easily dealt with. E_2 is called the *voltage clamp* of the circuit, and it can be labeled V_{clamp} (see Fig. A.17).

PROBLEM. Assume the source of current is a single channel opening with a current equal to $i = 1$ pA to show that we have the situation in Fig. A.15, since:

$$V = -IR_f + V_{clamp}$$

In Fig. A.15 the 1-mV downward deflection at the output implies a 1-pA current into the op-amp (the current into the op-amp is positive). We interpret the downward 1 mV at the output as a positive 1 pA at the input. The offset and the inversion are just nuisances that we can deal with.

PROBLEM. Suppose the single-channel current of 1 pA considered in Fig. A.14 comes through a 100 MΩ electrode (10^8 Ω). Show that the clamp voltage the channel actually sees is not 10 mV but 10.1 mV (see Fig. A.16).

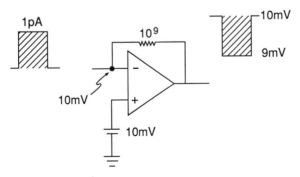

Figure A.15. Current-to-voltage converter: The input current (left) is converted to a voltage at the output (right). The dot represents a virtual 10 mV.

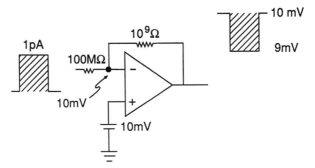

Figure A.16. Current-to-voltage converter: The input current (left) converts to the same voltage (right) as in Fig. A.15; however. the 100 MΩ resistor alters the voltage clamp of the cell.

The voltage at the channel is altered by the presence of the 100-MΩ resistor from 10 to 10.1 mV; output offset is still 10 mV and the downward deflection is still 1 mV. The channel does not see the clamp voltage that we apply, but a voltage that also depends on current. Consider that we are measuring from 100 channels with a peak inward current of −100 pA. What is the error in the voltage clamp?

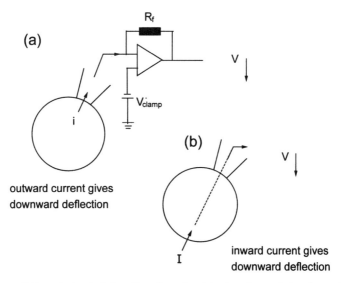

Figure A.17. Cell-attached and whole-cell configuration: (a) outward current gives downward deflection; (b) inward current gives downward deflection.

A patch clamp (SCRb, p. 3) setup uses an op-amp as a current-to-voltage converter (SCRa, pp. 4, 120; SCRb, p. 95). In this arrangement we record the current as a voltage, which is convenient for virtually all instruments in the laboratory; for example oscilloscopes measure voltages. Once we have the voltage, we can buffer it, amplify it, invert it, etc., all with the same basic op-amp device in different configurations. Using a current-to-voltage converter, we can also voltage clamp the cell; however V_{clamp} is the voltage we apply. It appears at the top of the patch electrode; it is not identical to the voltage that the channel or the cell sees (see Fig. A.16). The actual voltage depends on the size of the current and the resistors between virtual V_{clamp} (the dot in Fig. A.16) and the place where the current originates. We defined an inward current as negative and an outward current as positive; this means into or out of the cell membrane. Since op-amps invert the signal, we see from the preceding arguments that when we press the electrode to the cell surface in the cell-attached configuration, an *outward* current through the patch (which we identify as a single-channel current i) appears as a negative deflection in the voltage. However an *inward* current through the whole cell (I in Fig. A.17) looks the same to the amplifier with regard to its sign (current is flowing into the amplifier), so it too appears as a negative deflection. The best guide to patch clamps is *The Axon Guide for Electrophysiology and Biophysics Laboratory Techniques*, Axon Instruments, Inc., Foster City, CA 94404.

Appendix 2

Solution to Nernst–Planck

In the text we have often come across the equation:

$$-\phi = D\left[\frac{dn}{dx} + an\left(\frac{dV}{dx}\right)\right]$$

In this equation, D and a are constants. For Nernst–Planck theory, ϕ is a flux measured in units of #/cm^2·sec, that is, the number of particles moving across a unit area per unit time; n is a concentration (θ #/vol.), the number of particles per unit volume; x is the spatial dimension (positive moving from left to right), and $V(x)$ and $n(x)$ are functions of x. In this case D is the diffusion constant and a is ze/kT. The equation describes the movement of particles (#) in response to osmotic $n(x)$ and electric $V(x)$ forces.

One useful approach is to do some algebra before we go further; thus we write the two terms in the brackets [ ] as:

$$\frac{dn}{dx} + an\left(\frac{dV}{dx}\right) = e^{-aV}\frac{d}{dx}(ne^{aV})$$

Multiplying by e^{aV}:

$$e^{aV}\left[\frac{dn}{dx} + an\left(\frac{dV}{dx}\right)\right] = \frac{d}{dx}(ne^{aV})$$

Now we can proceed in many ways; recognize that the above equation is:

$$-\phi e^{aV}dx = dD(ne^{aV})$$

This yields:

$$-\phi\int_1^2 e^{aV}dx = D\int_1^2 d(ne^{aV})$$

223

Note: We remove ϕ from the integral by assuming $\phi \neq \phi(x)$. That is, we are in a steady state, so and there can be no increase or decrease of particles at any x. We notice that:

$$\int_1^2 e^{aV}dx \quad \vartheta \text{ length}$$

We have defined this integral as:

$$\ell = \int_1^2 e^{aV(x)}dx$$

where we write $V = V(x)$ explicitly. In general we cannot solve the integral because we do not know $V(x)$. However, we can write

$$\int_1^2 d(ne^{aV}) = n_2 e^{aV_2} - n_1 e^{aV_1}$$

Therefore:

$$\phi = -p\,(n_2 e^{aV_2} - n_1 e^{aV_1})$$

$$p = \frac{D}{\ell}$$

Since $D \; \vartheta \; \text{cm}^2/\text{sec}$, we see that:

$$p \quad \vartheta \; \text{cm/sec}$$

We think of this as a limiting velocity of fluxing particles as they move under these forces in the steady state. If $V_1 = 0$ (reference) as we agreed, then $V = V_2 - V_1$ and:

$$\phi = -p\,(n_2 e^{aV} - n_1)$$

Although we cannot solve the integral ℓ, in a famous chapter of membrane biophysics, a simple form for $V(x)$ was assumed (ICEMb, p. 266). This is the constant field assumption, which leads to the Goldman equation (ICEMb, p. 245).

If we assume that:

$$V(x) = \frac{xV}{\delta}$$

where δ is the thickness of the membrane, then when $x = 0$, $V(x) = 0$ (outside); when $x = d$, $V(x) = V$ (inside). Within the membrane itself, voltage is a straight line from 0 to V, which gives the name constant field, i.e., constant voltage slope. Now we have

$$\int_1^2 e^{a(xV/\delta)} \, dx$$

This is easy to solve: First multiply and divide by δ/aV, which changes nothing:

$$\left(\frac{\delta}{aV}\right)\int_1^2 e^{a(xV/\delta)} \, d\left(\frac{axV}{\delta}\right)$$

Then let $u = axV/\delta$ be the dummy variable of integration; thus we have

$$\left(\frac{\delta}{aV}\right)\int_1^2 e^u du = e^{u_2} - e^{u_1}$$

Since $u_1 = ax_1 V_1/\delta = 0$ and $u_2 = ax_2 V_2/\delta = aV$, $x_1 = 0$ and $x_2 = \delta$ (the thickness of the membrane), then:

$$\ell = \int_1^2 e^{a(xV/\delta)} dx = \frac{\delta(e^{aV} - 1)}{aV}$$

where $a = ze/kT$; therefore:

$$\phi = -\left(\frac{D}{\ell}\right)(n_2 e^{aV} - n_1)$$

$$\phi = -\frac{D}{[\delta(e^{aV} - 1)/aV]}(n_2 e^{aV} - n_1)$$

Let $I = -ze\phi A$; then:

$$\frac{I}{A} = (zeD/\delta) \times \frac{(zeV/kT) \times (n_2 e^{zeV/kT} - n_1)}{(e^{zeV/kT} - 1)}$$

This is the equation for the current per unit area (it could be the area of a cell, for example) as a function of concentration and voltage under the constant field assumption. It has the correct sign using $I = -ze\phi A$. To check let $V = 0$ and $n_2 < n_1$. Now we run into a slight problem because when $V = 0$ in the preceding equation.

$$\frac{V}{(e^{zeV/kT} - 1)} \rightarrow \frac{0}{0}$$

However if we use (l'Hopital's rule IMN, p. 48), then:

$$\frac{V}{e^{aV} - 1} \rightarrow \frac{1}{ae^{aV}} \rightarrow \frac{1}{a}$$

when $V = 0$; then:

$$\frac{I}{A} = \left(\frac{zeD}{\delta}\right)(n_2 - n_1) < 0$$

for $n_2 < n_1$. Now n_2 is the concentration inside, so if $z = +1$ (e.g., a K ion), the (+) ions flux into the cell (in the positive direction), and the current is negative, as it should be.

Let us consider a Cl current ($z = -1$) for a change. If $Cl_2 = 100$ mM, $Cl_1 = 10$ mM, and a $= ze/kT \sim -1/25$ mV, for the current per unit area A (A = cell area for example) we can write:

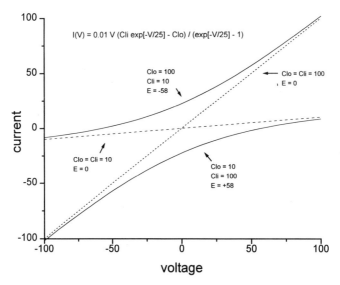

Fig. A.18. Cl current under different electrochemical conditions

$$\frac{I(V)}{A} = \frac{\mathcal{A}\,(V/25)(100\,e^{-V/25} - 10)}{(e^{-V/25} - 1)}$$

where $\mathcal{A} = (eD/\delta)$ is a constant. Note: z appears twice in the equation for $I(V)$, so the sign does not change even if $z = -1$. In Fig. A.18 we plot a series of graphs to show how Cl current behaves under different conditions assuming a constant field in the membrane. Remember: An inward Cl current means that Cl is moving out, and an outward Cl current means that Cl is moving in. Note: In Fig. A.18 we let $\mathcal{A}/25 = 0.01$ to give a convenient range. Try some other values, keeping in mind the definition of $\mathcal{A}$. We also indicated the reversal potential of the current (E), which is the potential when $I = 0$.

Problem: Show that another way of writing the constant field equation is:

$$\frac{I}{A} = \frac{(zeD/\delta)(zeV/kT)\,n_2\,(e^{ze(V-E)/kT} - 1)}{(e^{zeV/kT} - 1)}$$

where E in the preceding equation is given by:

$$E = -\left(\frac{kT}{ze}\right)\ln\left(\frac{n_2}{n_1}\right)$$

Appendix 3

All Kinds of Averages

Suppose we have a set of n numbers $\{a, b, c, \ldots\}$ and we wish to find the average. What springs to mind is:

$$\frac{a + b + c \ldots n}{n} = A$$

But there are other ways of finding the average value of the set. If we are not interested in A but in $1/A$, we could take the regular average, then take $1/A$; for example:

$$\frac{4 + 6 + 8 + 6}{4} = \frac{24}{4} = 6$$

$$1/A = \frac{4}{24} = \frac{1}{6}$$

But suppose we calculate $1/a$, $1/b$, etc., then perform the following operation:

$$\frac{1/4 + 1/6 + 1/8 + 1/6}{4} = \frac{6 + 4 + 3 + 4}{(24)4} = \frac{17}{96}$$

The two averages are not the same:

$$\frac{17}{96} \neq \frac{1}{6}$$

The inverse of the average is not equal to the average of the inverse. We see this from:

$$\frac{a + b}{2} = \frac{a}{2} + \frac{b}{2} \neq \frac{\dfrac{1}{a} + \dfrac{1}{b}}{2} = \frac{ab}{2(a + b)}$$

Now $(a + b)/2$ is an average, but so is $(ab/2)(a + b)$; and there are other kinds of averages, too. These are summarized below:

$$\frac{a + b}{2} \qquad \text{Arithmetic}$$

$$(ab)^{1/2} \qquad \text{Geometric}$$

$$\frac{ab}{2(a + b)} \qquad \text{Harmonic}$$

$$\frac{a - b}{\ln(a/b)} \qquad \text{Diffusional}$$

The name of last average is not standard. I used this name because it results from mixing two solutions of concentrations [a] and [b] by diffusion to produce an average concentration (see Kedem and Kalchalsky, Biochimica et Biophysica Acta 27: 229, 1958). This average also comes up in a well-known filtering problem (IMN, p. 177). Substitute some sample numbers, rank these averages in order; i.e., calculate $(3 + 5)/2 = 8$, etc., then see which is the largest. Try to determine how to generalize these averages for more than two numbers. Almost by inspiration, we can write

$$\frac{a + b + c}{3}, \quad \text{etc.}$$

$$(abc)^{1/2}, \quad \text{etc.}$$

$$\frac{ab + bc + ac}{3(a + b + c)}$$

What about the diffusional average? The diffusional average appears in the theory of prime numbers. If we plot the number of prime numbers P in the first N numbers, P falls off with N. Furthermore the average line through these points is:

$$P = \frac{N}{\ln N}$$

This is called the Prime Number Theorem. But if N is large it is also true that:

$$P \cong \frac{N - 1}{\ln(N/1)}$$

This is the diffusional average of N and 1. Can you think of a formula for the number of prime numbers between two arbitrary numbers? Can you test it?

Appendix 4

How Money Grows

Suppose we have a certain amount of money m (assume $m = \$100$). If the money increases by a certain percentage p after a period of time t (for example $p = 10\%$ and $t = 1$ year), at the end of the first time period, the money increases to:

$$m + pm = m(1 + p)$$

For example after one year:

$$\$100(1 + 0.1) = \$110$$

We let the compounding period be n. In the last problem, we really had $m(1 + p)^n$, where $n = 1$, but we did not write the exponent 1. Let money that we want to take out periodically be x. In the first problem, we really had $m(1 + p)^n - x$, where $n = 1$ and $x = 0$. Now let the two parameters n and x be variables.

After the first period, we have this much money left:

$$m(1 + p) - x$$

This is the new money to be compounded and subtracted from. Therefore after the second period we have this much money:

$$[m(1 + p) - x]\,(1 + p) - x$$

The amount of money in brackets is the amount of money gained after one period with x subtracted. In the second period, that net amount grows by $(1 + p)$, but we must again subtract the amount x that we take out. We see that the expression makes sense.

In the third period (Note: We have not yet fixed how long a period; it can be a day or a year), we use the same rule. Thus after Period 3, we have this formula:

$$\{[m(1+p)-x]\,(1+p)-x\}\,(1+p)-x$$

and so on. It looks complicated, but it is the simple rule applied over and over. We are running out of types of brackets, so we must find a compact way of writing the formula. We expand the preceding expression to see if we can generalize.

$$m(1+p)^3 - x(1+p)^2 - x(1+p)^1 - x$$

We have worked on *three* periods, and we have superscripts 3, 2, 1 in the expression. This suggests what to do next. We write down an expression for the *n*th period, using the summation sign Σ:

$$m(1+p)^n - x \sum_{i=1}^{n} (1+p)^{n-i}$$

We see this is true if we expand the expression for $n = 3$. We assume the equation is true for $n = 4$, and so on. If we wrote down this expression, it would be difficult to understand right away, but actually it is no more complicated than the original idea that $100 + 10\% = 110$.

Now what does compounded daily mean? If $m = \$100$, $p = 10\%$ ($= 0.10$) and $x = 0$, then compounded yearly means at the end of the year, we have

$$M = m(1+p)^n = \$100(1+0.1)^1 = \$110$$

If we compounded daily, after one year do we have $m(1 + p)^{365}$? No! We are generally given the value of p for 1 year, so, $p = 10\%$, means *for one year*. Then to compound daily, we use $p/365$ as the daily percentage, where p/n is the percent increase in the period n, p is the yearly percentage; therefore $n = 1$, then:

$$m(1+p) \Rightarrow \text{Yearly compound (by convention)}$$

Therefore:

$$m(1 + p/365)^{365} = \text{daily compound}$$

where $p/n = p/365$. Which one of these expressions is larger? We let $n = 1/2$:

$$m(1 + p/2)^2 = m(1 + p + p^2/4) = m(1 + p) + m(p^2/4)$$

This is larger than $m(1 + p)$, so compounding half-yearly is better than yearly, and compounding daily is even better.

We return to the general problem to see what happens if we remove money at a regular rate so that none is left after a while. Let us compound yearly. The general formula for M is:

$$M = m(1 + p)^n - x \sum_{i=1}^{n} (1 + p)^{n-i}$$

where M is the money after n years if the yearly percent increase is p and we remove x dollars each year. (We think of a period as a year, but we can change this equation if we compound differently.) No money left means $M = 0$. We ask how much can we remove to have nothing left in n years. To answer we let $M = 0$, then solve for x:

$$x = \frac{m(1 + p)^n}{\sum_{i=1}^{n} (1 + p)^{n-i}}$$

If we invest \$100,000 at the yearly rate of 10%, retire at 65, and want to spend all the money by age 75, 10 years later, then the equation is

$$x = \frac{10^5 (1.1)^{10}}{\sum_{i=1}^{10} (1.1)^{10-i}}$$

We can therefore calculate x, the amount to take out each year, given that the money also grows each year, so that nothing remains in 10 years. But who wants to calculate ten terms? What can we do? Let us take another look at the general formula:

$$m(1 + p)^n - x \sum_{i=1}^{n} (1 + p)^{n-i}$$

If we expand the Σ in this formula, we have:

$$m(1 + p)^n - x[(1 + p)^{n-1} + (1 + p)^{n-2} + \ldots 1]$$

The term in brackets can be written as:

$$(1 + p)^0 + (1 + p)^1 + (1 + p)^2 + \ldots + (1 + p)^{n-1} = \frac{(1 + p)^n - 1}{p}$$

To show this we expand the brackets; for $n = 1$:

$$(1 + p)^0 = 1$$

For $n = 2$:

$$(1 + p)^1 + (1 + p)^0 = 1 + p + 1 = 2 + p$$

For $n = 3$:

$$(1 + p)^2 + (1 + p)^1 + (1 + p)^0 = 1 + 2p + p^2 + 2 + p = 3 + 3p + p^2$$

These formulas remind us of Pascal's triangle (see p. 107):

$$1 + p$$

$$1 + 2p + p^2$$

$$1 + 3p + 3p^2 + p^3$$

$$1 + 4p + 6p^2 + 4p^3 + p^4$$

$$\vdots$$

As an example, for $n = 5$ the term in brackets becomes:

$$5 + 10p + 10p^2 + 5p^3 + p^4$$

This looks familiar because:

$$(1 + p)^5 = 1 + 5p + 10p^2 + 10p^3 + 5p^4 + p^5$$

which is equal to:

$$\frac{(1 + p)^5 - 1}{p}$$

Thus we see that:

$$[(1 + p)^{n-1} + (1 + p)^{n-2} + \ldots + 1] = \frac{(1 + p)^n - 1}{p}$$

Therefore a compact general formula for M is

$$M = m(1+p)^n - x\left[\frac{(1+p)^n - 1}{p}\right]$$

This is easier to solve than $m(1+p)^n - x[(1+p)^{n-1} + (1+p)^{n-2} + \ldots + 1]$.

Note: $(1+p)^n$ is in the new expression for M twice. Remember: $(1+p)^n$ means yearly, where p is the yearly percent and n is the number of years. For any other period, say, daily, it is $(1+p/365)^{365}$. This suggests the expression:

$$\left(1 + \frac{p}{y}\right)^{yn}$$

where y is the number of divisions in n, so if n and p refer to one year, $y = 12$ months, 52 weeks, or 365 days, etc. The definition of the exponential is:

$$\lim\left(1 + \frac{p}{y}\right)^y = e^p \quad \text{as } y \to \infty$$

Therefore:

$$\left(1 + \frac{p}{y}\right)^{yn} = (e^p)^n = e^{np} \quad \text{as } y \to \infty$$

If we think of the year as being divided into infinitely small bits, then we have a new equation for how money grows. In summary:

$$M = m(1+p)^n - x \sum_{i=1}^{n} (1+p)^{n-i}$$

$$= m(1+p)^n - x\left[\frac{(1+p)^n - 1}{p}\right]$$

compounded yearly. If we compound continuously then:

$$M = me^{np} - x\left(\frac{e^{np} - 1}{p}\right)$$

To know how much to take out each year after investing \$100,000 for 10 years, and to have nothing left after 10 years, we let $M = 0$ in this case:

$$x = \frac{pme^{np}}{e^{np} - 1}$$

$$= \frac{(0.1)\,(10^5)e^{10(0.1)}}{e^{10(0.1)} - 1}$$

$$= \frac{10^4 e}{e - 1} \simeq 1.6 \times 10^4$$

We can take out \$16,000/year for 10 years, then there will be no money left. This means we earned \$60,000, since we started with \$100,000. This would have been difficult to guess because the money is growing and shrinking at the same time.

Problem: Rework this problem compounding yearly.

Index